BASIC OKINAWAN

From Conversation to Grammar

RUMIKO SHINZATO
and **SHOICHI IWASAKI**

University of Hawaiʻi Press
Honolulu

© 2024 University of Hawai'i Press

All rights reserved

Printed in the United States of America

First printed, 2024

Library of Congress Cataloging-in-Publication Data

Names: Shinzato, Rumiko, author. | Iwasaki, Shōichi, author.
Title: Basic Okinawan : from conversation to grammar / Rumiko Shinzato, Shoichi Iwasaki.
Description: Honolulu : University of Hawai'i Press, [2024] | Includes bibliographical references. | In English and Central Okinawan.
Identifiers: LCCN 2023032337 | ISBN 9780824893651 (trade paperback)
Subjects: LCSH: Ryukyuan language—Textbooks for foreign speakers—English. | Ryukyuan language—Conversation and phrase books. | Ryukyuan language—Grammar—Problems, exercises, etc. | Ryukyuan language—Vocabulary—Problems, exercises, etc.
Classification: LCC PL693.R9 S55 2024 | DDC 495.67—dc23/eng/20231204
LC record available at https://lccn.loc.gov/2023032337

University of Hawai'i Press books are printed on acid-free paper and meet the guidelines for permanence and durability of the Council on Library Resources.

Cover design: Mardee Melton

Cover image: Payless Images.
The cover art is inspired by bingata, a traditional Okinawan stenciled dyeing technique. Bingata typically features motifs drawn from the natural world, such as flowers rendered in bright colors.

BASIC OKINAWAN

*For the beautiful land
and
people of Okinawa*

BRIEF CONTENTS

Acknowledgments		xix
Introduction		xxi
Abbreviations		xxix
Preliminary Lesson		xxxi
Note on Online Content		xxxv

PART I Conversation

Cast of Characters			2
Lesson	1	Okinawan New Year	3
Lesson	2	Okinawan New Year Family Gathering	21
Lesson	3	Making *Muuchii* Cake	45
Lesson	4	Do You Have Pain Somewhere?	69
Lesson	5	Riding in a Taxi / Grocery Shopping at the Market	93
Lesson	6	Cherry Blossom Festival	117
Lesson	7	Beach Outing	143
Lesson	8	Visit to an Ancestral Grave in Celebration	165
Lesson	9	Tug of War Festival	197
Lesson	10	Farewell: "Once We Meet, Brothers and Sisters Forever"	215

PART II Grammar

Topic	1	Typological Introduction	249
Topic	2	Case Marking	253
Topic	3	Verbs	259
Topic	4	Adjectives	267
Topic	5	Questions	273
Topic	6	Clause Combining	277
Topic	7	Sentence Final Particles	283
Topic	8	Focus Concord	289
Appendix 1		*Vocabulary List*	295
Appendix 2		*Construction List*	323
References			331

CONTENTS

Acknowledgments — xix
Introduction — xxi
   The Structure of the Book — xxiii
   Romanization Conventions — xxiv
Abbreviations — xxix
Preliminary Lesson — xxxi
Note on Online Content — xxxv

PART I   Conversation

Cast of Characters — 2

Lesson 1   Okinawan New Year — 3
Dialogue A — 3
Grammar A — 4
  1   Demonstratives: *kur*i 'this', *uri* 'that', *ari* 'that over there' — 4
  2   Topic Particle: *ya* — 5
  3   Particle: *(s)shi* 'by means of' — 5
  4   Complementizer: *ndi* — 5
  5   Sentence Final Particles: *doo* and *yaa* — 6
Exercises A — 7
Dialogue B — 10
Grammar B — 11
  1   Copula: Plain and Polite Forms — 11
  2   Verbs: Plain and Polite Forms — 12
  3   Adjectives: Plain and Polite Forms — 13
  4   Wh-Words: *nuu* 'what?', *chaa* 'how?', and the Wh-Question Particle *ga* — 14
  5   Particle: *nu* genitive marker — 14
Exercises B — 15
Applications — 16
Cultural Notes — 17
  1   New Year's Greetings in Okinawan — 17
  2   New Year's Dishes — 18

x   Contents

       3   "Okinawa: *Ganjuu naganuchi Okinawa-ken*" Prefecture
of a Healthy and Long Life   18
       4   "*Kwatchii sabira*" and "*Nifee deebiru*"   19

Lesson 2   Okinawan New Year Family Gathering   21

    Dialogue A   21
    Grammar A   22
       1   Personal Pronouns (First Person)   22
       2   Family Terms   23
       3   Additive Topic Particle: *n*   24
    Exercises A   25
    Dialogue B   26
    Grammar B   27
       1   Personal Pronouns (Second Person)   27
       2   Numbers   27
       3   Particles: *ga* and *nu* (Subject Markers)   28
       4   Verbs of Existence: *wun* (*wuibiin*) vs. *an* (*aibiin*)   28
       5   Location Demonstratives: *kuma* 'here', *ʔnma* 'there', *ama* 'over there'   28
       6   Particle: *nkai* 'at, in, on'   28
       7   Sentence Final Particle: *sa*   29
       8   Wh-Word: *ikuchi* 'how old?' / 'how many things?'   29
    Exercises B   30
    Dialogue C   31
    Grammar C   32
       1   Personal Pronouns (Third Person)   32
       2   Negative Form: The Copula and the Existential Verbs   32
       3   Negative Forms: Other Verbs   34
       4   Negative Forms: Adjectives   35
       5   Wh-Words: *taa* 'who?/whose?', *iku-tai* 'how many people?'   36
       6   Particle: *tu* 'and'   37
    Exercises C   37
    Applications   39
    Cultural Notes   40
       1   Family Terms: *wikii* vs. *wunai*   40
       2   Okinawan Family Name Jokes: *Yafuso*   40

Review Exercises: Lessons 1 and 2   41

Lesson 3   Making *Muuchii* Cake   45

    Dialogue A   45
    Grammar A   46
       1   Gerund Form   46
       2   Transitive vs. Intransitive Verbs   47
       3   Progressive and Resultative/Stative: [G.ROOT—*(t)oon*]:
'someone is doing something' and 'something has been done / is done'   48

	Exercises A	50
	Dialogue B	53
	Grammar B	54
	1 Simple Past vs. Extended Past	54
	2 Yes/No Question (Nonpast) with the Question Particle -*i*	56
	3 Yes/No Question (Past) with the Question Particle -*i*	56
	4 Invitation with the Question Particle -*i*	57
	5 Sentence Final Particle: *gayaa*	58
	Exercises B	58
	Dialogue C	60
	Grammar C	61
	1 Adjectives and Copulas: Past	61
	2 Particles: *nkai* 'into', *kara* 'from'	62
	3 Gerund Forms: Combining Function	62
	Exercises C	63
	Applications	64
	Cultural Notes	66
	1 *Muuchii biisa*	66
	2 Yes and No	66
	3 *Nankuru nai sa*	67
	4 Homophones	68
Lesson 4	**Do You Have Pain Somewhere?**	**69**
	Dialogue A	69
	Grammar A	70
	1 Body Parts	70
	2 *Wh-* vs. Indefinite: *maa* 'where?' vs. *maagana* 'somewhere'; *nuu* 'what?' vs. *nuugana* 'something'	71
	3 Adnominal Form	71
	4 Focus Construction 1: [… *du* … ADNOM.FORM]	73
	5 Sentence Final Particles: [APO.FORM + *ssaa*] vs. [FINITE.FORM + *tee*]	74
	Exercises A	76
	Dialogue B	77
	Grammar B	78
	1 Conjunctive Particles: [APO.FORM + *kutu*] 'so' vs. [APO.FORM + *shiga*] 'but'	78
	2 Expression of Causes: [APO.FORM (Adj.) + *nu*] '(adj.) so ~'	80
	3 Nominalization: [APO.FORM + *shi*]	80
	Exercises B	81
	Applications	84
	Cultural Notes	86
	1 Spirits: *shii* and *mabui*	86
	2 "God Bless You!" in Okinawan	86
Review Exercises: Lessons 3 and 4		**87**

Lesson 5   Riding in a Taxi / Grocery Shopping at the Market — 93
Dialogue A — 93
Grammar A — 95
1. Verbs of Motion: *ichun* 'to go' and *chuun* 'to come' — 95
2. Expressions of Ease and Difficulty: [ADV.FORM + *yassan*] 'easy to do something'; [ADV.FORM + *gurisan*] 'hard to do something' — 96
3. Particles: *nkai* 'to' and *madi* 'as far as (time/space)' — 97
4. Particle: *kara* 'by means of' and 'through' — 98
5. Diminutive Suffix: *gwaa* — 98
6. Wh-Word: *jiru* 'which?' — 98

Exercises A — 99
Dialogue B — 101
Grammar B — 102
1. Particles: *wuti/wutooti* 'in, at' — 102
2. Wh-Word: *chassa* 'how much?' — 102
3. Request: [G.FORM + *kwimisooree*]: 'Please do ~' — 102
4. Useful Expressions for Giving Directions — 103

Exercises B — 104
Dialogue C — 105
Grammar C — 107
1. Exalting Verbs — 107
2. Intentional Form — 107
3. Change of State: [Adj. (*-ku* form) / Noun] + *nain* 'to become' — 109
4. Sentence Final Particles: [INT.FORM + *na*] and [FINITE.FORM + *naa*] — 110

Exercises C — 110
Applications — 112
Cultural Notes — 114
1. *Ishigantoo* — 114
2. Liver and Heart — 114
3. Okinawan Humor — 115

Lesson 6   Cherry Blossom Festival — 117
Dialogue A — 117
Grammar A — 118
1. Desire Expressions: [ADV.FORM + *busan*] 'want to do'; [noun {*nu* / Ø} *fu(u)san*] 'I want (something)' — 118
2. Purposive: [ADV.FORM + (*i*) + *ga* + *ichun/chuun*] 'go/come in order to do V' — 119
3. The *aani* Clause: [B.ROOT + *(y)aani*] 'doing ~, and/then ~' — 120
4. Representative Actions [[G.ROOT + *(t)ai*] + [G.ROOT + *(t)ai*] + *sun*] 'doing X...doing Y...' — 121
5. Particles: *saani* (a) 'by means of', (b) 'with (everyone/everything)' — 123

Exercises A — 123

Dialogue B		125
Grammar B		126
1	Obligation [N.FORM + {*daree/nee*} *naran*] 'must'	126
2	The *(r)ee* Conditional: 'If/when S$_1$, then S$_2$'	127
3	Use of *gutu*	129
4	Conjecture: [Finite Form + *nee sun*] 'I have a feeling that ~'	130
5	Color Words	130
Exercises B		131
Applications		133
Cultural Notes		135
1	Northern Dynasty, Central Dynasty, Southern Dynasty	135
2	*Churasan* and Okinawan Poetry (*Ryūka*)	135

Review Exercises: Lessons 5 and 6   137

Lesson 7   Beach Outing   143

Dialogue A		143
Grammar A		145
1	Directional Motion: [G.FORM + *ichun / chuun*] 'do something and go / come'	145
2	Focus Construction 2: […*nu/ga ga*…RA.FORM] 'I wonder…'	145
3	Comparison of Items	147
Exercises A		149
Dialogue B		151
Grammar B		152
1	Potentials: Situational Possibility vs. Agent's Ability	152
2	Concessive Conditionals	152
3	Double Particle: [Subject Particle {*nu/ga*} + Topic Particles {*ya/n*}]	153
Exercises B		154
Dialogue C		156
Grammar C		157
1	Resultative: [G.ROOT + *(t)een*] 'have done'	157
2	Preparatory aspect: [G.ROOT + *(t)oochun*] 'do it for future use'	158
3	Total Negation: [Numeral (one) + *n* + NEG] 'not even one' / [Wh + *n* + NEG] 'no one, nothing…'	159
Exercises C		160
Applications		161
Cultural Notes		162
1	*Urijin* and *Wakanachi*	162
2	*Diigu* (Deigo) 'Erythrina'	162
3	The Musical *Tumai Aakaa*	163

Lesson 8 Visit to an Ancestral Grave in Celebration 165

Dialogue A 165
Grammar A 166
  1 Verbs of Giving 166
  2 Benefactive: [G.FORM + verbs of giving] 'do something for someone' 167
  3 Imperative Forms: [NEG.ROOT + (r)ee] and [N.ROOT + (r)i] + yoo 'Do it!' 168
  4 Negative Imperative: [NEG.FORM + kee] and [NEG.FORM + ki yoo] 'Don't do it!' 170
  5 Passive Constructions 171
Exercises A 174
Dialogue B 176
Grammar B 177
  1 Exalting Expressions: [ADV.FORM + misheen] / [ADV.FORM + misooran] 177
  2 Exalting and Humble Forms 177
  3 Provisional Conditionals: [APOCO.FORM + raa] 'if that is the case,…' 179
  4 Speaker Conjecture: [ADNOM.FORM + haji] 'something is expected (to happen / have happened)' 180
Exercises B 181
Dialogue C 183
Grammar C 184
  1 Simultaneous Actions: [V$_1$ (ADV.FORM) gachii, V$_2$] 'While doing V$_1$, do V$_2$' 184
Exercises C 185
Applications 187
Cultural Notes 188
  1 The Day to Pay Respect to One's Ancestors: Shiimii / U-shiimii (Seimei sai) 188
  2 Shiimii vs. U-shiimii 188
  3 Kamekoo-baka 'turtleback tombs' 188

Review Exercises: Lessons 7 and 8 191

Lesson 9 Tug of War Festival 197

Dialogue A 197
Grammar A 199
  1 Wh-Word: nuunchi? 'why?' 199
  2 Purpose Expression: [V$_1$ ADNOM.FORM + tami ni V$_2$] 'in order to do V$_1$, do V$_2$' 199
  3 Contrast/Reason: [V$_1$ ADNOM.FORM + munnu V$_2$] (a) 'V$_1$ but V$_2$' (b) 'V$_1$ so V$_2$' 199
Exercises A 200
Dialogue B 201
Grammar B 203
  1 Causatives 203
  2 Causative-Passives 204

Exercises B		206
Dialogue C		207
Grammar C		208
1	Completive Aspect: [G.FORM + *neen*] 'end up'	208
2	Concessive Conditional 2: [G.FORM (V/ADJ.) + *n*] 'even if…'	209
3	Sentence Final Particle: *ee sani*	209
Exercises C		210
Applications		212
Cultural Notes		212
1	Tug of War Festival	212
2	East-West-South-North	213
3	Summer Events: *O-bon* and *Eisaa*	213

Lesson 10 Farewell: "Once We Meet, Brothers and Sisters Forever" — 215

Dialogue A		215
Grammar A		217
1	Verbs of Clothing	217
2	Temporal Clause: [G.FORM + *kara*] 'since/after doing ~'	218
3	The *gutu* Expressions	219
Exercises A		220
Dialogue B		222
Grammar B		223
1	*Naa* 'already' and *maada / naaa* 'still'	223
2	Habitual Conditional: [ADV.FORM + *(i)nee*] 'when/whenever'	224
3	"Difficulty" Expression: [ADV.FORM + *kantii sun*] 'difficult to ~'	225
4	Derived verbs: [(adj. of emotion/sensation) APO.FORM + *sun*]	226
Exercises B		226
Dialogue C		228
Grammar C		229
1	Temporal Relations	229
2	Speech Act Expressions	231
3	Experiential Expressions	233
4	Visual Evidential	234
Exercises C		235
Applications		237
Cultural Notes		238
1	*Kugani kutuba* ('Words of Wisdom')	238
2	*Kajimayaa*	238
3	*Choodee gwaa bushi*	239
4	*Yamanokuchi Baku*	240

Review Exercises: Lessons 9 and 10 — 241

PART II Grammar

Topic 1 Typological Introduction — 249
- 1.1 Demonstratives — 249
- 1.2 Personal Pronouns — 249
- 1.3 Constituent Orders — 250
- 1.4 Subject and Topic — 251
- 1.5 Agglutinating Morphology — 252
- 1.6 Other Points — 252

Topic 2 Case Marking — 253
- 2.1 Subject: *ga, nu* — 253
- 2.2 Possessor: *ga, nu,* Ø — 255
- 2.3 Modifier: *nu* — 255
- 2.4 Object: Ø (zero marking) — 256
- 2.5 Goal 1: *nkai* — 256
- 2.6 Goal 2: *madi* — 256
- 2.7 Locative: *wuti / wutooti / nji* — 257
- 2.8 Temporal: *ni* — 257
- 2.9 Origin: *kara* 1 — 257
- 2.10 Passage: *kara* 2 — 257
- 2.11 Means of Transportation: *kara* 3 — 258
- 2.12 Instrument: *(s)shi / saani* — 258
- 2.13 Companionship: *tu* — 258

Topic 3 Verbs — 259
- 3.1 Preliminary — 259
- 3.2 Building Blocks — 259
- 3.3 Predicate Forms — 263

Topic 4 Adjectives — 267
- 4.1 Finite Form — 268
- 4.2 Adnominal Form — 269
- 4.3 Adverbial Form — 269
- 4.4 Apocopated Form — 270

Topic 5 Questions — 273
- 5.1 Yes/No-Question Particles — 273
- 5.2 Wh-Questions — 275
- 5.3 Self-addressing Questions — 276

Topic 6 Clause Combining — 277
- 6.1 Simple Clause Combining — 277
- 6.2 Adverbial Clause Combining — 279

Topic 7 Sentence Final Particles — 283
- 7.1 Information Oriented Particles — 284
- 7.2 (Inter)action Oriented Particles — 287

Topic 8	**Focus Concord**	**289**
8.1	…*du*…*ru*	289
8.2	Quasi-Focus Concord	292
8.3	…*ga*…*ra*	292

Appendix 1	*Vocabulary List*	295
Appendix 2	*Construction List*	323
	Sorted by Lesson	323
	Sorted by Building Blocks	327
References		331

ACKNOWLEDGMENTS

In the process of writing this textbook, we have greatly benefited from many existing scholarly works, including *Okinawago Jiten* (Uemura Yukio, ed. *Kokuritsu Kokugo Kenkyūjo*), *Okinawago Jiten* (Uchima Chokujin and Nohara Mitsuyoshi), *Okinawan-English Wordbook* (Sakihara Mitsugu), *Ryūkyūgo Jiten* (Handa Ichirō), *Uchināguchi Katsuyō Jiten* (Miyara Shinshō), and several published textbooks in Japanese, in addition to numerous journal papers, book chapters, and books.

We are extremely grateful for the careful reading and thoughtful comments by the three anonymous reviewers, without which the book could have never been published in this form. We are also indebted to many people who contributed in various ways to improve the original manuscript. Professor Kanemoto Madoka read the earlier version of the manuscript in its entirety and enlightened us with many invaluable comments and corrections. Mr. Kuniyoshi Tomohisa checked the entire set of dialogues and offered us extensive feedback which saved us from rudimentary errors. We also benefited from Professors Leon A. Serafim, Shimabukuro Moriyo, and Arakaki Tomoko for their linguistic consultation. Our heartfelt thanks go to many native speakers of Okinawan, who participated in this project as consultants, always with unfailingly willing spirits.

In addition, we would like to extend our special thanks to those who participated in the recordings of the main dialogues of this textbook: Okinawa Hands-On NPO Youth Club (Ms. Higa Nanase, Mr. Nema Hiroto, Mr. Sakiyama Rin, and Mr. Ishikawa Hiroto), and Mr. Kuniyoshi Tomohisa and Ms. Nishizato Katsuko. We also appreciate the generous support we received from Okinawa Hands-On NPO, especially Mr. Agena Tatsuya (founder) and Mr. Miyazato Jun (manager), who also encouraged their junior members to participate in recordings and granted us the use of their facility. We are also indebted to Dr. Kikuchi Masato for his artistic contribution in providing us with many illustrations, which made the book more user-friendly.

We would like to acknowledge various grants we received before and during this project from the Georgia Tech Dean's Office grants, Japan Foundation, Okinawa Ginkō Furusato Shinkō Kikin grants, and Terasaki Center for Japanese Studies at UCLA. The very first draft of the manuscript was pilot-tested at UCLA in the winter of 2020. We are grateful to Professor Seiji Lippit, the chair of the Department of Asian Languages & Cultures and the associate director of the Terasaki Center for Japanese

Studies at UCLA, for making the offering of this course possible. We are also indebted to the students who took the course and gave us much useful feedback, which has been reflected in our later versions.

Rumiko Shinzato would like to express deep gratitude to the late Professor Handa Ichirō, whose influence on her linguistic work is beyond what words could express. She extends her gratitude also to her late parents for passing on to her the treasure of Okinawan heritage, including the very language she now feels to be her mission to preserve and propagate. Last but not least, she would also like to express her appreciation to her husband, who has been a source of inspiration, a driving force, and a well of positive energy. Thanks also goes to her children and their spouses for their moral and technical support throughout the project, and to her grandchildren for their innocent smiles and burgeoning multilingual skills, which have given her the joy of life!

Shoichi Iwasaki acknowledges his wife (Pensy) and son (Stan-Shogo), who gave much needed moral support during this project. His thanks also goes to many people he met in Okinawa and in Hawaiʻi who encouraged him to start working on this textbook project. Professor Karimata Shigehisa and Dr. Sakihara Masashi introduced him to various aspects of the language and culture of Okinawa. Professor William O'Grady of the University of Hawaiʻi at Mānoa introduced us to the University of Hawaiʻi Press, which took up this book project.

Thanks also go to Christianne Ono for her excellent editing, Tsuyoshi Ono for his technical consultation, and Hiroko Nakama for providing many beautiful photos. Stephanie Chun, Gianna Marsella, Lori Paximadis, and Wanda China from the University of Hawaiʻi Press have been generous and supportive from the beginning to the end of this project. Finally, it would be greatly remiss of us not to mention Marc Miyake's expert assistance during the final stage of manuscript preparation.

Needless to say, all faults remaining in this monograph are ours and ours alone.

INTRODUCTION

The Ryukyuan languages are spoken on various islands between Amami and Yonaguni along an archipelago in the southwest of Japan (see Map 1). These languages constitute a separate branch of the Japonic language family with Japanese as the other main branch. The Okinawan language introduced in this book is one of the six endangered Ryukyuan languages designated by UNESCO (Moseley 2010). It belongs to the northern group of Ryukyuan along with Amami and Kunigami. Languages belonging to the southern Ryukyuan group are Miyako, Yaeyama, and Yonaguni.

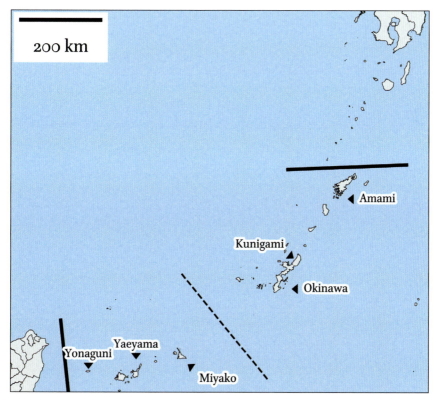

Map 1. The Ryukyuan Islands (created by Kanji Kato and based on information from the Geospatial Information Authority of Japan (https://www.gsi.go.jp/kankyochiri/gm_jpn.html).

There is a vast difference between the northern and southern groups, and even languages within the northern or southern groups are mutually unintelligible.

The variety of Okinawan introduced in this book is the Naha-Shuri dialect of Okinawan. It is the variety spoken in the old capital and commercial center of the old Ryukyu Kingdom (1429–1879), which is located in the south-central region of the main island of Okinawa (see Map 2). This variety, albeit with some dispute, is referred to as *Uchinaaguchi* by some (Nishioka and Nakahara 2006:7).

Fluent speakers of Okinawan were mostly born before the 1950s—currently about seventy years old or older (Ishihara 2014:141; Heinrich 2015:620; among others). According to Okinawa Prefecture's 2019 resident registry (Okinawa Prefecture 2019), the number of this age group in Naha City is 55,042, which is roughly 17.2% of the

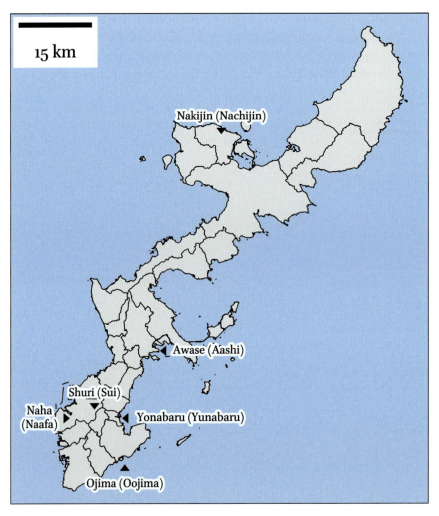

Map 2. The Island of Okinawa (created by Kanji Kato and based on information from the Ministry of Land, Infrastructure, Transport, and Tourism (https://mlit.go.jp).

total population of 320,319 (Okinawa Prefecture 2019). In reality, however, fluent speakers in and around Naha and Shuri are mostly over eighty years old (25,057 or 7.8%), though slightly younger speakers may be found in some peripheral areas of the city. Intergenerational transmission of the local language has been disrupted, making Okinawan a "severely endangered" language according to UNESCO's vitality and endangerment scale (Ishihara 2014:145). In recent years, however, various revitalization efforts have been made with an aim to bring the vitality of the Okinawan language back. In 2000, the *Uchināguchi Fukyū Kyōkai* (Society of Okinawan Language Revitalization) was established. In 2006, the Okinawa Prefectural Government enacted an ordinance to designate September 18 as *Shimakutuba nu hi* 'Local Language Day.' The prefectural government also published *Shimakutuba* readers for elementary through high school students and a *Shimakutuba* handbook for the general public. Various NPOs have been organizing *Shimakutuba* seminars, speech contests, and other activities (Okinawa Prefecture 2020; Heinrich 2008). While the future of the Okinawan language depends on the will of the people in Okinawa, external encouragement may make some contribution toward their efforts. It is the authors' hope that a textbook such as this one will encourage young students to become interested in Okinawa and will play a small part toward the preservation of the Okinawan language and culture. It is also hoped that textbooks like this will be published for other Ryukyuan languages to reinvigorate them in the future.

THE STRUCTURE OF THE BOOK

This book aims to provide comprehensive resources for studying Okinawan language and culture. Part I of the book uses model conversations to provide a context for language use and offers many exercises to enhance the student's understanding of grammar, while Part II gives more detailed descriptions of selected grammar points presented throughout Part I.

Part I embraces the **5C** objectives in the US National Standards in Foreign Language Education: **Communication**, **Cultures**, **Connections**, **Comparisons**, and **Communities**. In addition, it takes a user-centered approach bearing on the following traits to make language learning easy, effective, and fun via:

- A systematic organization of grammar and vocabulary to provide scaffolding for the students, so they gradually add to and build upon knowledge they have already gained;
- The inclusion of examples from categories such as music, pop culture, films, theater, etc.;
- A comprehensive vocabulary list with cross-references to grammar and dialogue sections in Part I;
- The inclusion of humorous anecdotes and exercise questions;
- The creation of authentic dialogues with a developing storyline about the

life of a foreign exchange student in Okinawa, from his first encounter to his poignant departure from his host family, who remind him of a well-known Okinawan saying, *Ichariba choodee* "Once we meet, we are friends forever," which is seen by many as a reflection of the character of the Okinawan people.

More specifically, Part I consists of the following five sections: Dialogue; Grammar; Exercises; Applications; and Cultural Notes. **Dialogues** are designed to echo how speakers actually use the language in daily life [i.e., **C**ommunication in the 5C's]. Through these dialogues, the book presents new vocabulary and grammatical constructions. Each dialogue in a lesson has its own particular focus on a certain cultural theme, blended with festivals and seasonal events through the year [i.e., encouraging **C**ommunity participation]. The **Grammar** section describes grammatical structures in an accessible, user-friendly fashion. **Exercises** utilize various formats from simple mechanical drills to conversational exchanges to narratives. **Applications** take a task-based approach, giving students opportunities to deal with novel situations by applying all the grammar and vocabulary at their disposal. These two sections are designed not only to test students' mastery of their newly acquired knowledge, but also to help their learning through review, repetition, and application to new contexts. To solidify their grammatical knowledge, more summative and comprehensive exercises are also provided every two lessons. **Cultural Notes** present relevant cultural information associated with the themes of each dialogue, encompassing a wider range of disciplines such as history, geography, religion, pop culture, etc. [i.e., **C**ulture and **C**onnection]. This section also poses questions to encourage critical thinking from a cross-cultural perspective, prompting comparisons between Okinawan and other cultures, and also historical comparisons of the present day with the past [**C**omparison].

Part II presents eight chapters arranged by grammar topics which are cross-referenced with the corresponding sections in Part I. Given the topical organization of Part II, students are encouraged to use this part of the textbook whenever they need to review grammar points that may be distributed over multiple lessons in Part I.

ROMANIZATION CONVENTIONS

Okinawan words and sentences are presented in the romanization conventions used in the *Okinawan-English Wordbook* (Sakihara 2006), with adjustments made for the notation of the glottal stop sound. *Wordbook* uses an apostrophe to indicate this segment, but the notation in this book uses the phonetic notation [ʔ] in order to achieve clarity in exposition.

The table below summarizes the romanization of syllables adopted in this book based on the conventions used in WB and OGJ2. Those in parentheses are rare syllables. The dash (—) marks syllables that generally do not appear, except for special cases such as interjections.

					Notes
a	i	u	e	o	see Note 1
ka	ki	ku	ke	ko	
kwa	kwi	—	kwe	—	
ga	gi	gu	ge	go	
gwa	gwi	—	gwe	—	
sa	—	su	se	so	
(za)	—	—	(ze)	(zo)	
(sha)	shi	shu	(she)	(sho)	
ja	ji	ju	je	jo	
ta	ti	tu	te	to	
da	di	du	dee*	do	*/de/ does not exist
cha	chi	chu	—	cho	
na	ni	nu	nee*	no	*/ne/ does not exist
ha	hi	hu	(he)	(ho)	
fa	fi	fu	(fe)	—	
ba	bi	bu	be	bo	
pa	pi	pu	pe	po	
(hya)*	—	—	—	(hyo)*	
—	—	—	—	(byo)*	
ma	mi	mu	me	mo	
ʔya	—	—	—	—	see Note 1
ya	yi	yu	—	yo	see Note 1
ra	ri	ru	re	ro	In Naha, /d/ is mostly pronounced as /r/, cf. OGJ2, p. xix
ʔwa	ʔwi	—	ʔwe	—	see Note 1
wa	wi	wu	—	wo	see Note 1
nna	nni	—	—	—	
ʔnna	ʔnni	—	—	—	see Note 2
ʔnma	—	—	—	—	see Note 2
n-					initial nasal before /b/, /ch/, /d/, /j/, /k/
moraic nasal [n, m, ŋ]					see Note 3
Gemination.					see Note 4
Long vowel					see Note 5

Notes

1. Glottal Stop (with Vowels and Semivowels). A vowel at the word-initial position is always accompanied by a glottal stop, e.g. [ʔa], [ʔi], [ʔu]. Since this is always predictable, a vowel is simply written without a mark, e.g. *a, i, u*, in the romanization adopted in this book. In contrast, semivowels may or may not be accompanied by the glottal stop, thus it is crucial to indicate the presence of the glottal stop in this environment. We use the symbol [ʔ] to indicate a glottal stop. Note that WB uses an apostrophe instead.

Glottalized Semi-Vowel	
Romanization	IPA
ʔya	[ʔja]
ʔwa	[ʔwa]
ʔwi	[ʔwi]

Smooth Semi-Vowel	
Romanization	IPA
ya	[ja]
wa	[wa]
wi	[wi]

- ʔyaa ('you') vs. yaa ('house')
- ʔwaa ('pig') vs. waa ('I')
- ʔwii ('up') vs. wii ('drunk')

In addition, the vowels *i* [ʔi] and *u* [ʔu] contrast with smooth semi-vowels *yi* [ji] and *wu* [wu], respectively.

Vowel	
Romanization	IPA
i	[ʔi]
u	[ʔu]

Smooth Semi-Vowel	
Romanization	IPA
yi	[ji]
wu	[wu]

- ii ('yes') vs. yii ('good')
- iin ('say') vs. yiin ('sit')
- inaka ('countryside') vs. yinagu (cf. OGJ2) ('woman') [Note: *winagu* (WB)]
- utu ('sound') vs. wutu ('husband')

2. Glottal Stop (with Initial Nasals). The initial nasal consonants may or may not be initiated with a glottal stop.

Glottalized Nasal	
Romanization	IPA
ʔn	[ʔn]
ʔm	[ʔm]

Smooth Nasal	
Romanization	IPA
n	[n]
m	[m]

Spellings differ in different dictionaries:

English (Japanese)	This book	WB	OGJ1	OGJ2 (phonetic)
rice plant (ine)	ʔnni	′nni	ʔNni	ʔnni
chest (mune)	nni	nni	ʽNni	Nni
everyone (mina)	n(n)na	nnna	ʽNna	n:na
sea (umi)	umi	′nmi	ʔumi	ʔumi
horse (uma)	ʔnma	′nma	ʔNma	ʔmma

3. Moraic Nasal *n* [n, m, ŋ]. This book follows WB and uses *n* to represent the moraic nasals because the sound quality is predictable.

- [n] *sannin* ‘ginger plant’ (*gettoo* in Japanese)
- [ŋ] *sangwachi* ‘the third month (= March)’
- [m] *sanmin* ‘calculation’

4. Geminate Consonants. Geminate consonants are two identical sequential consonants. When written, they are represented by repeating the consonant in question:

- *ippee* ‘very’
- *ussan* ‘happy’
- *sakkwii* ‘cough’

However, note that this book adopts *tch* instead of the geminate *cc*.

- **tch**u (not *cch*u) ‘person’
- *mu***tch**an ‘had, held’

5. Long Vowels. Long vowels are written with two vowels.

- *mii* ‘eyes’
- *uubi* ‘sash’
- *teegee* ‘generally’
- *maasan* ‘delicious’

ABBREVIATIONS

add = additional vocabulary
adj. = adjective
ADNOM.FORM = Adnominal Form
adv. = adverb
ADV.FORM = Adverbial Form
AFF = affirmative
ANIM = animate
APOCO = Apocopated Form
ASP = aspect
AUX = auxiliary verb
B.ROOT = Basic Root
CAUS = causative
CAUS.PASS = causative-passive
COND = conditional
conj. = conjunction
COP = copula
Cul = Cultural Notes
C-verb = consonant verb
Dial = Dialogue
Dic. = dictionary
DIM = diminutive suffix
Eng. = English
EXAL = exalting verb
FC = Focus Concord
FINITE = Finite Form
GEN = genitive
G.FORM = Gerund Form
G.ROOT = Gerund Root
HON = honorific
HUM = humble verb
IMP = imperative
INANIM = inanimate

inj. = interjection
INT.FORM = Intentional Form
INTR = intransitive
IPA = International Phonetic Alphabet
IRG = irregular
Jp. = Japanese
N = noun
NEG = negative
N.FORM = Negative Form
N-proper = proper noun
N.ROOT = Negative Root
N-wh = noun wh-word
NOM = nominalizer
OBJ = object
OGJ1 = *Okinawago Jiten* (Uemura, Kokuritsu Kokugo Kenkyūjo 1963)
OGJ2 = *Okinawago Jiten* (Uchima and Nohara 2006)
PASS = passive
PAST-1 = simple past tense form with *-an*
PAST-2 = extended past tense form with *-tan*
pl. = plural
pol. = polite auxiliary
POL.COP = polite copula
POT = potential auxiliary
Prel. = Preliminary Lesson
PROG = progressive
Pron. = pronoun
PRT = particle
PST = past
Q = question

QP = question particle
RA.FORM = *Ra* Form (the ending of Focus Construction II)
RES = resultative
S = sentence
SFP = sentence final particle
sg. = singular
s.o. = someone
s.t. = something
SUBJ = subject
TOP = topic
TR = transitive
V = verb
V_1 = first verb
V_2 = second verb
V-c = consonant verb
V-hon. = honorific verb
V_{intr} = intransitive verb
V-IRG = irregular verb
V_{tr} = transitive verb
V-v = vowel verb
V-verb = vowel verb
wh = wh-question or wh-word
WB = *Okinawan-English Wordbook* (Sakihara 2006)
ʔ = glottal stop
o = accepted word or sentence
x = unaccepted word or sentence

PRELIMINARY LESSON

CLASSROOM EXPRESSIONS

Here are a few useful expressions your instructor will use.

	Okinawan	English
1	Yuu chiki yoo.	Please listen.
2	X nkai chichi ndee.	Please (try) asking X.
3	Ichi ndee.	Please (try) saying it.
4	Naa chukeen ichi ndee.	Please (try) saying it once more.
5	Wakaim-i?	Do you understand?

For 5, you will respond with:
 'Yes' = Uu
 'No' = Wuu wuu

SELF-INTRODUCTION

Here are a few different ways you can introduce yourself. These are all formulaic expressions, and the English translations are rough equivalents which are provided as a guide. The translation in the parentheses are more literal translations. See further explanations after the model dialogues.

A: *Hai {tai/sai}. Hajimiti yaa {tai/sai}.* Hello. Nice to meet you. (It is the first time.)
 Wannee A yaibiin.   I'm A.
B: *Hai {tai/sai}. Wannee B ndi ichoo-ibiin.* Hello. I'm B. (I am called B.)
 Hawai daigaku nu shiitu yaibiin. I'm a student at the University of Hawaii.

A: *Hajimiti deebiru. A ndi iy-abiin.* Nice to meet you. (It is the first time.) I am A.
   Yutasarugutu unigee sabira. Nice to meet you. (Please take care of me well.)

B: *Hajimiti ya-ibiin yaa {tai/sai}.* Nice to meet you. (It is the first time.)
   Wannee B ndi ichoo-ibiin. I am B. (I am called B.)
   Yutasarugutu unigee sabira. Nice to meet you. (Please take care of me well.)

Notes

1. **Sai** and **Tai.** These two are gender-specific polite sentence-final particles. *Sai* is used by men while *tai* is used by women. They soften utterances and can be used with both plain and polite predicate endings, but it is not required that speakers end their sentences with them.

2. **Hajimiti** 'for the first time'. This word can appear with a few different ending expressions, and is appropriate to be used when you meet people for the first time.

- *Hajimiti yaibiin.*   'It is the first time.'
- *Hajimiti deebiru.*   'It is the first time.'
- *Hajimiti yaa {sai/tai}.*   'It is the first time.'

3. **Wannee [A] yaibiin**. *Wannee* means 'I' in the topic form (Lesson 1). *Wannee A yaibiin* means 'I am A.' This is a common way to introduce yourself: *Wannee Niko yaibiin* 'I am Niko'; *Wannee Kaya yaibiin* 'I am Kaya.' You can use the same construction to describe what you do (i.e., occupation): *Wannee [Hawai daigaku nu shiitu] yaibiin* 'I am [a student at the University of Hawaii].'

4. **X nu Y.** X in this construction modifies Y, e.g., 'Y of/in/at/from X'. *Hawai daigaku nu shiitu* means 'a student at University of Hawaii.' A few examples are:

- *UCLA nu shinshii*   'a teacher at UCLA'
- *Hawai nu hana*   'flowers in Hawaii'
- *Uchinaa nu uta*   'songs of Okinawa'

5. **Wannee [B] ndi iyabiin / ichooibiin.** This is another way to introduce yourself, using the phrase *ndi iyabiin/ichooibiin* 'is called', so *Wannee Ooshiro ndi iyabiin/ichooibiin* means 'I am called Oshiro (= I am Oshiro).'

6. **Yutasarugutu unigeesabira.** Literally, this expression means 'Please take care of me well.' It is a good expression to end your self-introduction. It expresses your hope for future smooth human relations with a newly acquainted person.

EXERCISES

1. Practice introducing yourself with the [*Wannee [A] yaibiin*] construction. Substitute [A] with your own name.

- *Wannee [A] yaibiin.*

Common Okinawan last names include: Ōshiro, Higa, Kinjō, Nakama, and Shinzato. Pretend that you have one of these names and introduce yourself. If you have an Okinawan name, use it.

- *Wannee Ooshiro yaibiin.* etc.

2. Practice introducing yourself with the [*Wannee [B] ndi iyabiin / ichooibiin*] construction. Substitute B with your own name.

- *Wannee B ndi {iyabiin / ichooibiin}.*

Pretend your name is one of the common Okinawan names above and practice these sentences. If you have an Okinawan name, use it.

- *Wannee Ooshiro ndi {iyabiin / ichooibiin}.*

3. You can use the [*Wannee [A] yaibiin*] construction to describe what you do (i.e., occupation). Expand your sentence above with the [*X nu Y*] construction following the first sentence.

- *Wannee UCLA nu shinshii yaibiin.* etc.   'I am a teacher at UCLA.'

4. Have a conversation with your partner following the format below.

A: *Hai {sai / tai}.*
B: *Hai {sai / tai}.*
A: (Say your name with *ndi iyabiin*). 'Nice to meet you.'
B: (Say your name with *ndi ichooibiin*). 'Nice to meet you.'
A: (Say your occupation with X *nu* Y)
B: (Say your occupation with X *nu* Y)
A: '*Yutasarugutu unigeesabira.*'
B: '*Yutasarugutu unigeesabira.*'

NOTE ON ONLINE CONTENT

An answer key to the exercises and audio files for lesson dialogues may be accessed at https://go.hawaii.edu/7Xn or by using the QR code below.

PART I

CONVERSATION

CAST OF CHARACTERS

Niko (an exchange student) and his host family

Niko — Yuna — Host Mother — Host Father

Host Great-Grandmother — Host Grandfather

People in Niko's circle:

Teacher — Amy — Pensy — Shogo

LESSON 1

Okinawan New Year

DIALOGUE A

An international student, Niko, is spending his first New Year's Day in Okinawa with his homestay family. He is now talking to Yuna, his host sister, who is a college student in Okinawa.

Niko:	Happy New Year!	Happy New Year!
Yuna:	**Uree**, Uchinaaguchi **shee** "yii soogwachi deebiru" **ndi iin**. Anshikara, "uwakaku naimisoochii?" **ndi iin doo**.	For that, in Okinawan we say, "*yii soogwachi deebiru.*" Then (we say), "*uwakaku naimisoochii?*"
Niko:	Umu(s)san **yaa**.	That's interesting!

CORE VOCABULARY

Notes on vocabulary: (a) The arrow (←) means "derived from"; (b) the plus sign (+) after the arrow indicates the breaks in words and phrases for easy understanding of their composition; (c) [A2] means "Grammar note (2) in section (A)" in the current lesson. If, for example, L5 is added before A2 (e.g. [L5(A2)]), it means the grammar note is found in Lesson 5.

uree	← *uri* 'that' + *ya* (TOP = topic)
ya	Topic particle [A2]
Uchinaaguchi	'Okinawan language' (*Uchinaa* = 'Okinawa'; *guchi* = 'language')
(s)shi	'by means of'
shee	← *shi* 'means' + *ya* (top)
yii soogwachi deebiru	Okinawan phrase for 'Happy New Year'
ndi	'that' (complementizer)
iin (or *ʔyun, iyun*)	'to say'
anshikara	'then'
Uwakaku naimi-soochii?	'You grew younger?'
u-wakaku	← *u* 'prefix' + *wakasan* 'young'[1]
doo	SFP [A5]
umu(s)san	'interesting'
yaa	SFP [A5]

[1] This *u-* is a prefix indicating politeness. This prefix is situation-dependent, and optional in some cases.

GRAMMAR A

1. Demonstratives: *kuri* 'this', *uri* 'that', *ari* 'that over there'

When we point at an object/person around us, we use demonstratives. While English has a two-way contrast, 'this' and 'that', Okinawan has a three-way contrast, *kuri, uri,* and *ari*. *Kuri* is similar to 'this' and used when an object/person is close to the speaker. *Uri* is similar to 'that' and used when it is close to the addressee. *Ari* can be expressed by 'that over there' in English and is used when an object/person is far away from both speaker and addressee [Part II, Topic 1].

There is another difference between English and Okinawan demonstratives. The Okinawan demonstratives *kuri, uri, ari* change shapes to *ku**nu**, u**nu***, and *a**nu***, respectively, when they precede a noun, while English *this* and *that* do not.

- *kunu u-cha*   'this tea'   (referring to the tea the speaker is drinking)
- *unu u-cha*   'that tea'   (referring to the tea the hearer is drinking)
- *anu hushi*   'that star over there' (referring to the star in the sky)

2. Topic particle: *ya*

Uree in the dialogue is a contracted form of *uri + ya*. *Ya* is a topic particle. Topics indicate what a sentence is about, roughly paraphrasable as 'as for' and 'speaking of'. Topic is an important grammatical concept in Okinawan. It often corresponds to the subject, but they are not the same [Part II, Topic 1]). In natural conversation, *uree* is by far more common than *uri ya*. *Ya* variously changes its form as shown below, but if the preceding noun ends with a **long** vowel as in *rafutee* 'Okinawan dish', *ʔwaa* 'pig', *ya* does NOT contract.

- *rafutee + ya* → *rafutee ya* [*rafutee* is an Okinawan dish. See Dialogue [B].]

There are four patterns and one exception.

- *a + ya* → **aa**   *Naafa*   + *ya* → *Naaf**aa*** (Capital of Okinawa)
- *i + ya* → **ee**   *kuri*   + *ya* → *kur**ee*** (this)
- *u + ya* → **oo**   *u-shiru* + *ya* → *u-shir**oo*** (soup);
                       iyu 'fish' + *ya* → *iy**oo*** (fish)
- *n + ya* → **noo**   *hun*   + *ya* → *hu**noo*** (book)
- Special form: **wan** 'I' + *ya* → *wan**nee*** (it is NOT *wanoo*)

3. Particle: *(s)shi* 'by means of'

Uchinaaguchi shi means 'in Uchinaaguchi'. However, this phrase is often topicalized with *ya*. So *Uchinaaguchi + shi + ya* comes out as '*Uchinaaguchi sh**ee***'. When the topic *ya* is followed, *shi,* instead of *sshi* is used.

- *Eego* **shee**   'in English'
- *Supeingo* **shee**   'in Spanish'
- *Hawaigo* **shee**   'in Hawaiian'
- *Kankokugo* **shee** 'in Korean'
- *Yamatuguchi* **shee** 'in Japanese'

4. Complementizer: *ndi*

The complementizer *ndi* corresponds to English 'that,' as in *John said **that** he would be late.* It is used with verbs of speech (*iin, iyun* or *ʔyun* 'to say') and thought (*umuin* 'to think'). In the dialogue, the construction [X *shee* Y *ndi iin*] '{It is called / We call it} Y in X' is used.

- *Uchinaaguchi shee "yii soogwachi deebiru"* **ndi iin**. 'In Okinawan (we) say, "*yii soogwachi deebiru*."'
- *Kuree Eego shee "starfish"* **ndi iin**. 'This is called "starfish" in English.'
- *Umu(s)san* **(n)di umuin**. 'I think it is interesting.' (Note: The initial *n* of *ndi* is fused with the final *n* of *umusan*.)

5. Sentence Final Particles (SFP): *doo* and *yaa*

a. *Doo*

This is one of many sentence final particles in Okinawan. It is used by the speaker when he/she thinks that the hearer does not yet know the information. It conveys the meaning something like, 'I tell you,' or 'Believe me!'

- *Kuree Eego shee "starfish" ndi iin* **doo**.
  'This is called "starfish" in English.'
- *Kuree Yamatuguchi shee "hitode" ndi iin* **doo**.
  'This is called "*hitode*" in Japanese.'
- *Kuree Hawaigo shee "pe'a" ndi iin* **doo**.
  'This is called "*pe'a*" in Hawaiian.'

b. *Yaa*

This is another sentence final particle. This particle adds the nuance of 'right?', 'you know', or 'I know you agree with me' at the end of a sentence. *Umusan yaa* as a whole means something like 'It's interesting, isn't it!' Here are a few more examples with different adjectives.

- *maasan* **yaa** 'It's delicious, isn't it?'
- cf. *maasan* **doo** 'It's delicious, I tell you (you should try it).'
- *achisan* **yaa** 'It's hot, isn't it?'

- *churasan* **yaa**   'It's beautiful, isn't it?'
- *muchikasan* **yaa**   'It's difficult, isn't it?'

ADDITIONAL VOCABULARY

achisan 'hot'
biiru 'beer'
churasan 'beautiful'
Eego 'English'
Hawaigo 'Hawaiian'
hun 'book'
hushi 'stars'
iyu 'fish'
kuri 'this'
maasan 'delicious'
muchikasan 'difficult'
Naafa 'Naha, the capital of Okinawa'
Orion '(the name of a popular Okinawan beer)'
saki '*sake*, rice wine'
sashimi 'sashimi (raw fish cuisine)'
shiitu 'student'
shiru 'soup'
sumuchi 'book'
sushi 'sushi'
tako raisu 'taco rice—Okinawan-American dish with a taco shell replaced by rice'
(u-)cha 'tea'
umi 'ocean'
uri 'that'
umuin 'to think'
wan 'I'
ʔwaa 'pig'
Yamatuguchi 'Japanese (language)'

EXERCISES A

1. Write the contracted form with *ya* for the following words. If the contraction is not possible, then write the uncontracted form.

    a. *uchinaaguchi* + *ya* → _____

    b. *sashimi* + *ya* → _____

    c. *u-cha* + *ya* → _____

    d. *sushi* + *ya* → _____

    e. *tako raisu* + *ya* → _____

    f. *Orion* + *ya* → _____

    g. *biiru* + *ya* → _____

    h. *ʔwaa* + *ya* → _____

    i. *iyu* + *ya* → _____

8   PART I   Conversation

2. Complete the following sentences using the words provided.

   a. "Turtle" ya (_____) "honu" (_____).
      [Hawaiigo, ndi, shee, iin]

   b. "Ocean" ya (_____) "umi" (_____).
      [ndi, Yamatuguchi, shee, iin]

   c. "Sake" ya (_____) "saki" (_____).
      [iin, shee, ndi, Uchinaaguchi]

3. Translate the following into *Uchinaaguchi*. Start each sentence with ' "Star" ya'.

   a. "Star" is called "*hushi*" in Okinawan.

   _____

   b. "Star" is called "*hoshi*" in Japanese.

   _____

   c. "Star" is called "*hōkū*" in Hawaiian.

   _____

   d. "Star" is called "*xīngxīng*" in Chinese (= *Chuugokugo*).

   _____

4. Complete the following sentences using the correct demonstrative form (*kuree/kunu, uree/unu, aree/anu*) (see [A1]).

   a. Referring to the sushi the speaker is eating.

      i. (_____) *maasan*.
      ii. (_____) *sushee maasan*.

LESSON 1 Okinawan New Year

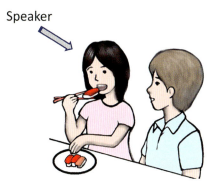

b. Referring to a student (*shiitu*) wearing a UCLA T-shirt over there, away from both the speaker and the hearer.

　i. (＿＿＿＿) *shiitoo UCLA nu shiitu yaibiin yaa.*

　ii. (＿＿＿＿) *UCLA nu shiitu yaibiin yaa.*

c. Referring to the Orion beer the hearer is drinking.

　i. (＿＿＿＿) *maasan.*

　ii. (＿＿＿＿) *biiroo maasan.*

10　PART I　Conversation

DIALOGUE B

Niko's host mother is explaining Okinawan New Year's food to him. Niko is trying different food items.

(Looking at the food on the table)

Niko:	*Ai, kwatchii* **yaibiin yaa**.	Wow, what a feast!
Mother:	*Uri, uri.*	Go ahead. (Try some.)
Niko:	*Nifee deebiru.*	Thank you.
	Anshee, kwatchii sabira.	Then, I will eat.
Mother:	**Chaa ya ga**?	How is it?
Niko:	*Ippee* **maasaibiin**.	It's very delicious.
	Kuree nuu *ndi iyabii* **ga**?	What do you call this?
Mother:	**Uree**, *nakami* **nu** *u-shiru, anshikara, rafutee, kubushimi, irichii…*	That is *nakami* soup and *rafutee, kubushimi* (cuttlefish sashimi), and *irichii* (stir-fried dish)…

CORE VOCABULARY

Notes on vocabulary (cont.): (d) [Cul2] means "Cultural note (2) in this lesson." If, for example, L5 is added before Cul2 (e.g. [L5(Cul2)], it means the cultural note is found in Lesson 5.

ai	exclamatory expression
kwatchii	'feast'
yaibiin	copula (POL.COP) [B1]
uri, uri	'here, here (go ahead)'
nifee deebiru	'thank you'
anshee	'then'
kwatchii sabira	expression said before meal

chaa	'how?' [B4]
ippee	'very'
maasaibiin	← *maasan* 'delicious' [B3]
nuu	'what?' [B4]
nakami	'pig intestines' [Cul2]
nu	genitive particle (GEN)
u-shiru	← *u* (polite prefix) + *shiru* 'soup'
rafutee	a traditional Okinawan dish in which chopped pork is slow cooked with soy sauce, sugar, and awamori liquor (WB) [Cul2]
kubushimi	'cuttlefish', often served as sashimi [Cul2]
irichii	'simmered vegetables' [Cul2]

GRAMMAR B

1. Copula: Plain and Polite Forms

The English copula *be* (*am, is, are*) appears between two nouns as in 'This *is* a feast' or 'A *is* B.' The Okinawan copula appears at the end of a sentence, [A B is]. Furthermore, Okinawan has two forms of the copula, *yan* (Plain Form) and *ya-ibiin* (Polite Form). Niko's first line, *kwatchii ya-ibiin* means '(It) is a feast.' Omission of a subject ('it' in this case) is quite common in Okinawan. Niko is using the Polite Form because he is talking to an older addressee, his host mother. If Niko is talking to a friend, he can use the plain form **yan** as in *kwatchii yan*. We may use a hyphen as in *ya-ibiin* occasionally to show the composition of a word, but the hyphen does not change the meaning of the word.

	Plain	Polite	English
Copula (COP)	*yan*	*ya-ibiin*	'be'

Here are a few examples of the copula construction [X-TOP Y-COP] 'X is Y' in the plain and polite copulas. The examples below use the contracted topic forms (e.g., *kuri + ya* → *kuree*).

- *Kuree rafutee* **yan***.*   'This is *rafutee*.' (plain)
- *Kuree rafutee* **yaibiin***.*   'This is *rafutee*.' (polite)

- *Uree sashimi **yan**.*   'That is sashimi.' (plain)
- *Uree sashimi **yaibiin**.*   'That is sashimi.' (polite)

- *Aree Ninufa-bushi **yan***   'That over there is the North Star.' (plain)
- *Aree Ninufa-bushi **yaibiin**.*   'That over there is the North Star.' (polite)

2. Verbs: Plain and Polite Forms

The plain-polite distinction is very regular for verbs, too. First, let's learn a few basic grammatical terms. The **Dictionary Form** is the form you find in a dictionary like the *Wordbook*. All dictionary verb forms end in either *-in* (e.g., *tu-in* 'to take') or *-un* (e.g., *chich-un* 'to listen/ask'). The form without *-in* or *-un* of the Dictionary Form is called the **Basic Root** (e.g., *tu-* and *chich-*). Verbs of the first type (with the *-in* ending) are called **vowel verbs** (or **V-verbs**), and verbs of the second type (with the *-un* ending) **consonant verbs** (or **C-verbs**), because the sound before a hyphen is a vowel or a consonant, respectively. The short form without the final *-n* of the Dictionary Form is called the **Apocopated Form** (e.g., *tui-* and *chichu-*). Here is a comparison of V- and C-verbs.

	Dictionary Form (= DIC.FORM)	Basic Root (= B.ROOT)	Apocopated Form (= APO.FORM)
V-verb ('to take')	*tu-in*	*tu-*	*tui-*
C-verb ('to listen')	*chich-un*	*chich-*	*chichu-*

The Dictionary Form is used for the Plain Form. For the Polite Form, *-in* and *-un* are changed to *-ibiin* and *-abiin*, respectively.

	Plain	Polite
V-verb ('to take')	*tu-in*	*tu-**ibiin***
C-verb ('to listen')	*chich-un*	*chich-**abiin***

In Dialogue [A], Yuna used the plain verb ***i-in*** (interchangeable with ***iy-un, ?y-un***) 'to say' because she is talking to her friend, Niko. In Dialogue [B], Niko used its Polite Form ***iy-abiin*** (or ***?y-abiin***) because he is talking to his host mother. The following table shows a comparison of the copula and different types of verbs. (The irregular verb *s-un* is also added.)

	Plain	Polite Form	English
Copula	ya-n	ya-*ibiin*	'to be'
V-verb	tu-in	tu-*ibiin*	'to take'
C-verb	chich-un	chich-*abiin*	'to listen, hear'
IRR	s-un	s-*abiin*	'to do'
IRR	i-in	iy-*abiin* / ʔy-*abiin*	'to say'

Here are a few more important V-verbs and C-verbs in the Plain and Polite Forms.

- waka-in → **waka-ibiin** (V-verb) 'to understand'
- na-in → **na-ibiin** (V-verb) 'to become/to be able to'
- kam-un → **kam-abiin** (C-verb) 'to eat'
- yum-un → **yum-abiin** (C-verb) 'to read'
- kach-u → **kach-abiin** (C-verb) 'to write'

3. Adjectives: Plain and Polite Forms

The plain-polite distinction is regular for adjectives, too. In [A], Niko used the Plain Adjective Form *umu(s)sa-n* 'interesting.' In (B), talking to his host mother, he used *maasa-ibiin* [Part II, Topic 4]. Here is a list of more adjectives.

Meaning	Plain	Polite
'hot'	achisa-n	achisa-ibiin
'cold'	hiisa-n	hiisa-ibiin
'big'	magisa-n	magisa-ibiin
'small'	gumasa-n	gumasa-ibiin
'high/expensive'	takasa-n	takasa-ibiin
'cheap'	yassa-n	yassa-ibiin
'fast'	feesa-n	feesa-ibiin
'slow'	niisa-n	niisa-ibiin
'young'	wakasa-n	wakasa-ibiin
'beautiful'	churasa-n	churasa-ibiin

 yii 'good' is exceptional [Part II, Topic 4]

4. Wh-Words: *nuu* 'what?', *chaa* 'how?', and the Wh-Question Particle *ga*

We introduce two wh-question words in this lesson: **nuu** 'what?' and **chaa** 'how?'. With these and other wh-words, you can make wh-questions ('What is this?', 'How is it?'). Unlike English, you don't need to bring the wh-word at the beginning of a question, but you must add a question particle at the end. The question particle for a wh-question is *ga*, while that for a yes/no question is *-i* (see [L3(B2)]). Note that before the question particle *ga*, the final *n* of the **Dictionary Forms** of the copula (*yan*), verbs (*iin*), and adjectives (*maasan*) drops. We learned that this form is called the **Apocopated Form** in [B2] above (see also Part II, Topic 3). The final *n* of *-ibiin/-aibiin* also drops before *ga*. Study the use of *ga* below (the superscript x indicates ungrammatical sequences).

- Wh + *yan* → Wh…*ya ga?* (ˣ *yan ga?*)
- Wh + *ya-ibiin* → Wh…*ya-ibii ga?* (ˣ *yaibiin ga?*)
- Wh + *iin* → Wh…*ii ga?* (ˣ *iin ga?*)
- Wh + *iy-abiin* → Wh…*iy-abii ga?* (ˣ *iyaibiin ga?*)
- Wh + *chichun* → Wh…*chichu ga?* (ˣ *chichun ga?*)
- Wh + *chich-abiin* → Wh…*chich-abii ga?* (ˣ *chich-abiin ga?*)
- Wh + *maasan* → Wh…*maasa ga?* (ˣ *maasan ga?*)
- Wh + *maasa-ibiin* → Wh…*maasa-ibii ga?* (ˣ *maasaibiin ga?*)

Here are a few examples.

- *Chaa ya ga?*   'How is it?' (Plain)
- A: *Kubushimee chaa ya-ibii ga?*   'How is *kubushimi*?' (Polite)
  B: *Ippee maasan.*   '(It) is very good.' (Plain)
- *Uree nuu ndi iy-abii ga?*   'What is that called?' (Polite)
- A: *Kuree nuu ya-ibii ga?*   'What is this?' (Polite)
  B: *Uree kubushimi yan doo.*   'That is *kubushimi*.' (Plain)

5. Particle: *nu* (genitive marker)

This particle is used between two nouns. The first noun modifies the second with various semantic relationships (Part II, Topic 2).

- *Nakami **nu** ushiru*   '*nakami* soup'
- *soogwachi **nu** kwatchii*   'New Year dishes'

ADDITIONAL VOCABULARY

bideo geemu 'video game'
chichun 'hear, listen'
gooyaa 'bitter melon'
gurukun 'popular fish in Okinawa'
kuruma 'car'

Ninufa-bushi 'pole star, North Star'
shiisaa 'lion-dog statue'
shinshii 'teacher'
tinsagu 'balsam flower'

EXERCISES B

1. Put either *chaa* or *nuu* in the parentheses, and translate each question into English.

   A: *Unu u-shiroo* (_____) *nu u-shiru yaibii ga?* [English: _____

   _____]

   B: *Nakami nu shiru yan doo.*
   (B serves the soup to A.)

   B: (_____) *ya ga.* [English: _____

   _____]

   A: *Ippee maasaibiin.*

2. Change the plain form in **bold** to the Polite Form, or the Polite Form to the Plain Form. Check the chart in [B3] above. Translate each sentence into English.

   a. *Tamaki-sanoo* **wakasan**. → _____.

      English: _____

   b. *Kunu tako-raisoo* **maasaibiin**. → _____.

      English: _____

   c. *Anu hushee* **churasan**. → _____.

      English: _____

   d. *Higa shinshii nu kurumaa* **magisaibiin**. → _____.

      English: _____

16   PART I   Conversation

3. Put the appropriate particle (*ga, nu, doo, yaa*) in the blank, and translate each sentence into English.

   a. A and C are talking to each other while playing a video game, *Final Fantasy*.

   A&C: *Ippee umusan* (_____). _____

   (B arrives and joins the conversation.)

   B: *Uree nuu ya* (_____)? _____

   A: *Bideo geemu yaibiin.*

   B: *Uree nuu* (_____) *geemu ya* (_____)? _____

   A: *Final Fantasy ndi iyabiin. Ippee umusaibiin* (_____). _____

   b. A and B met on New Year's Day.

   A: *Yii soogwachi yaibiin* (_____) *sai.* _____

   B: *Yan* (_____). _____

APPLICATIONS

1. Referencing the example conversation and illustrations below, talk to your partner about locating and identifying various objects around you. You can use English words such as 'desk' or 'pencil' for this exercise (but you already know how to say 'books').

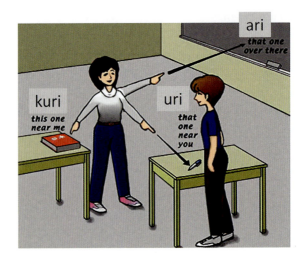

Example:

Q: *Aree **nuu** ya **ga**?*   ('What is that over there?')
A: *Aree _____ yaibiin.*   ('That over there is _____.')

2. Following the model dialogue between Amy and her host parent below, and using the pictures shown, make a conversation with your partner. Use the Polite and Plain forms appropriately. In addition, find pictures of Okinawan food on the internet, and make similar conversations.

   Model Dialogue:

   Amy: *Kuree nuu yaibii ga?*   'What is this?'
   Host parent: *Kubushimi yan. Maasan doo.*   'This is cuttlefish sashimi. It's delicious.'

Tinsagu   *Gooyaa*   *Gurukun*   *Shiisaa*

3. Using the images in (2), ask your partner how to say a word in Okinawan/English (*Eego*), or any other language.

   Example:

   A: *Kuree Uchinaaguchi shee nuu ndi ii ga?*   'What is this called in Okinawan?'
   B: *Uree tinsagu ndi iin doo.*   'It is *tinsagu*.'

4. There are many Okinawan foods with unique Okinawan names, such as *duruwakashi, ashitibichi, mimigaa, andaagii,* etc. Look up what they are on the internet, and share your findings with your classmates.

CULTURAL NOTES

1. New Year's Greetings in Okinawan

The Okinawan New Year's Day greeting, "*Uwakaku naimisoochii?*" (You grew younger?), may be puzzling to you. It may make more sense if you know a custom of scooping of *waka-miji* '(lit.) young-water'. On New Year's Day, in some villages, the (first-born) son goes to a sacred well to fetch some water. This water is *waka-miji* or 'young-water'.

The embedded concept, 'young' is very important in Okinawan culture, signifying 'birth' and 'fullness of energy'. There are compounds such as *waka-nachi* '(lit.) young (i.e., early) summer' and *waka-tiida* '(lit.) young (rising) sun at dawn'.

- Do you know any other interesting New Year customs from around the world?
- Do you know any other unique greetings from other cultures or in other languages?

2. New Year's Dishes

Below are some typical dishes Okinawan people have for the New Year. *Nakami* soup is soup with pork intestines.

Nakami soup   *Rafutee*   *Kubushimi* (cuttlefish sashimi)   *Irichii* (simmered vegetables and seaweed)

- Do you eat/drink something special on New Year's Day?
- Are there any traditional auspicious dishes in your culture?

3. "Okinawa: *Ganjuu naganuchi Okinawa-ken*" (Prefecture of a Healthy and Long Life)

Okinawa has been often referred to as the prefecture of long life, which has in turn drawn attention to Okinawan cuisine. For example, when an NHK program advocated for *gooyaa* as a healthy food, everyone rushed to supermarkets to buy it. As a result, stores completely sold out of *gooyaa*.

- How does your diet compare to the typical Okinawan diet?
- Do some research on the Okinawan diet. What more can you tell us about the healthy foods Okinawan people consume?

✏️ Okinawa was known worldwide for its longevity. The phrase 健康・長寿の沖縄県 ('Prefecture of a healthy and long life') was coined at that time. The Okinawan translation was adopted from Takara Ben, 沖縄生活誌 [Okinawa Lifestyle Magazine], (Tokyo: Iwanami Shoten, 2005b), 62–63.

4. *"Kwatchii sabira"* and *"Nifee deebiru"*

Kwatchii sabira is an expression used right before your meal. *Kwatchii* means a 'feast' and *sabira* means 'let's do ~' or 'let me do ~'. It signifies your gratitude for the provider of the meal, such as the chef, cook, or your family member who cooks for you. *Nifee deebiru* is a standard way of saying "Thank you." It came from *mi-fai* 'three bows' followed by *-du-ya-ibiiru* 'the focus particle and polite copula' (Kinjō [1944] 1974: 141). This means '(something) is worthy of bowing three times'. The initial *mi* went through a phonological change to become *ni*.

LESSON 2

Okinawan New Year Family Gathering

DIALOGUE A

Niko's host family is having a New Year family gathering at their house with all their relatives. Niko's friend Amy is also there. It is very lively.

Niko:	*Taarii sai, kuree/kumaa waa dushi yaibiin.*	Father, this is my friend.
Amy:	*Amy yaibiin.* **Wan nin** *UCLA nu shiitu yaibiin. Yutasaru gutu unigee sabira.*	I am Amy. I am also a UCLA student. Nice to meet you.
Father:	*ʔyaa n Uchinaaguchi jooji yan yaa.*	You are good at Okinawan, too.
Amy:	*Kuree Amirika nu u-kwaashi yaibiin.*	These are some sweets from America.
Father:	**Nifee** *doo.*	Thanks.

CORE VOCABULARY

taarii	'father, dad'
sai/tai	polite suffix (cf. Preliminary Lesson)
kumaa	this person, more polite than *kuree* [B5]
waa	'my'
dushi	'friend'
wan nin	'I also' [A1]
ʔyaa	'you, second person singular' [B1]
n	'also' [A3]
jooji	'skillful, good'
u-kwaashi	← *u* polite prefix + *kwaashi* 'sweets'
nifee doo	'Thank you', less formal than *nifee deebiru* [L1(DialA)]

GRAMMAR A

1. Personal Pronouns (First Person)

The table below summarizes the first person pronouns of singular (sg.) and plural (pl.) forms. (The second and third person pronouns will be discussed in [B] and [C], respectively.)

	First Person			
sg.	*wan* 'I'	*wannee* 'I-TOP'	*wan nin* 'I also'	*waa/wan* 'my'
pl.	*wattaa* 'we'	*wattaa ya* 'we-TOP'	*wattaa n* 'we also'	*wattaa* 'our'

The basic singular first person form ('I') is *wan*, which changes to *wannee* (the topic form) and *wan nin* (the additive topic form) 'I also' (see [A3]). The plural first person ('we') is *wattaa*, which has the topic form *wattaa ya* and the additive topic form *wattaa n* 'we also'.

- *wannee* Amy yaibiin. 'I am Amy.'
- *wannee* Amirikajin yaibiin. 'I am an American.'
- *wan nin* Amirikajin yaibiin. 'I am American, too.'

- *wattaa ya* Hawai daigaku nu shiitu yaibiin.   'We are UH students.'
- *wattaa n* Hawai daigaku nu shiitu yaibiin.   'We are UH students, too.'

The possessive form for the first person singular ('my') is *waa/wan* (but we only use *waa* below, if *wan* is not possible, it is noted), and the plural form ('our') is *wattaa*. It is important to remember that these forms do not use the typical linking particle (*nu*): **waa** / ˣ **wan** *nu dushi* [Part II, Topic 2].

- *waa dushi*   'my friend'
- *waa kuruma*   'my car'
- *waa computer*   'my computer'
- *waa mun* / ˣ *wan mun*   'my thing'
- *wattaa shinshii*   'our teacher'

2. Family Terms

In Dialogue [A], *taarii* 'father' is used, and more family terms appear in Dialogue [C]. Kinship terms in Okinawan are organized differently from English. For example, the gender of younger siblings is irrelevant as both younger brothers and younger sisters are called *uttu*. On the other hand, the genders of older siblings are crucial; an older brother is *yatchii* and an older sister *ʔnmii*. See the family tree and a summary table below.

It is also important to note that family terms show great variations by region, social class, historical period, and so forth. The family terms adopted in this textbook reflect the traditional Shuri regional variety, which may not be used widely today. In fact, *suu* 'father' may be more popular than *taarii* 'father', and *anmaa* 'mother' more popular than *ayaa* 'mother'. Furthermore, the use of terms originating from Japanese are widespread in Modern Okinawan. Thus, the following terms are commonly heard: *ojii* 'grandfather', *obaa* 'grandmother', *otoosan/toochan* 'father', *okaasan/kaachan* 'mother', *nii nii* 'big brother', and *nee nee* 'big sister'.

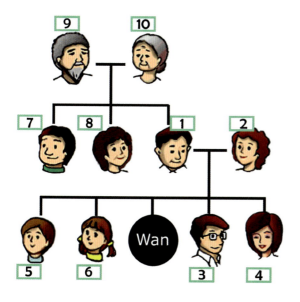

1	taarii	father
2	ayaa	mother
3	yatchii	older brother
4	ʔnmii	older sister
5	wikiga uttu	younger brother
6	winagu uttu	younger sister
7	wujasaa	uncle
8	wubamaa	aunt
9	tanmee	grandfather
10	ʔnmee	grandmother

At the beginning of this section, we explained that *uttu* is used for both male and female younger siblings, but they can be distinguished by adding *wikiga* 'male' and *winagu* 'female'; *wikiga uttu* 'younger brother' and *winagu uttu* 'younger sister'. We also noted older siblings are distinguished by gender. However, there is also the term *shiija*, which refers to both male and female older siblings. These terms may be also combined with *wikiga* 'male' and *winagu* 'female' to create innovative labels, though such uses are not very common.

| 11 | (wikiga/winagu) | shiija | (male/female) older sibling |
| 12 | (wikiga/winagu) | uttu | (male/female) younger sibling |

There is another interesting cultural fact associated with the family terms. To say 'my father/mother', the first person PLURAL form (*wattaa* 'our') is used instead of the first person SINGULAR form (*waa*). It is strange to say *waa taarii* 'my father' and you should instead say *wattaa taarii* 'our father'. Also, *ʔyaa shinshii* 'your (sg.) teacher' sounds awkward, and instead *ittaa shinshii* 'your (pl.) teacher' should be used (see *wattaa shinshii* in [A1] [Part II, Topic 1]).

3. Additive Topic Particle: *n*

We introduced the topic particle *ya* in Lesson 1. Here, we introduce the additive topic particle *n*, which means 'also/too'. Unlike the topic particle, this particle does not contract to change its shapes.

- kuri   'this'   + **n** → kuri **n**   'this also'
- uri   'that'   + **n** → uri **n**   'that also'
- ari   'that over there'   + **n** → ari **n**   'that over there also'

However, there are two exceptions you should remember:

a. If the final sound of the preceding word is **n** as in *Orion*, **un** is used instead of **n**.

- Orion   + **n** → Orion **un** 'Orion, too'
- hun   + **n** → hun **un**   'book, too'
- in   + **n** → in **un**   'dog, too'

- *Orion* **un** *maasan doo.*   'Orion Beer is also delicious, you know.'
- *Kunu hun* **un** *umu(s)san doo*   'This book is also interesting, you know.'

b. For *wan* 'I', *nin* is used instead of *n*.

- wan   + **n** → wan **nin**   'I also'

ADDITIONAL VOCABULARY

in 'dog' (see also **first person pronouns** in G1 and **family terms** in G2.)

EXERCISES A

1. Give the opposites of the following family terms.

   a. *uttu*   ↔ _____

   b. *taarii* ↔ _____

   c. *yatchii* ↔ _____

   d. *ʔnmee*   ↔ _____

2. Complete a script for the following scene by filling in the blanks. Yuna is introducing her friend Niko to her Okinawan teacher, *Higa shinshii* 'Prof. Higa'.

   Yuna: *Higa shinshii* (_____). *Kumaa* (_____)

   dushi (_____).

   Niko: *Hajimiti yaa* (_____). (_____)

   Niko ndi (_____). (_____)

   unigee sabira.

   Higa: *Hajimiti yaa.* (_____) *Higa ya sa.* (See [B7] for *sa*.)

3. Fill in the blanks with the appropriate word + topic/additive topic particle. If a contraction is possible, use the contracted form (e.g., *uree* instead of *uri + ya*). The two speakers in each conversation are friends.

   a. Lina is pointing to the Orion constellation **far away** in the sky.

   Lina: *Anu* (_____) *Orion ndi iin doo.*

   Leo: (Pointing to the Orion beer **near** him) (_____) *Orion ndi iin doo.*

   b. Edie: (_____) *maasaibiin yaa.* 'Kirin is good.'

   Mr. Takushi: (_____) *maasan doo.* _____ 'Orion is good, too.'

26　PART I　Conversation

c. Ms. Goya:　　Hajimiti deebiru. (＿＿＿＿＿)
　　　　　　　　 Goya ya-ibiin.

　Mr. Nigauri:　(＿＿＿＿＿) Nigauri ndi iyabiin doo.

✎ Both *Goya* and *Nigauri* are real family names. *Goya* in Okinawan and *Nigauri* in Japanese both mean bitter melon.

DIALOGUE B

Niko's host father is talking to Niko and Amy.

Father:	***Ittaa** ya **ikuchi** nai ga?*	How old are you (plural)?
Niko:	*Nijuuichi yaibiin.*	Twenty-one.
Amy:	*Wannee hatachi yaibiin.*	I am twenty.
Father:	*Anshee, uri. Kirin biiru **nu a** sa.*	Then, here is a Kirin beer.
	*Orion**un an** doo.*	There is also Orion beer.
Niko:	*Nifee deebiru.*	Thank you very much.
(Niko noticing Father pouring beer into a tall glass)		
	Too too too, yutasaibiin.	Oh, it's too much!

CORE VOCABULARY

ittaa	2nd person plural [B1]
ikuchi	'how old?' [B8]
nai (APO.FORM)	← *nain* 'to become'
nijuuichi	'21' [B2]
hatachi	'20 years old'

Kirin	'Kirin beer'
nu	subject particle [B3]
a (APO.FORM)	← *an* 'to exist, there is' [B4]
sa	SFP [B7]
too too (too)	exclamation
yutasa-ibiin	← *yutasan* 'fine' + *ibiin* 'polite'

GRAMMAR B

1. Personal Pronouns (Second Person)

	Second Person			
sg.	*unju* (polite) / *ʔyaa* (plain) 'you'	*unjoo* / *ʔyaa ya* 'you TOP'	*unju n* / *ʔyaa n* 'you also'	*unju {ga/nu}* / *ʔyaa* 'your'
pl.	*unju naa taa* (polite) / *ittaa* (plain) 'you (pl.)'	*unju naa taa ya* / *ittaa ya* 'you (pl.) TOP'	*unju naa taa n* / *ittaa n* 'you (pl.) also'	*unju naa taa* / *ittaa* 'your' (pl.)

- The second person pronoun *unju* is more polite than *ʔyaa*. The same is true for *unju naa taa* vs. *ittaa*.
- *taa* and *naa* in *unju naa taa* are both plural-making suffixes (OGJ1: 559). Thus, *unju naa taa* actually involves two plural-forming suffixes. It is possible to use only *naa*, i.e., *unju naa*.
- *Unju* requires a possessive particle, *ga* or *nu*, as in *unju ga / unju nu*, but its plural form, *unju naa taa*, does not [Part II, Topic 1].

2. Numbers

Okinawan uses both the indigenous and the Sino-Japanese number systems. The indigenous system is used when counting up to ten:

(1) *tiichi*   (3) *miichi*   (5) *ichichi*   (7) *nanachi*   (9) *kukunuchi*
(2) *taachi*   (4) *yuuchi*   (6) *muuchi*   (8) *yaachi*   (10) *tuu*

After ten, Sino-Japanese numerals are used, as in (11) *juuichi*, (12) *juuni*, etc.

Traditionally, however, *tuu tiichi* (ten-one) for 11, *tuu taachi* (ten-two) were used. In literature, *nanachi kasabitaru* (seven doubled) for 14 (*Kumiodori, Shūshin Kaneiri*) is used.

3. Particles: *ga* and *nu* (Subject Markers)

There are two subject particles, *ga* and *nu* [Part II, Topic 2]. *Ga* marks human subjects while *nu* marks non-human (animal) or inanimate subjects, as shown in the next section.

4. Verbs of Existence: *wun* (*wuibiin*) vs. *an* (*aibiin*)

There are two verbs of existence: *wun* is used for animate subjects (both humans and animals), while *an* is used for inanimate subjects. Their polite counterparts are *wuibiin* and *aibiin*, respectively. The choice of subject particle and those of existential verb are coordinated as shown in the examples below.

- *Shiitu **ga** wun.*   'There is a student.'   human subject
- *Shinshii **ga** wuibiin.*   'There is a teacher.'   human subject

- *Nuu **nu** wu ga?*   'What (animal) is there?'   animate (non-human) subject
- *Mayaa **nu** wun.*   'There is a cat.'   animate (non-human) subject

- *Kirin **nu** an.*   'There is Kirin beer.'   inanimate subject
- *Uchinaaguchi nu hun **nu** aibiin.* 'There is an Okinawan language book.' inanimate subject

5. Location Demonstratives: *kuma* 'here', *ʔnma* 'there', *ama* 'over there'

Lesson 1 introduced demonstratives (*kuri, uri, ari; kunu, unu, anu*). Location demonstratives (*kuma, ʔnma, ama*) are related to these words [Part II, Topic 1]. These could be used referring to people, and they are more polite than *kuri* 'this', *uri* 'that person', *ari* 'that person over there'.

6. Particle: *nkai* 'at, in, on'

This particle follows a location word, and is used with verbs of existence:

LOCATION ***nkai*** + {*an* / *wun*} = '(something/someone is) at/in/on LOCATION'

- *ʔyaa hunoo **kuma** nkai **an** doo.*   'Your book is here.'
- *Ittaa inoo **ama** nkai **wu** sa.*   'Your dog is over there.'

- *Ama* nkai Amy ga **wun**.   'There is Amy over there.'
- *Kuma* nkai mayaa nu **wun**.   'There is a cat here.'
- *Ugushiku ya Sui* nkai **an**.   'Shuri Castle is in Shuri.' (*Sui* = capital of Ryukyu Kingdom, *Ugushiku* = Shuri castle)

7. Sentence Final Particle: *sa*

Like *doo* introduced in Lesson 1 [A5], the Sentence Final Particle (SFP) *sa* conveys some information to the addressee which they suspect he/she does not know. In a simplistic comparison, *sa* is more emphatic/exclamatory and assertive compared to *doo*. Moreover, they are also different because they attach to different forms. As shown below, *doo* simply attaches to the dictionary form of a verb/adjective (e.g. *an doo* 'There is one, you know'; *churasan doo* 'It's beautiful, you know'), while *sa* attaches to Apocopated Forms (e.g. *a sa* 'Oh, there is one!'; *churasa sa* 'I tell you, it's beautiful!').

- A: *Anshee, uri. Kirin nu **a sa**.*   'Then, here, we have Kirin!'

  B: *Orion un **an doo**.*   'We have Orion, too, you know.'
- A: *Ai! **Achisa sa**!*   'Oh, it's hot!'

  B: ***Achisan doo.***   'I am telling you it's hot.'

8. Wh-Word: *ikuchi* 'how old?' / 'how many things?'

The question word *ikuchi* can be used to ask both 'How many?' as well as 'How old?'. As explained in [L1(B4)], a question with a question word ends with *ga* which follows the Apocopated Form.

- A: *ʔyaa ya **ikuchi** nai ga?*   'How old are you?'

  B: ***Nijuuichi** yaibiin.*   'Twenty-one.'
- A: *Orionoo **ikuchi** a ga?*   'How many bottles of Orion are there?'

  B: ***Yaachi** aibiin.*   'There are eight (bottles).'

For *iku tai* 'how many people', see [C5].

ADDITIONAL VOCABULARY

aakeejuu 'dragonfly'
haabeeruu 'butterfly'
mayaa 'cat'
nkai 'in, at, on'
tui 'bird'

ugushiku 'Shuri castle'
warabi 'child'
ʔwenchu 'mouse'
warabi-n-chaa 'children'
yaa 'house, family'

EXERCISES B

1. How do you say the following numbers in Okinawan?
   a. One
   b. Three
   c. Five
   d. Two
   e. Four

2. Select the correct word

   a. Higa: *ʔyaa ya uttu { **nu** / **ga** } { **an** / **wun** } yaa.* 'You have a sibling (at your house), right?'

   Niko: *Uu, uttu ga {**aibiin** / **wuibiran** / **wuibiin** } doo.*

   'Yes, (I have) a younger brother.'

   *Shiija (**ya/n**) { **aibiran** / **wuibiran** / **wuibiin** }.*

   '(I) do not have an older sibling.'

   b. Higa: *ʔyaa ya { **nuu** / **ikuchi** } nai ga?* 'How old are you?'

   Amy: *Nijuu ichi naibiin.* 'I am twenty-one years old.'

   Higa: *Orion { **nu** / **ga** } a sa. Kirin { **n** / **un** } an doo. Uri, Uri.* 'There is Orion beer. Kirin beer, too. Here, go ahead.'

3. Insert *ga, nu, nkai, n,* or *ikuchi* in the parentheses. For the other spaces, fill in the numbers in Okinawan.

   a. Picture A

   A: *Ama (_____) nuu (_____) wu ga?*

   B: *Tui (_____) wuibiin doo.*

   A: *(_____) wu ga?*

   B: _____ *wuibiin.*

   b. Picture B

   A: *ʔnma (_____) Gooyaa (_____) ikuchi a ga?*

   B: _____ *aibiin.*

c. Modeling after conversations (a) and (b) above, and using the words in the Word Bank, create your own dialogues. Draw appropriate pictures as well.

Word Bank: [dragonfly and butterfly (or plurals); mouse (mice)]

DIALOGUE C

Niko:	*Anu tchoo taa yaibii ga?*	Who are those people?
Father:	*Attaa ya yatchii tu ʔnmii yan.*	They are my older brother and my older sister.
	Shiija nu chaa ya tai gakkoo nu shinshii yan doo.	They are both schoolteachers.
Niko:	*Wattaa uya n tai shinshii yaibiin doo.*	My parents are also schoolteachers.
Father:	*ʔyaa ya choodee ya **iku tai** wu ga?*	How many siblings do you have?
Niko:	*Uttu ga chui wuibiin.*	I have one younger brother.
	*Tanmee n ʔnmee n **wuibiran**.*	I do not have a grandfather or grandmother.
	Yaaninjoo uya tu uttu tu wan… *Yu **ttai** yaibiin. Ikirasaibiin.* ***Ufukoonee(ya)biran**.*	With my parents, my younger brother, and myself, there are four people in my family. It's a small one. It's not big.

CORE VOCABULARY

tchoo	← *tchu* 'person' + *ya* (TOP)
taa	'who?'
attaa	'they' [C1]
yatchii	'older brother' [A2]
tu	'and'
ʔnmii	'older sister' [A2]
shiija	'older sibling' [A2]
chaa	plural suffix used as in kinship terms

tai (ttai, tchai)	classifier for people [C5]
gakkoo	'school'
uya	'parents'
choodee	'siblings'
iku tai	'how many (people)?' [C5]
uttu	'younger sibling' [A2]
chui	'one (person)'
tanmee	'grandfather'
ʔnmee	'grandmother'
yaaninjoo	← yaaninju 'family' + ya (TOP)
yu ttai	'four (people)'
ikirasaibiin	← ikirasan 'few, small quantity'
ufukoonee(ya)biran	'not many' ← negative of ufusan 'many', 'much' [C4]
wuibiran	'not exist' ← negative of wuibiin 'exist' [C2]

GRAMMAR C

1. Personal Pronouns (Third Person)

	\multicolumn{4}{c}{3rd Person}			
sg.	ari 'he/she'	aree 'he/she-TOP'	ari n 'he/she also'	ari ga 'his/her'
pl.	attaa 'they'	attaa ya 'they-TOP'	attaa n 'they also'	attaa 'their'

Notice *ari* 'he/she' has the same form as the demonstrative *ari* 'that one over there'. A word of caution: *Ari* cannot be used if one refers to elders or respected people like a teacher. Instead, *anu tchu* is used as in Dialogue C.

2. Negative Forms: The Copula and the Existential Verbs

The negative form of *wun* (the existential verb for humans and animals) is regular. Use the negative suffix, *-ran* (Plain) or *-ibiran* (Polite):

- *wu* + *-ran* → *wu-ran* (Negative Plain)
- *wu* + *-ibiran* → *wu-ibiran* (Negative Polite)

In contrast, the Negative Form of *an* (the existential verb for inanimate nouns) is completely irregular:

- **neen (or nee-ran)** (Negative Plain)
- **nee-biran/nee-yabiran** (Negative Polite)

The negative form of *yan* (copula) is also irregular:

- **aran** (Negative Plain)
- **a-ibiran** (Negative Polite)

Below is a comparative chart. As noted, there are irregularities for *ya-n* and *a-n*, marked by *.

Affirmative		Negative		Meaning
Plain	Polite	Plain	Polite	
wu-n	wu-ibiin	wu-ran	wu-ibi-ran	'to exist' (animate)
a-n	a-ibiin	neen*/nee-ran*	nee-bi-ran/nee-yabi-ran	'to exist' (inanimate)
ya-n	ya-ibiin	a-ran*	a-ibi-ran	'copula'

There is one more thing to keep in mind. Compare the affirmative and negative copula sentences below. Changing *yan/yaibiin* to *aran/aibiran* is not enough. The topic particle *ya* also has to be added to the noun before the negative copula forms. This applies to other verbs as well [Part II, Topic 3].

- *Wannee shinshii* **yan**. 'I am a teacher.'
- *Wannee shinshii* **ya aran**. 'I am not a teacher.'
- *Kuree Uchinaaguchi* **yaibiin**. 'This is Okinawa.'
- *Kuree Uchinaaguchee* (←Uchinaaguchi + **ya**) 'This is not Okinawa.'
  aibiran.

The topic particle *ya* is also used with the subject when the negative forms of the existential verbs, *wun* and *an*, are used.

- *Shiitoo* (←shiitu + **ya**) **wuibiran**. 'There is no student.'
- *Mayaa* **ya wuran**. 'There is no cat.'
  (cf. *Mayaa* **nu** wun 'There is a cat.')
- *Kirinoo* (←Kirin + **ya**) **neen/neeran**. 'There is no Kirin beer.'
- *Uchinaaguchi nu hunoo* (←hun + **ya**) **nee(ya)** 'There are no Okinawan books.'
  biran.

3. Negative Forms: Other Verbs

a. Polite Negative Forms

The Polite Negative forms of the other verbs are mostly regular. For both V-verbs and C-verbs, replace the final *-in* with *-ran*.

V-verbs		
Finite Form	Negative Form	Meaning
tu-ibi-**in**	tu-ibi-**ran**	'to take'
na-ibi-**in**	na-ibi-**ran**	'to become'
waka-ibi-**in**	waka-ibi-**ran**	'to understand, to know'

C-verbs		
Finite Form	Negative Form	Meaning
ʔwiij-abi-**in**	ʔwiij-abi-**ran**	'to swim'
kunj-abi-**in**	kunj-abi-**ran**	'to tie up'
kach-abi-**in**	kach-abi-**ran**	'to write'

b. Plain Negative Forms

To make the Plain Negative Form of a V-verb, add *-ran* to the Negative Root (N.ROOT).

Finite Form	Negative Form	Verb Class	Meaning
tu-in (L1)	tu-**ran**	V-verb	'to take'
na-in (L2)	na-**ran**	V-verb	'to become'
waka-in (L1)	waka-**ran**	V-verb	'to understand'

To make the Plain Negative Form of a C-verb, add *-an* to the Negative Root (N.ROOT). The Basic Root (i.e., the Dictionary form without the final *-un*) and the Negative Root are identical for #6–9, but they are different for #1–5 and must be memorized. For Verb Classes, see the classification used in the *Wordbook*.

	Dictionary Form	Negative Form	Verb Class	Meaning
1	ʔwii*j*-un	ʔwii*g*-an	IIa1	'to swim'
2	nin*j*-un	nin*d*-an	IIa2	'to sleep'
3	kun*j*-un (L4)	kun*d*-an	IIa3	'to tie up'
4	ka*ch*-un	ka*k*-an	IIb1	'to write'
5	mu*ch*-un	mu*t*-an	IIb2	'to hold'
6	turas-un (L4)	turas-an	IIc	'to give'
7	yu*b*-un	yu*b*-an	IId	'to invite'
8	yu*m*-un	yu*m*-an	IIe	'to read'
9	shin-un	shin-an	IIf	'to die'[1]

[1] *shinun* 'die' is used only for animals except for certain circumstances (cf. *Wordbook*, pp. xv, 161). For humans, *maasun* is used. In addition, *shinun* is the only verb that belongs to this category. Therefore this verb will not be included for the rest of the tables in this textbook.

Here are some examples:

- *Wannee chuu ya ʔwiigan. Achaa ʔwiijun.* 'I will not swim today. I will swim tomorrow.'
- *Yaaninju ya yubun. Dushee yuban doo.* 'I will invite my family. I will not invite my friends.'

4. Negative Forms: Adjectives

To make negative adjectives, you change the **-san** of the dictionary form to **-kooneen/-kooneeran**. There is no difference in meaning or use between the two forms.

- *achi-san*   'hot'   → *achi-kooneen* / *achi-kooneeran*   'not hot'
- *hii-san*   'cold'   → *hii-kooneen* / *hii-kooneeran*   'not cold'
- *chura-san* 'beautiful' → *chura-kooneen* / *chura-kooneeran* 'not beautiful'

Polite negative adjectives are formed by changing **kooneen/kooneeran** to **koonee(ya)biran**.

- *achi-kooneen/-kooneeran*   → *achi-koonee(ya)biran*   'not hot (polite)'
- *hii-kooneen/-kooneeran*   → *hii-koonee(ya)biran*   'not cold (polite)'
- *chura-kooneen/-kooneeran* → *chura-koonee(ya)biran* 'not beautiful (polite)'

The adjective forms are summarized below.

Affirmative		Negative		Meaning
Plain	Polite	Plain	Polite	
achi-san	achi-saibiin	achi-kooneen/achi-kooneeran	achi-koonee(ya)biran	'not hot'

Here are some examples:

- *Hawai ya hiikooneen.*   'Hawaii is not cold.'
- *Uchinaa n hiikooneen.*   'Okinawa is not cold either.'
- *Wattaa yaaninjoo ufukooneen.*   'Our family is not big.'
- *Kubushimee yashikooneen*[1]   'Cuttlefish sashimi is not cheap.'

[1] *yassan* 'cheap' → *yashikooneen* 'not cheap' (This negative form is irregular)

5. Wh-Words: *taa* 'who?/whose?', *iku tai* 'how many people?'

We learned three wh-words so far: *nuu* 'what?', *chaa* 'how?', and *ikuchi* 'how many/how old?'. We introduce two more wh-words here: *taa* 'who?' and *iku tai* 'how many people?'. When *taa* appears before a noun, it means 'whose?' as in *taa mun* 'whose (thing)?' *taa sumuchi* 'whose book?'. *Tai* in *iku tai* is a general classifier for people. Recall the sentence final question particle *ga* must be used after the Apocopated Form (APO.FORM) [Part II, Topic 3].

    taa 'who', 'whose'

- *Anu tchoo **taa** yaibii ga?*   'Who is that person over there?' (Polite)
- *Aree **taa** ya ga?*   'Who is that over there?' (Plain)
- *Kuree **taa** u-shiru ya ga?*   'Whose soup is this?' (Plain)

    iku tai 'how many people'

- A: *ʔyaa ya choodee ya **iku tai** wu ga?*   'How many siblings do you have?'
  B: *Uttu ga chui wuibiin.*   'I have one younger sibling.'
- A: *Yaaninjoo **iku tai** ya ga?*   'How many people are in your family?'
  B: *yu ttai yaibiin.*   'There are four people in my family.'

✏️ To count one and two people, use ***chui*** 'one person' and ***tai*** 'two people'. For three to five people, use the classifier ***tai/chai***: *mit chai* [← *tai*], *yu ttai*, and *ichu tai*. After five, use the classifier ***nin***: *gu nin*, *ruku nin*, etc.

6. Particle: *tu* 'and'

This particle connects two nouns with the meaning of 'and'.

- *Uri tiichi **tu** ari taachi...*   'One of these and two of those...' (e.g. when shopping at a store)

- *Wattaa yaa nkai ya mayaa **tu** in nu wuibiin.*   'There are a cat and a dog at our house.'

- *Wattaa yaaninjoo uya tu uttu tu wan...yu ttai yaibiin.*   'There are four people in my family: my parents, a younger sibling and myself.'

ADDITIONAL VOCABULARY

achaa 'tomorrow'
chuu 'today'
isatuu 'praying mantis'
kachun 'write'
mun 'thing'

neen/neeran 'negative of *an*'
nin (classifier for people)
tiida 'the Sun'
ujiraasan 'cute'
yaaruu 'gecko'

EXERCISES C

1. Indicate if the following statements are true (T) or false (F).

    a. (___) *ʔunju* is more polite than *ittaa*.

    b. (___) Okinawan for 'your father' is *ittaa taarii*.

    c. (___) Okinawan for 'your thing' is *ʔunju mun*.

    d. (___) *ari ga mun* is the correct way to say 'his thing'.

2. Insert *ga*, *tu*, or *nkai* in the parentheses. For the other spaces, fill in the appropriate numbers in Okinawan based on the picture to the right.

    A: *Ama (_____) warabi-n-chaa (_____) wun yaa.*

    B: *Uu. Wikiga warabi (_____) ____ (_____)*

       winagu warabi (_____) ____wu-ibiin.

    A: *Ujiraasan yaa.*

3. Select the correct choice.

   a. The speaker (*Higa shinshii*) is pointing to an umbrella close to himself.

   Higa: *Kunu kasaa { taa / taa ga } mun ga?*

   Pensy: *Uree { ari / ari ga } mun ya-ibiin.*

   Higa: *{ ari n / ari mun } yam-i?* 'Is that one there also hers?' [*yam-i* is the question form of *yan.* (See [L3(B2)]).]

   Pensy: *Wuu wuu, aree { aibiin / aibiran / yaibiin }.*

   b. S: *Anu tchoo { taa / taa ga } yaibii ga?*

   H: *{ waa / wattaa } ʔnmii ya sa.*

   S: *{ unjoo / ʔyaa ya } choodee ya { ikuchi / iku tai } wuibii ga?*

   H: *Mitchai.* (showing a picture) *Kuree { waa / wattaa } ʔnmii yan doo.*

4. Give the Negative Forms and their English meanings.

   a. *kachun* _____

   b. *kamun* _____

   c. *iin* _____

   d. *ninjun* _____

5. Change the following into negative sentences. Pay attention to the use of *ya* [C2].

   a. *Anu tchoo wattaa shinshii yaibiin.* → _____

   _____

   b. *Anu tchu-taa yaa nkai in nu wu-ibiin.* → _____

   _____

   ('There is a dog at the house of those people.' For the change of *nu* → *ya*, see [C2])

   c. *Ama nkai ya tinsagu nu aibiin.* → _____

   _____

LESSON 2   Okinawan New Year Family Gathering   39

6. Using the *Wordbook*, find the meanings of the following adjectives and give their English counterparts as well as their Negative Forms.

Example: *magisan* 'big' → *magikooneen* 'not big'

a. *achisan* '_____' → _____

b. *gumasan* '_____' → _____

c. *fiisan* '_____' → _____

d. *feesan* '_____' → _____

e. *niisan* '_____' → _____

f. *takasan* '_____' → _____

APPLICATIONS

1. Let's sing a song in Okinawan about numbers!

   https://youtu.be/JDwOJwrbCEg

   Write the English name for the following items in the parentheses (__) and the number referred to in the song in the square brackets [__].

 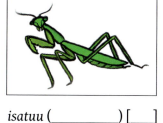 

tiida (_____) [__]   *isatuu* (_____) [__]   *yaaruu* (_____) [__]

2. Partner activity: Have one person say a family term in English. The other person will give the equivalent Okinawan family term.

3. Using the verbs in Grammar [C3], do the following activity: Student A says the positive form and Student B responds with the negative form.

4. Discuss your family with your partner.
   a. How many people are in your family?
   b. Who are they? How are they related to you?
   c. How old are you?
   d. Do they live in Los Angeles?

CULTURAL NOTES

1. Family Terms: *wikii* vs. *wunai*

You learned sibling terms in this lesson. In addition to those, there are also traditional Okinawan sibling terms distinguished by gender: male siblings are *wikii* and female siblings *wunai*. This word *wunai* appears in *Omoro Sōshi*, the oldest piece of Okinawan literature. During the time of the Ryukyu Kingdom, the king's sister, *wunai*, assumed the role of *Kikoe Ookimi*, the tutelary priestess to the king. Reflecting this, in the world of *Omoro Sōshi* female siblings were called *wunai-gami* 'female deity' and prayed for the smooth and safe travel/voyage of their male siblings.

- Does this aspect of Okinawan religious practice remind you of any other legends or stories from other cultures you know?

2. Okinawan Family Name Jokes: *Yafuso*

There are several Okinawan last names in this lesson. Some are unique and written in unfamiliar combination of Chinese characters so that it is difficult for Japanese people to get the correct readings right away. Some Okinawan names are almost homophonous with other Okinawan/Japanese common nouns (e.g., Tamanaha ≈ *tamanaa* [cabbage], Takushi ≈ *takushii* [taxi]). The following episode should be understood in this context. It also depicts the time when the use of Okinawan at school was prohibited.

At the beginning of the school year, a teacher came into the class and introduced himself. "I'm Yafuso. Glad to meet you" in Japanese. Upon hearing it, one student repeated his name, *ya-fu-so*, as "ʔyaa ufusoo?". This incited a roar of laughter from his fellow students. This episode comes from the time when Okinawan was prohibited at school. The boy was 'repeating' the teacher's name with a spin, which turns the name into an Okinawan sentence, 'You are...' This can be interpreted as a student's resistance towards a strict language policy. Check the meaning of *ufusoo* in WB to figure out why the class burst into laughter.

- Discuss the humor in Exercise A(3c).

REVIEW EXERCISES

Lessons 1 and 2

1. Complete blanks a–f below with the appropriate demonstrative pronouns.

Close to the Speaker	Close to the Hearer	Far Away
kuri	c. _____	e. _____
a. _____	unu	f. _____
b. _____	d. _____	ama

2. Complete the blanks a-h below with the appropriate personal pronouns.

Singular			Plural		
1st Person	2nd Person	3rd Person	1st Person	2nd Person	3rd Person
a. _____	b. (plain) _____	d. _____	e. _____	f. (plain) _____	h. _____
	c. (polite) _____			g. (polite) _____	

3. Choose the correct pronoun form. Choose X if nothing is required.

    a. Kuree { taa / taa ga / taa nu } mun ga? // Waa { ga / nu / X } mun yan doo. Uri n ?yaa { ga / nu / X } mun yami? // Wuu wuu. Kuree ari { ga / nu / X } mun yaibiin.

b. { *Waa / Wattaa* } *shinshii ya Higa shinshii yaibiin.*

c. *Higa shinshii,* { *?yaa / unju* } *n ?wiijabiimi?* 'Mr. Higa, are you going to swim, too?'

d. *Anu tchoo* { *unju / unju naa taa* } *yaaninju ya-ibiimi?*

e. *Higa Shinshii sai,* { *?yaa / unju* } *n achisaibiimi?*

4. For the following terms, give Okinawan words for English and English words for Okinawan.

   a. Grandfather_____   e. Younger sister_____

   b. Mother_____   f. *Wikii*_____

   c. Older brother_____   g. *Wunai*_____

   d. Older sister_____   h. *Wikiga warabi*_____

5. Give the contracted forms. If a contraction does not occur, write the appropriate result of the combination.

   a. *kuri + ya* →_____   e. *ari + ya* →_____

   b. *unu tchu + ya* →_____   f. *wan + ya* →_____

   c. *Uchinaa nu umi + ya* →_____   g. *hun + ya* →_____

   d. *biiru + ya* →_____

6. Write the following numbers in Okinawan.

   a. One_____   f. Six_____

   b. Two_____   g. Seven_____

   c. Three_____   h. Eight_____

   d. Four_____   i. Nine_____

   e. Five_____   j. Ten_____

7. Complete the charts.

   a. Verbs & Copula

| Affirmative | | Negative | | |
Plain	Polite	Plain	Polite	Meaning
wakain	e. _____	h. _____	k. _____	p. _____
a. _____	ninjabiin	i. _____	l. _____	q. _____
b. _____	f. _____	mutan	m. _____	r. _____
c. _____	g. _____	yuman	n. _____	s. _____
d. _____	yaibiin	j. _____	o. _____	t. _____

   b. Adjectives

| Affirmative | | Negative | | |
Plain	Polite	Plain	Polite	Meaning
churasan	e. _____	i. _____	m. _____	p. _____
a. _____	f. _____	fiikooneen	n. _____	q. _____
b. _____	achisaibiin	j. _____	o. _____	r. _____
c. _____	g. _____	k. _____	feekoonee(ya) biran	s. _____
d. _____	h. _____	l. _____	yashikoonee(ya) biran	t. _____

8. Fill in the parentheses with the appropriate subject particle (*ga* or *nu*) and write the appropriate verb of existence (*wun* or *an*) in the other spaces.

   a. *Arakaki-san taa yaa nkai ya in* (_____) _____. *Yohina-san taa yaa nkai ya, mayaa* (_____) _____.

   b. *Ama nkai UH nu shiitu* (_____) _____ *yaa. UCLA nu shiitu* _____ *doo.*

   c. *Ai, sushi* (_____) _____ *yaa. Kwatchii sabira.*

   d. *Ooshiro san taa ya wikiga warabi* (_____) *tai, winagu warabi* (_____) *chui* _____.

   e. *Orion* (_____) _____ *doo. Uri uri.*

9. Based on the answers given after //, fill in the blanks with the appropriate question words.

   a. *Orion biiroo* (_____) *a ga?* // *Miichi aibiin.*

   b. *Ittaa yaaninjoo* (_____) *ya ga?* // *Yu ttai yaibiin.*

   c. *?yaa ya* (_____) *nai ga?* // *Nijuuichi naibiin.*

   d. *Uree* (_____) *ya ga?* // *Gurukun yaibiin.*

   e. *Aree* (_____) *ya ga?* // *Wattaa yatchii yaibiin.*

10. Fill in the blanks with the appropriate particle from the following list: *nu, nkai, shee (shi+ya), ndi, yaa,* and *sa.*

    a. *Ama* (_____) *nuu* (_____) *wu ga?* // *Isatuu* (_____) *wuibiin.*

    b. *Mayaa ya eego* (_____) *nuu* (_____) *ii ga?* // *Cat yaibiin.*

    c. *Anu tchoo ippee feesan* (_____) // *Yan* (_____).

    d. *Kuree maasa* (_____). *Uri uri.* // (after tasting it) *Yaibiin* (_____). (Note: *maasa* is an APOCOPATED FORM, not a Dictionary Form)

    e. *Ai, ama* (_____) *tui* (_____) *wu* (_____). // *Aree Yanbaru Kuina* [endangered species] *ya* (_____).

LESSON 3

Making *Muuchii* Cake

DIALOGUE A

People in Okinawa celebrate *Muuchii* (see Cultural Note 1) on December 8 according to the lunar calendar. Niko's host family's daughter, Yuna, is making *muuchii* cake.

Niko:	*Fiisan yaa!*		It's cold!
Yuna:	*Ii. Muuchii biisa ya sa.*		Yeah. It's a *muuchii* cold wave.
Niko:	*Nuu **soo** ga?*		What are you doing?
Yuna:	*Muuchii Ø **chukutoon**.*		I'm making *muuchii*.

45

CORE VOCABULARY

ii	'yes' (plain)
muuchii	'rice cake'
muuchii biisa	'cold wave' ← *muuchii* + *fiisa* (APO.FORM) 'cold'
soo (APO.FORM)	← *s* 'do' + *oon* (progressive) 'am/are/is doing' [A3]
chukutoon	← *chuku* 'make' + *toon* (progressive) 'am/are/is making' [A3]

GRAMMAR A

1. Gerund Form

The Gerund Form (G.FORM) is similar to *-ing* in English. It is used to form a variety of constructions in Okinawan ([A3], [B1]). For V-verbs, the gerunds are made by simply adding *-ti* to the Gerund Root (G.ROOT).

Dictionary Form	Gerund Root	Gerund Form	Meaning
chuku-in	*chuku*	*chuku-ti*	'to make'
na-in	*na*	*na-ti*	'to become'
waka-in	*waka*	*waka-ti*	'to understand'

For C-verbs, you must first memorize the Gerund Root (G.ROOT) and add *-i* to make the Gerund Form (see Part II, Topic 3).
Study the chart below together with the *Wordbook* (pp. xiii-xv).

	Dictionary Form	Gerund Root	Gerund Form	Meaning
1	*ʔwiij-un*	*ʔwiij*	*ʔwiij-i*	'to swim'
2	*ninj-un*	*nint*	*nint-i*	'to sleep'
3	*nnj-un*	*nnch*	*nnch-i*	'to see'
4	*kach-un*	*kach*	*kach-i*	'to write'
5	*much-un*	*mutch*	*mutch-i*	'to hold'
6	*turas-un*	*turach*	*turach-i*	'to give'
7	*yub-un*	*yud*	*yud-i*	'to invite'
8	*yum-un*	*yud*	*yud-i*	'to read'
IRG	*s-un*	*s*	*ssh-i**	'to do'

2. Transitive vs. Intransitive Verbs

Verbs can be classified into transitive and intransitive verbs. Transitive verbs (TR) require a subject and an object. They are arranged in the following sentence structure (Part II, Topic 1). Ø in the transitive structure stands for no particle. That is, an object is not marked by any particle.

- [SUBJ- *ga/nu*] [OBJ- Ø] [VTR]

Intransitive verbs (INTR) require only a subject.

- [SUBJ- *ga/nu*] [VINTR]

Ga/nu are subject-marking particles [L2(B3)]. They will change to *ya* when the subject is a topic [L1(A2)].

In Dialogue [B], ***iriin*** 'someone puts something' (TR) and ***iin*** 'something gets in' (INTR) are used.

- *Wannee saataa Ø **iriin**.* 'I put in sugar.' transitive
- *Saataa nu **iin**.* 'Sugar gets/is in.' intransitive

A transitive sentence reports an action that is performed by an agent to someone/something (e.g. '**Yuna boils water**'), while an intransitive sentence reports an event where an agent does an action alone ('**John slept**'), or where something happens without an agent's involvement ('**The water boiled**'). Okinawan has many pairs of transitive and intransitive verbs. English also has such pairs, but it often uses the same verb transitively and intransitively. See the next comparison chart.

Transitive	Intransitive
agiin 1. '(someone) raises (a flag)' 2. '(someone) fries (food)'	**again** 1. '(the sun) rises' 2. '(the food) is fried'
sagiiin '(someone) lowers (a flag)'	**sagain** '(the flag) comes down'
akiin '(someone) opens (the door)'	**achun** '(the door) opens'
michiin '(someone) closes (the door)'	**michain** '(the door) closes'
iriin '(someone) puts (sugar)'	**iin** '(sugar) goes in'
ʔnjasun '(someone) takes out (money/child)'	**ʔnjiin** '(a child) comes/goes out'

3. Progressive and Resultative/Stative: [G.ROOT-*(t)oon*] '(someone) is doing (something)' and '(something) has been done/is done'

Progressive and resultative/stative are different phases of an event. The term 'aspect' is used to discuss such a distinction. The progressive aspect refers to an ongoing action, e.g., 'Chris is drawing a picture'), and the resultative/stative aspect refers to a state brought about by some action, e.g., 'the plate is clean (after someone cleaned it).' You can make the *(t)oon* form by adding *-toon* to the Gerund Root (G.ROOT) for V-verbs and *-oon* to the G.ROOT for C-verbs. (In the table below, 'X' represents any subject such as 'I, you, he/she'.

	DIC.FORM	G.ROOT	-(t)oon	Aspect	Translation
V	chuku-in	chuku	chuku-**toon**	Progressive	'X is making ~'
V	na-in	na	na-**toon**	Resultative	'X has become ~'
V	waka-in	waka	waka-**toon**	Resultative	'X understands ~'
C-1	ʔwiij-un	ʔwiij	ʔwiij-**oon**	Progressive	'X is swimming'
C-2	ninj-un	nint	nint-**oon**	Progressive	'X is sleeping'
C-3	nnj-un	nnch	nnch-**oon**	Progressive	'X is seeing ~'
C-4	kach-un	kach	kach-**oon**	Progressive	'X is writing ~'
C-5	much-un	mutch	mutch-**oon**	Progressive	'X is holding ~'
C-6	turas-un	turach	turach-**oon**	Progressive	'X is giving ~ to someone'
C-7	yub-un	yud	yud-**oon**	Progressive	'X is inviting ~'
C-8	yum-un	yud	yud-**oon**	Progressive	'X is reading ~'
IRG	s-un	s	s-**oon**	Progressive	'X is doing ~'

There is a tendency for a transitive verb with *(t)oon* to indicate the progressive aspect ('is doing something') while an intransitive verb with *(t)oon* indicates the resultative/stative aspect ('is done').

Note that the following three verbs have gone through irregular sound changes.

LESSON 3 Making *Muuchii* Cake

D.FORM	Meaning	Intr/Tr	G.ROOT	-(t)oon Form	Aspect
iri-in	'to put in'	TR	iri	ittoon	progressive
i-in	'to enter/be put in'	INTR	itch	itchoon	resultative
i-in (iyu-n/ ʔyun)	'to say'	INTR	ich	ichoon	progressive

A few illustrations will help you to understand the difference.

Progressive		Resultative	
	*Ayaa ga tinjoo kara muuchii **sagi-toon**.* 'Mom is hanging *muuchii* from the ceiling.'		*Muuchii nu tinjoo kara **saga-toon**.* '*Muuchii* is hung from the ceiling.'
	*Tinpura **agi-toon**.* 'I am deep-frying *tempura*.'		*Tinpura **aga-toon**.* '*Tempura* is deep-fried.'
	*Saataa **ittoon** (← iri-toon).*[1] 'I'm putting sugar in.'		*Saataa ya **itch-oon**.* 'Sugar is put in.'

[1] The alternative form *ittoon* is a result of the following phonological change: *iri-toon* > ('i' deletion) > *ir-toon* > (assimilation of 'r' to 't') > *it-toon*.])

Here are more comparisons.

Transitive + *(t)oon* = Progressive	Intransitive + *(t)oon* = Resultative
aki-in > **aki-toon** '(someone) is opening (the door)'	ach-un > **ach-oon** '(the door) is opened'
michi-in > **michi-too**n '(someone) is closing (the door)'	micha-in > **micha-toon** '(the door) is closed'
ʔnjas-un > **ʔnjach-oon** '(a child) is taking (toys) out'	ʔnji-in > **ʔnji-toon** '(toys) are taken out'

ADDITIONAL VOCABULARY

achun 'to open (INTR)'
agiin 'to rise (INTR)'
agiin 'to be fried (INTR)'
agiin 'to raise'
agiin 'to fry (TR)'
akiin 'to open (TR)'
bentoo 'boxed lunch'
chitu 'gift'
michain 'to close (INTR)'
michiin 'to close (TR)'
miruku 'milk/cream'
naagi 'gift'

nama 'now'
ʔnjasun 'to take out (TR)'
ʔnjiin 'to go/come out (INTR)'
numun 'to drink'
tigami 'letter'
tinpura 'tempura, deep fried fish/vegetables etc., (cf. *andaagii* [← *anda* 'oil' + *agi* 'fry'] is also used, especially as in *saataa andaagii* 'Okinawan-style donut')
uta 'song'
utain 'to sing (TR)'

EXERCISES A

1. Fill in the blanks. (Consult WB. The last three are irregular. See [A(3)] above.)

Dictionary	Meaning	INTR/TR	G.ROOT	*-(t)oon* form	Aspect
sagi-in					
saga-in					
tu-in					
s-un					
kam-un					

LESSON 3   Making *Muuchii* Cake   51

Dictionary	Meaning	INTR/TR	G.ROOT	*-(t)oon* form	Aspect
num-un					
yub-un					
iri-in					
i-in					
i-in (iyu-n)					

2. Describe what a person is doing both in plain and polite forms.

Ex   *uta* {*utatoon.* (plain) / *utatooibiin.* (polite)}

a.   *shinbun* {_____. (plain) / _____. (polite)}

b.   *J-pop* {_____. (plain) / _____. (polite)}

c.   *tigami* {_____. (plain) / _____. (polite)}

d.		terebi {_____. (plain) / _____. (polite)}
e.		nama {_____. (plain) / _____. (polite)}

3. Select the correct form, and translate the whole sentence into English.

   a. *Miruku* (a. *iriin* / b. *iin*)._____

   _____

   b. *Miruku ya* (a. *ittoon* / b. *itchoon*)._____

   _____

   c. (I don't like milk, so) *miruku ya* (a. *irian* / b. *iriran*)._____

   _____

4. Using one of the verbs in (2), create exchanges where A asks B what he/she is doing.

   a. A & B are friends

      A: *Nuu* _____ *ga?*   B: _____.

   b. A is older than B

      A: *Nuu* _____ *ga?*   B: _____.

   c. A is younger than B

      A: *Nuu* _____ *ga?*   B: _____.

DIALOGUE B

Yuna:	*Ai, wannee saataa Ø **itta gayaa**.*	Ah, I wonder if I put in sugar.
Niko:	***Iriitan** doo.*	I saw you putting it in.
(Niko tasting *muuchii* dough)		
	***Itchoon**.*	It is in.
Yuna:	*Ya**mi**? Naa ufee **iriimi**?*	Is it? Should I put in some more?
Niko:	***Yii yii**. Choodu yii saku ya sa.*	No. It's just right.

CORE VOCABULARY

saataa	'sugar'
itta	← *irta* ← *irita* ← *iri* 'put in (TR.)' + *ta* (PAST-1) [B1]
gayaa	SFP [B5]
irii-tan	← *irii* 'put in (TR)' + *tan* (PAST-2) [B1]
itch-oon	← *itch* 'be put in (INTR)' + *oon* (ASP) [A3]
ufee	'little'
naa ufee	'little more'
iriim-i	← *iriin* 'put in' + *i* (QP) [B2]
yii yii	'no' (plain)

GRAMMAR B

1. Simple Past (PAST-1) vs. Extended Past (PAST-2)

Okinawan has two past tense forms, -(t)an and -tan. These two have different meanings and formations. First, we start with the formation of these forms:

- Simple past (PAST-1): [GERUND.ROOT + -(t)an] (t only appears after V-verbs)

    iri + **tan**   → (i deletion) → ir[ ]-**tan**   'I put something in.'
                 (r to t assimilation) → it-**tan**

    mutch + **an** → mutch-**an**   'I held something.'
    chich + **an** → chich-**an**   'I listened to something.'

- Extended past (PAST2): [APOCOPATED.FORM + -**tan**] (t appears both after V- and C-verbs)

    irii-**n**   → irii-**tan**   '(someone) put something in.'
    muchu-**n** → muchu-**tan**   '(someone) held something.'
    chichu-**n** → chichu-**tan**   '(someone) listened to something.'

Study the chart below together with the *Wordbook*.

	DIC.FORM	G.ROOT	PAST-1	APO.FORM	PAST-2	Meaning
V	na-in	na	na-**tan**	nai	nai-**tan**	'to become'
V	waka-in	waka	waka-**tan**	wakai	wakai-**tan**	'to understand'
V	iri-in	iri	it-**tan**	irii	irii-**tan**	'to put in'
C-1	ʔwiij-un	ʔwiij	ʔwiij-**an**	ʔwiiju	ʔwiiju-**tan**	'to swim'
C-2	ninj-un	nint	nint-**an**	ninju	ninju-**tan**	'to sleep'
C-3	nnj-un	nnch	nnch-**an**	nnju	nnju-**tan**	'to see'
C-4	chich-un	chich	chich-**an**	chichu	chichu-**tan**	'to listen to'
C-5	much-un	mutch	mutch-**an**	muchu	muchu-**tan**	'to hold'
C-6	ʔnbus-un	ʔnbuch	ʔnbuch-**an**	ʔnbusu	ʔnbusu-**tan**	'to steam'
C-7	yub-un	yud	yud-**an**	yubu	yubu-**tan**	'to invite'
C-8	chichim-un	chichid	chichid-**an**	chichimu	chichimu-**tan**	'to wrap'
IRG	s-un	s	s-**an**	s-u	su-**tan**	'to do'

LESSON 3   Making *Muuchii* Cake   55

There is an interesting difference in meaning between the two past tense forms. In a statement sentence, PAST-1 is used only with first person subjects, and expresses the first person subject's (i.e., the speaker's) **direct experience**. On the other hand, PAST-2 is used for second or third person subjects and it reports the **speaker's observation of other people's actions**. See the following examples.

*Saataa iri-**tan**.* → *it-**tan**.* 'I put sugar in.'   *Saataa irii-**tan**.* '(I saw) you/her putting sugar in.'

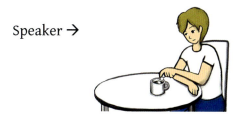

*Muuchii chichid-**an**.* 'I wrapped *muuchii*.' (Dial[C])   *Muuchii chichimu-**tan**.* '(I saw) you/him wrapping *muuchii*.' (Dial[C])

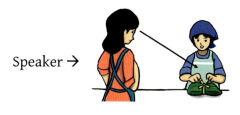

*Wannee binchoo s-**an**.* 'I studied.'   *Aree binchoo su-**tan**.* '(I saw) you/her studying.'

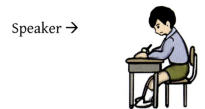
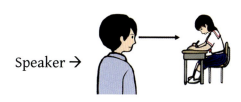

What this shows is that Okinawan past tense forms are sensitive to the "evidential" distinction between "directly experienced information" vs. "observed information". However, the <u>negative</u> past tense has only one form: [NEG.FORM + *tan*] (e.g. *iriran-tan* 'I/he/she did not put in'; *kaman-tan* 'I/he/she did not eat.')

2. Yes/No Question (Nonpast) with the Question Particle (-i)

In order to form yes/no questions (nonpast tense), the question particle *-i* is added to the Dictionary/Finite Form of verbs and adjectives. This is different for wh-questions, which require *ga* as a question particle and the Apocopated Form before it [L1(B4)]. It is important to remember that when *-i* is added to the Dictionary/Finite Form, the final **n** changes to **m** as in the following examples (for exceptions, see [B4] below):

- *Ya**m**-i?* (← *yan -i*) 'Is that so?'
- *Naa ufee irii**m**-i?* (← *iriin -i*) 'Shall I put in a bit more?'
- *Kuri n muuchii yaibii**m**-i?* (← *yaibiin -i*) 'Is this also *muuchii* cake?'
- *Shinshii ya yamatunchu yaibii**m**-i?* (← *yaibiin -i*) 'Are you (= teacher) Japanese?'
- *Kunu kwaashee maasaibii**m**-i?* (← *maasaibiin -i*) 'Is this sweet good?'

3. Yes/No Question (Past) with the Question Particle (-i)

To ask about actions in the past, *-i* is attached to the Gerund Forms of PAST-1 and PAST-2.

a. 'Did *you*...?'

Attach the question particle *-i* to the Gerund Forms of PAST-1, which ends in *-(t)i* instead of *-(t)an*. For example:

	Verb	PAST-1 → G.FORM		PAST Q	Translation
		→ -(t)an	→ -(t)i		
V	*iriin* 'put in'	→ *it-tan*	→ *it-ti*	→ *it-ti-i?*	'Did you put it in?'
1	*ʔwiijun* 'swim'	→ *ʔwiij-an*	→ *ʔwiij-i*	→ *ʔwiij-i-i?*	'Did you swim?'
8	*kamun* 'eat'	→ *kad-an*	→ *kad-i*	→ *kad-i-i?*	'Did you eat?'

- *Saataa it**ti**-i?* (cf. *it-tan*) 'Did **you** put sugar in?'
- *Ka**di**-i?* (cf. *kad-an*) 'Did **you** eat?'
- *Chinuu ʔwiiji-i?* (cf. *ʔwiij-an*) 'Did **you** swim yesterday?'

To answer these questions affirmatively, the PAST-1 form (*itt-an* 'I put it in' and *kad-an* 'I ate') is used. The negative answer would be *iriran-tan* 'I did not put it in' and *kaman-tan* 'I did not eat.'

The negative past questions ('Didn't you...?') are formed by adding *-ti-i* to the negative forms.

- *tuin* → *tu-ran* → *turan-**ti-i*** (NEGATIVE PAST QUESTION) 'Didn't you take...?'
- *yubun* → *yub-an* → *yuban-**ti-i*** (NEGATIVE PAST QUESTION) 'Didn't you invite...?'

b. 'Did (you *see*) *him/her/them*...? / Did (you *see*) *me*...?'

To form these questions, attach the question particle *-i* to the Gerund Forms of PAST-2, which ends in *-(t)i* instead of *-(t)an*. For example:

	Verb	PAST-2 → G.FORM		PAST Q	Translation (x= *him/her/them/me*)
		→ *-(t)an*	→ *-(t)i*		
V	*iriin* 'put in'	→ *irii-**tan***	→ *irii-**ti***	→ *irii-**ti-i**?*	'Did (you see) X putting it in?'
1	*ʔwiijun* 'swim'	→ *ʔwiiju-**tan***	→ *ʔwiiju-**ti***	→ *ʔwiiju-**ti-i**?*	'Did (you see) X swimming?'
8	*kamun* 'eat'	→ *kamu-**tan***	→ *kamu-**ti***	→ *kamu-**ti-i**?*	'Did (you see) X eating?'

- *Saataa irii-**ti-i**?*   'Did (you see) me/him put sugar in?'   (V-verb)
- *Lewis ya chinuu ʔwiiju-**ti-i**?* 'Did (you see) Lewis swim yesterday?'   (C-verb, 1)
- *Munu kamu-**ti-i**?*   'Did (you see) me/him eat something?' (C-verb, 8)

To answer these questions affirmatively, the PAST-2 form (*irii-**tan*** 'I saw X put it in' and *kamu-**tan*** 'I saw X eating') is used. The negative answers would be *iriran-**tan*** 'I did not see X put it in' and *kaman-**tan*** 'I did not see X eat.'

4. Invitation and Negative Questions with the Question Particle (*-i*)

When the question particle *-i* described above is added to a negative sentence [L2(C3)], it can express, in addition to a negative, or a rhetorical question, an invitation ('Would you like to...?'). Unlike the ***n*** of the Dictionary/Finite Form (see (2) above), the negative ***n*** (as in *yuman*) does NOT change to ***m***. Further note that for the negative sentences to be interpreted as invitation, the verbs have to be volitional. For example, compare the first two verbs in the examples below as opposed to the last two, which do not express actions controllable by the speaker's will:

- A: *Kunu hun yuma**n-i**?* 'Would you like to read this book?'   (invitation)
  B: ***Uu**, nifee deebiru.* 'Yes, thank you.'

- *Orion numa**n-i**?* 'Would you like to drink Orion beer?'   (invitation)

- A: *Achaa ya muuchii ya ara**n-i**?* 'Isn't tomorrow *muuchii* day?' (negative question)
  B: ***Wuu wuu**, aibiran. / **Yii yii**, aran.* 'No, it is not. / No, it is not.'
  ***Uu, yaibiin**. / **Ii, yan** (doo).* 'Yes, it is. / Yes, it is.'

*Junni nara**n-i**?* 'You really can't do it? (I think you can).'   (rhetorical question)

👉 In addition to the meaning of 'become ', *na-in* can also express one's ability as shown in the last sentence above (more on this in (L8)). The verb *na-in* embodies a culturally important concept [Cul3].

To answer negative questions, affirmative answers take 'yes' with a positive ending (cf. [L5(DialA)]). The opposite is true for negative answers as above. This is straightforward for English speakers, but appears strange for Japanese speakers.

5. Sentence Final Particle: *gayaa*

The sentence-final particle *gayaa* expresses the speaker's self-doubt (i.e., 'I wonder'; 'I am wondering'). This is in contrast with the question particle *ga*, which clearly directs a question to the addressee. The particle *gayaa* follows the Apocopated Form of the Past and Nonpast Forms (i.e., the Dictionary Form without *n* for both verbs and adjectives).

- *Wannee saataa Ø itta **gayaa**.*   'I wonder if I put the sugar in?'
- *Aree nakami nu shiroo chukuta **gayaa**.* 'I wonder if he made *nakami* soup.'
- *Kunu muuchiii ya maasa **gayaa**.*   'I wonder if this *muuchii* is delicious.'

ADDITIONAL VOCABULARY

chinuu 'yesterday'   *naa* 'name'
junni 'really'   *uttii* 'day before yesterday'

EXERCISES B

1. Fill in the blanks.

Dictionary Form	Meaning	PAST-1	PAST-2
iri-in			
i-in			
ʔnbus-un (Dial[C])			
kunj-un (Dial[C])			
sagi-in			
s-un			

Dictionary Form	Meaning	PAST-1	PAST-2
kam-un			
tu-in			
waka-in			
yum-un			

2. Choose the correct form to match the translation.

   a. *Tinpura* { *agi-in* / *aga-in* }.   '(I) will deep-fry *tempura*.'

   b. *Tinpura ya* { *agi-toon* / *aga-toon* }.   '*Tempura* has been fried.'

   c. *Muuchii nu* { *sagi-toon* / *saga-toon* }.   '*Muuchii* is hung (there).'

   d. *Muuchii* { *sagi-toon* / *saga-toon* }.   '(I) am hanging *muuchii*.'

   e. *In ya yaa nkai* { *iriin* / *iin* / *itch-oon* }   'The dog is in the kennel.' (*nkai* 'into' Dial[C])

   f. *In ya yaa nkai* { *iriin* / *iin* / *itch-oon* }.   'The dog is going into the kennel.'

3. Select the correct verb form and translate each sentence into English.

   a. *Wannee uttii shukudai* { *s-an* / *su-tan* }.

      English: _____.

   b. *Aree tigami* { *kach-an* / *kachu-tan* }.

      English: _____.

   c. *?yaa ya chinuu sumuchi* { *yudi-i* / *yumu-ti-i* }?

      English: _____?

4. Complete the questions below using *gayaa* or *-i*.

   a. *Wannee naa* (_____). 'I wonder if I wrote my name (perhaps in some document).'

   b. *aree nakami nu shiru* (_____)? 'Was she making *nakami* soup?'

   c. *?yaa ya chinuu hun* (_____)? 'Did you read a book yesterday?'

   d. *Ari n* (_____). 'I wonder if we should invite him too.'

60 PART I Conversation

DIALOGUE C

Niko:	*Wan nin tiganee su sa.*	I will help you too.
	Sannin nu faa nkai chichimumi?	Shall I wrap them in *sannin* leaves?
Yuna:	*Ii, sannin nu faa* **nkai chichidi**, *anshikara,*	Yes, we will wrap them up with *sannin*,
	ʔnbusu sa.	and after that, steam them.

(Niko tried some *muuchii* that Yuna had just made)

Niko:	*Maasa**tan** yaa.*	It was good, wasn't it?
	*Waa munoo murasachi ʔnmu ya**tan**.*	Mine was purple sweet potatoes.

(Niko looked at Yuna who is chaining *muuchii*)

Niko:	*Nuu s**oo** ga?*	What are you doing?
Yuna:	*Muuchii Ø tushi nu kaji* **kunchi**, *tinjoo*	I am chaining as many *muuchi* as my
	kara *sagitoon.*	years of age, and hanging them from the ceiling.

✍ The plant *sannin* belongs to the ginger family. It is said to have antibacterial power and provide protection against bad spirits. The celebratory *muuchii* is shared with ancestors during prayers for health and longevity.

CORE VOCABULARY

tiganee	'help'
sannin	'*alpinia zerumbet*' (ginger family)
faa	'leaf'
nkai	'into, with' [C2]
chichimum-i	← *chichimun* 'to wrap' + *i* [B2]
chichidi (G.FORM)	← *chichimun* 'to wrap'
ʔnbusu (APO.FORM)	← *ʔnbusun* 'to steam'
murasachi	'purple'
ʔnmu	'potato'
tushi	'age'
kaji	'number'
kunchi (G.FORM)	← *kunjun* 'to chain'
tinjoo	'ceiling'

GRAMMAR C

1. Adjectives and Copulas: Past

To form the past tense adjectives and the copulas, change *-n* of the Dictionary Form to *-tan*. Here are examples (for Past Negative Forms, see Part II, Topic 4):

a. Adjectives

- *ʔwiirikisa-n* → *ʔwiirikisa-**tan*** 'it was fun'
- *achisa-n* → *achisa-**tan*** 'it was hot'
- *yassa-n* → *yassa-**tan*** 'it was inexpensive'
- *ufusa-n* → *ufusa-**tan*** 'it was too much'
- *ikirasa-n* → *ikirasa-**tan*** 'it was not enough'

b. Copulas

- *shinshii ya-n* → *shinshii ya-**tan*** '(he/she) was a teacher'
- *Uchinaa ya-n* → *Uchinaa ya-**tan*** '(As for the place that I went,) it was Okinawa.'

2. Particles: *nkai* 'into', *kara* 'from'

a. *nkai*

This particle was introduced in the construction [Location + *nkai* + Existential Verb] ([L2(B6)]). It also marks a location an activity is directed to, such as 'to/into/onto' as shown in the dialogue above.

- *Muuchii sannin nu faa **nkai** chichimun.*   '(We) wrap *muuchii* up **in** *sannin* leaves.' (lit. '(We) take *muuchii* **to** *sannin* leaves and wrap it up in them.')
- *Kuma **nkai** naa kachun.*   '(You) write your name here.'

b. *kara*

This particle marks an origin in space and time, similar to English 'from'.

- *Muuchii tinjoo **kara** sagiin.*   'I'll hang *muuchii* **from** the ceiling'
- *Acha **kara** sun.*   'I'll do it starting **from** tomorrow'

3. Gerund Forms: Combining Function

The Gerund Form was introduced in [A1], and its usages with *(t)oon* and *(t)an* were explained in [A3] and [B1], respectively. The Gerund Form has another important function of connecting verbs, adjectives and clauses. Note that *tu* 'and' introduced in [L2(C6)] connects two nouns, but cannot connect two verbs, adjectives, or clauses.

- *Sannin nu faa nkai **chichidi**, anshikara, ʔnbusu sa.*   'We will wrap this up with *sannin* leaves, and after that, steam them.'
- *Muuchii tushi nu kaji **kunchi**, tinjoo kara sagitoon.*   'I am chaining as many *muuchi* as my years of age, and hanging them from the ceiling.'

ADDITIONAL VOCABULARY

chin 'clothes'
daigaku 'university'
deekuni 'radish'
ʔnjiin 'to leave, graduate'
n(n)su 'miso, fermented beans'
ufutchu 'adult' [*Ufutchu* is a compound noun consisting of *ufu* 'big' + *tchu* 'person.' *Ufu* is related to *ufusan* 'many; big in quantity' introduced in (L2).]

ʔwiirikisan 'fun'
yuufuru 'bath'

LESSON 3 Making *Muuchii* Cake   63

EXERCISES C

1. Fill in the blanks with *nu*, *nkai*, or *kara*. Consult WB for unknown words.

   a. *Chuu ya Seijin nu Hii yan. ?yaa n chuu* (_____) *ya ufutchu yan yaa.* (hint: 'from this day on…') [Note: *Seijin nu Hii* = 'Coming of Age Day' celebrated on January 15.]

   b. *N(n)su jiru* (_____) (← *n(n)su + shiru*) *nu naaka* (_____) *deekuni tu toofu ittan.*

   c. *Aree yuufuru* (_____) *itchoon.*

2. Match the following by putting a number (1–5) in the blanks.

   a. (___) *Saataa iriin.*   1. 'I put sugar (in it).' (past tense)

      (___) *Saataa itchoon.*   2. 'I saw him putting sugar (in it).'

      (___) *Saataa ittan.*   3. 'Sugar is put in.'

      (___) *Saataa iriitan.*   4. 'Shall I put sugar (in it)?'

      (___) *Saataa iriimi?*   5. 'I am going to put sugar (in it).'

   b. (___) *Chin ya sagatoon.*   1. 'I hung up my coat.'

      (___) *Chin sagitan.*   2. 'I saw him hanging up his coat.'

      (___) *Chin sagiimi?*   3. 'My coat is hung up.'

      (___) *Chin sagiitan.*   4. 'Shall I hang (your) coat up?'

      (___) *Chin sagitoon.*   5. 'I am hanging up my coat.'

3. Change the adjectives into their past tense forms.

   a. *Chinuu nu geemu ya ippee ʔwiirikisan.* → _____

   b. *Chinuu ya ippee hiisan.* → _____

   c. *Waa munoo ikirasan.* (said by the girl in the picture to the right, who is drinking juice) → _____

   _____

   d. (Make one example of your own with a past tense adjective.) _____

   _____

APPLICATIONS

1. The dialogues in this lesson are all between Niko and Yuna, both of whom are college students. How would the dialogue change if it were between Niko and his host mother? Rewrite the dialogue by inserting the correct expressions in the parentheses. Note that the polite counterpart of *yii yii* ('no') is *wuu wuu* (more on this in [Cul2]).

   Niko: (_____) *yaa!* 'It's cold!'

   Mother: *Ii. Muuchii biisa ya sa.* 'Yeah. It's a *muuchi* cold wave.'

   Niko: *Nuu* (_____) *ga?* 'What are you doing?'

   Mother: *Muuchii chukut-oon.* 'I'm making *muuchi*.'

   Ai, wannee saataa Ø it-ta gayaa. 'Ah, I wonder if I put in sugar.'

   Niko: (_____) *doo.* 'I saw you putting it in.'

   (Tasting muuchii dough)

   Niko: (_____). 'It is in.'

   Mother: *Yami? Naa ufee iriimi?* 'Is it? Should I put in some more?'

   Niko: (_____). *Choodu, ii saku* (_____) *sa. Wan nin tiganee* (_____) *sa. Sannin nu faa nkai* (_____)*-i?*

   'No. It's just right. I will help you. Shall I wrap them in *sannin* leaves?'

   Mother: *Ii, sannin nu faa nkai chichidi, anshikara, ʔnbusu sa.*

   'Yes, we will wrap them up with *sannin,* and after that, steam them.'

LESSON 3 Making *Muuchii* Cake 65

(Niko tried some muuchii that the mother had just made)

Niko: *Maasa-(_____) yaa. Waa munoo murasachi ʔnmu (_____)-tan.*

'It was good, wasn't it? Mine was purple sweet potatoes.'

(Looking at the mother chaining muuchii with a string)

Niko: *Nuu (_____) ga?* 'What are you doing?'

Mother: *Nama,* muuchii Ø *tushi nu kaji, kunchi, tinjoo kara sagit-oon.* 'I am chaining as many *muuchi* as my years of age, and hanging them from the ceiling.'

2. The pictures below represent different flavors of *muuchii.* Find words for A (brown sugar), B (white sugar), C (pumpkin), D (purple sweet potato) from the *Wordbook.* [Look for 'sugar' in the "English-Okinawan Glossary Index" in WB to find 'brown sugar' and 'white sugar'.]

   a. Insert the Okinawan name in the parentheses under each picture.

   A (***kuru jaataa***)   B (_____)   C (_____)   D (_____)

   b. Using your answers for (a.), fill in the blanks below for (A) through (D).
   Q: *kumu muuchii nu naaka nkai ya nuu nu itchoo ga?*

   i. (A) *nkai ya* (_____) *nu* (_____).

   ii. (B) *nkai ya* (_____) *nu* (_____).

   iii. (C) *nkai ya* (_____).

   iv. (D) (_____).

3. Find the Okinawan words for different occupations using WB and answer A's question as in the example below. You may use occupation names in English if you cannot find them in WB.

   Example:

   A: *Daigaku ʔnjiti*[1] *atu, nuu nai ga?* 'After graduating from college, what will you be?'
   B: *Gakkoo nu shinshii* **nkai nain.**   '(I) will be a schoolteacher.'

[1] *ʔnjiti* = G.FORM of *ʔnjiin* 'to leave, graduate' More on *atu* 'after' in [L10(C1)].

CULTURAL NOTES

1. *Muuchii biisa*

Many Okinawan festivals and cultural activities are scheduled according to the lunar calendar (although most people celebrate New Year's Day according to the Gregorian calendar). *Muuchii* is celebrated on December 8 of the lunar calendar (which falls sometime in January of the Gregorian calendar, depending on the year). Since it is expected to be very cold (*hiisan*) on this day, this cold wave is usually referred to as *muuchii biisaa* (← *hiisan*). *Muuchii* is a rice cake seasoned with brown sugar and other flavors. It is wrapped in *sannin* leaves and steamed. *Muuchii* is presented to one's ancestors in front of the family altar and/or hung from the ceiling in quantities matching the ages of the children.

- How was the lunar calendar established? In what parts of the world is it used? Do they use it in Western countries?
- You may be familiar with the Western zodiac, which includes the following twelve signs: Aries, Taurus, Gemini, Cancer, Leo, Virgo, Libra, Scorpio, Sagittarius, Capricorn, Aquarius, and Pisces. The Western cycle is determined by the earth's orbit around the sun and the constellations' positions relative to the earth. In Okinawa and other Asian cultures, they use the Chinese zodiac animal signs, or *juunishi*, which are traditionally determined by the lunar calendar. Each year is assigned to one of the following twelve animals: rat, ox, tiger, rabbit, dragon, snake, horse, sheep, monkey, rooster, dog, and pig. Compare the beliefs associated with the Western zodiac versus the Chinese zodiac.

2. Yes and No

We learned Okinawan has polite and plain forms of sentence endings, such as *yaibiin* and *yan*. We have already learned the polite versions of 'yes' and 'no' in the preliminary lesson, and here their plain counterparts are introduced.

	Plain	Polite
'Yes'	ii	uu
'No'	yii yii	wuu wuu
'Yes' (when called)	hii	huu

You can use the plain forms when talking to a friend, but you must use the polite form when talking to elders and those with higher social status (e.g. your teachers or boss). An elder person may use the plain form when talking to you. The last pair, *hii* vs. *huu*, is interesting; these are specialized forms used when you respond when someone calls your name or gets your attention. The expression *uu-huu nu naran* in Okinawan means 'he/she does not know how to use polite/honorific language.'

- In general, the English language does not overtly indicate many vertical/hierarchical personal relationships. However, if you listen carefully, people use different styles of language talking to their friends, teachers, and superiors (e.g. *yes, sir; yes; yup; yah;* etc.). Explain the English system or share your observations of actual usage. Discuss your thoughts.
- In Asian cultures, it is not unusual for people to ask each other's ages when they meet the first time. This is considered rude in Western culture. Is this kind of question offensive to you? If so, how do you resolve the conflict?

3. *Nankuru nai sa*

The expression *nankuru nai sa* (Japanese characters in the inset image) is popularly used and is often seen on T-shirts and other souvenirs in Okinawa. The full expression is *makutu sookee nankuru nai sa,* and it means 'If you live honestly, things will turn out all right.' The verb *nain* 'to become' [A1] is often contrasted with *sun* 'to do' from a typological point of view (Ikegami 1981). A 'do'-type language emphasizes the agent's will in events, while a 'become'-type language emphasizes the occurrence of events without such intervention. Languages like Okinawan prefer to use 'become'-type verbs while Western languages such as English prefer to use 'do'-type verbs. Compare the two sentences below (Shinzato 2008). The Okinawan translation has the structure: [X] *nkai naibiin* 'X (= the situation of our getting married) became as such.'

- We **decided** to get married.
- *Wattaa niibichi suru kutu nkai **na-ibitan*** '[Our getting married] became as such.'

4. Homophones

Homophones are words that have the same sound but different meanings. For example, in English the 'bank' where you keep your money and the 'bank' along a river are homophones. You can find homophones in any language, including Okinawan (*agiin* 'to raise' and 'to fry' [A2]). Here are a few such examples. The first example, the past tense and the Negative Form of the very important verb *sun* 'to do', both of which are introduced in this lesson, is especially intriguing to some learners. Imagine a situation when A orders B "do it", and B says "*san doo*" with less prominent stress. You can also imagine the situation in which A asks B to circulate the paper using *maashee*, and B responds *what are you saying?*

- *san* 'will not do (something)' vs. *sán*[1] 'did (something)'
- *maashee*[2] 'circulate' and 'please die'
- *maasan* 'delicious' vs. *maasán*[3] 'passed away, died'

[1] The diacritical mark on *a* indicates it is accented.
[2] The verb *maasun* 'to die' is used for people, while *shinun* is usually used for animals [L2(C3)].
[3] In Naha this word is pronounced as *maachan*. Thus, this pair is not homophonous in the Naha dialect.

LESSON 4

Do You Have Pain Somewhere?

DIALOGUE A

Niko looks sick today. His host mother is worried.

Mother: *Chuu ya munoo ansuka kaman yaa.*   You haven't been eating much today.
        Maagana yami du surui?   Do you have pain somewhere?

Niko: *Uu.*   Yes.

Mother: ***Maa** nu yamu ga?*   Where does it hurt?
        *Wata nu **du** yamurui?*   You have a stomachache?

Niko: *Wuu wuu, **chiburu** nu **du** yamabiiru.*   No. I have a headache.
        Nichi nu ʔnjiti, ufee duu n achisaibii   I have a fever, and my body also feels
        ssaa.   hot.

Mother: *Anshee, hanafichi yan **tee**.*   Then it must be a cold.

CORE VOCABULARY

munu	'thing, food'
ansuka	'that much'
kaman (NEG)	← *kamun* 'eat'
maagana	'somewhere' [A2]
yami (ADV. FORM)	← *yamun* 'hurt, have pains'
du	focus particle [A4]
maa	'where' [A2]
wata	'stomach'
yamuru-i	← *yamuru* (ADNOM.FORM) + *i* (QP)
chiburu	'head'
yamabiiru (ADNOM.FORM)	← *yam* 'hurt' + *abiiru* (POL)
nichi	'fever'
ʔnjiti (G.FORM)	← *ʔnji-in* 'come out', 'run'
duu	'body' [A1]
achisa-ibii (APO.FORM)	← *achisa* 'hot' + *ibii* (POL)
ssaa	SFP [A5]
hanafichi	'(have) a cold'
tee	SFP [A5]

GRAMMAR A

1. Body Parts

Here are some major body parts.

- *chiburu* 'head'
- *kata* 'shoulder'
- *chinshi* 'knee'
- *chira* 'face'
- *mii* 'eye(s)'
- *mimi* 'ear(s)'
- *nuudii* 'throat'
- *kubi* 'neck'

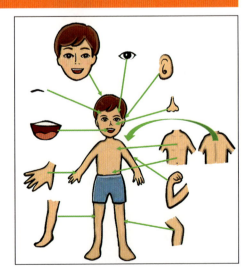

- *duu*   'body'
- *wata*   'stomach, belly'
- *kushi*   'lower back'
- *tii*   'hand'
- *hisa*   'foot, legs'

2. Wh- vs. Indefinite: *maa* 'where?' vs. *maagana* 'somewhere'; *nuu* 'what?' vs. *nuugana* 'something'

Okinawan has wh-word (who? where?) and indefinite ('someone', 'somewhere', etc.) pairs. Indefinites are formed by adding *gana* to wh-words. An exception to this is *ichi* 'when.' Its indefinite counterpart is *ichika* ('sometime'), not ˣ*ichigana*. *Maagana* 'somewhere' is used in Dialogue [A] and *nuugana* 'something' in Dialogue [B].

Wh-Word	Indefinite
maa 'where'	*maagana* 'somewhere'
nuu 'what'	*nuugana* 'something'
taa 'who'	*taagana* 'someone'
ichi 'when'	ˣ*ichigana* / °*ichika* 'sometime'

Wh-words and indefinites make different types of questions. Wh-words end with *ga* and form a wh-question, which cannot be answered with yes/no. Indefinites, on the other hand, make yes/no questions, which end with *i*.

- **Taa** ga wuibii **ga**?   'Who is there?' (Polite, wh-question)
  Taa ga wu **ga**?   'Who is there?' (Plain, wh-question)

- **Taagana** wuibii**mi**?   'Is someone there?' (Polite, yes/no question)
  Taagana wu**mi**?   'Is someone there?' (Plain, yes/no question) (inset)

- **Maa** nu yamabii **ga**?   'Where does (it) hurt?' (Polite, wh-question)
  Maa nu yamu **ga**?   'Where does (it) hurt?' (Plain, wh-question) [Dialogue (A)]

- **Maagana** yamabii**mi**?   'Does somewhere hurt?' (Polite, yes/no question)
  Maagana yamu**mi**?   'Does somewhere hurt?' (Plain, yes/no question)

3. Adnominal Form

The Adnominal Form (ADNOM.FORM) is the form taken by an adjective or a verb when it modifies a noun (e.g., 'a **red** flower', 'a **barking** dog') [Part II, Topics 3 and 4]. You can make this form by changing the **n** of the Finite Form (i.e., the Dictionary Form and other sentence-ending forms such as the past tense form) to **ru** both for adjectives and verbs.

Adjectives (nonpast tense):

- *churasan* → *churasaru* → *churasaru tui* 'a beautiful bird'
- *maasan* → *maasaru* → *maasaru iyu* 'a delicious fish'

Verbs (nonpast tense):

- *wakain* → *wakairu* → *wakairu kutuba* 'the language I understand'
- *yumun* → *yumuru* → *yumuru sumuchi* 'the book to read'

The Polite Form also has Adnominal counterparts.

- *wakaibii-n* → *wakaibii-ru*
- *yumabii-n* → *yumabii-ru*

Here is a table to show both nonpast and past plain adnominal forms of C-verbs.

	DIC.FORM	ADNOM.FORM (NONPAST)	PAST-2	ADNOM.FORM (PAST-2)	PAST-1	ADNOM.FORM (PAST-1)	Meaning
1	ʔwiiju-n	ʔwiiju-ru	ʔwiiju-tan	ʔwiiju-taru	ʔwiij-an	ʔwiij-aru	'to swim'
2	ninju-n	ninju-ru	ninju-tan	ninju-taru	nint-an	nint-aru	'to sleep'
3	kunju-n	kunju-ru	kunju-tan	kunju-taru	kunch-an	kunch-aru	'to tie up'
4	kachu-n	kachu-ru	kachu-tan	kachu-taru	kach-an	kach-aru	'to write'
5	muchu-n	muchu-ru	muchu-tan	muchu-taru	mutch-an	mutch-aru	'to hold'
6	ʔnbusu-n	ʔnbusu-ru	ʔnbusu-tan	ʔnbusu-taru	ʔnbuch-an	ʔnbuch-aru	'to steam'
7	yubu-n	yubu-ru	yubu-tan	yubu-taru	yud-an	yud-aru	'to call'
8	numu-n	numu-ru	numu-tan	numu-taru	nud-an	nud-aru	'to drink'

Here are a few examples.

- *Arabiago wakai**ru** tchoo Leo yan.*   'The **person** who understands Arabic is Leo.'
- *Edie ga wakai**ru** kutubaa chuugokugo yan.*   'The **language** Edie understands is Chinese.'
- *Churasa**ru** tchoo Lina yan.*   'The **person** who is pretty is Lina.'
- *Maasa**ru** muuchii ya murasachi ʔnmu yan.*   'The **muuchii** that is tasty is purple potato (flavor).'

4. Focus Construction (1): [...*du*... ADNOM.FORM]

The Adnominal Form (ADNOM.FORM) is used in the 'Focus Construction', in which one piece of information is given special attention. (e.g., In 'It's TARO who drank your juice!', TARO is emphasized) [Part II, Topic 8]. The focused element is marked by a focus particle (***du***). In this case, a sentence *must* end with an Adnominal Form. In a normal (i.e., nonfocus construction) sentence, the Dictionary Form or other Finite Forms are used. The focus particle *du* can immediately follow subject particles as *ga du* or *nu du* as in the examples below.'

- *Shogo ga **du** numuta**ru**.* 'It is **Shogo** who drank that (not me)!'
- *Wata nu **du** yamu**ru**.* 'It is my **stomach** that hurts (not other parts).'
- *Musarachi ʔnmu nu **du** maasa**ru**.* 'It is the **purple potato** (flavor) that is tasty.'
- *Uchinaa nu umi nu **du** churasa**ru**.* 'It is the **Okinawan ocean** that is pretty.'
- *Kuree nakami nu ushiru **du** ya**ru**. Chimu shinjee aran.* 'This is **nakami soup**, not *chimu shinji*.'

The particle ***du*** may also follow a verb. In that case, it is attached to the Adverbial Form of the verb (i.e., B.ROOT + *i*), and ends with *suru* for the nonpast tense. When it is attached to an adjective, it attaches to the adjective's Apocopated Form followed by *aru*. When ***du*** appears after a verb or an adjective, it is the verb or adjective that is in focus.

- Verb Adverbial Form (ADV.FORM) + ***du*** + ***suru*** (*chukui du suru*; ***numi*** *du suru*)
- Adj. Apocopated Form (APO.FORM) + ***du*** + ***aru*** (*achisa du aru*)

Compare (a) and (b).

(a) *Mii nu **du** yamu**ru**.* 'It is my **eyes** that hurt (not other parts).'
(b) *Mii nu yami **du** suru.* 'My eyes **hurt** (not itchy)' or 'It's that my eyes hurt, (so I can't go).'

To form a question, add the question particle *i*.

- Verb ADV.FORM + ***du*** + ***suru*** -*i?*
- Adj APO.FORM + ***du*** + ***aru*** -*i?*

Examples:

- **Focus** construction:
  (Situation: You look like you are in pain.)
  Regular sentence:
  (Situation: At a regular medical check-up.)

  *Maagana yami **du surui**?*
  'Is it that you have pain somewhere?'

  *Maagana yamum**i**?*
  'Do you have pain anywhere?'

- **Focus** construction:
  (Situation: You are sweating.)
  Regular sentence:
  (Situation: I'm not sure if you are hot or not.)

  *Achisa **du arui**?*
  'Is it that you feel hot?'
  *Achisam**i**?*
  'Are you hot? (I can adjust the thermostat)'

5. Sentence Final Particles:
[APO.FORM + *ssaa*] VS. [FINITE.FORM + *tee*]

These two Sentence Final Particles (SFP) could indicate a difference as to the source of information (Part II, Topic 7).

ssaa: attached to a verb/adjective's Apocopated Form to indicate directly obtained information

tee: attached to a verb/adjective's Finite Form to indicate information obtained through inferences or guesses.

First compare (a) and (b) below. (a)-sentence with ***ssaa*** is used when the speaker directly touches an object and exclaims, whereas the (b)-sentence with ***tee*** is used when, for example, the speaker is watching the object, perhaps a steaming kettle, and concludes that the kettle must be still hot.

LESSON 4   Do You Have Pain Somewhere?   75

(a)   *Achisa **ssaa**.*   '**Oh, boy!** It's hot. (I'm touching it now.)'

(b)   *Achisan **tee**.*   '**I believe** / It's hot, I'm sure.'

Now, confusing as it may be, there is another SFP *sa* which is attached to the Apocopated Form shown in (c) and (d) sentences below (see [L2(B7)]). As in (c), it can express a sense of discovery for the speaker, and also as in (d), it can communicate new information to the hearer.

(c)   *Achisa sa.*   'It's hot. (I didn't think that was the case.)'

(d)   *Achisa sa.*   '**You know**, it's (still) hot. (So you can make tea.)'

The difference with *ssaa* is that first, *ssaa* is more emphatic than that with *sa*. Second, a sentence with *ssaa* is not necessarily uttered with the hearer in mind (see the picture (a)) while that with *sa* could be directed to the hearer (see the picture (d)), though this hearer-orientation may not be as strong as *doo* [L1(A5)].

Here is another set of similar sentences.

a. *Nai ssaa.*   '**Oh, my!** He/she indeed can do it.'
b. *Nain tee.*   '**I believe/guess** he/she can do it.'
c. *Nai sa.*   '**I assure you** that I/you/he/she can do it.'

ADDITIONAL VOCABULARY

See [A1] for body parts.
gumasan 'small'
hikusan 'low'
inchasan 'short'

magisan 'big'
nagasan 'long'
takasan 'expensive / tall / big (nose)'
yin 'yen' (Japanese currency)

76   PART I   Conversation

EXERCISES A

1. Each picture frame has two people. According to the description under each frame, choose either the left or the right person (circle R or L), and complete the blanks as shown in the example. Then find the appropriate adjective from the Word Bank below and write it in ___. Finally, translate each sentence in [___].

   Example: (R / L) (*Hisa nu*) <u>*nagasan*</u>. [(He) has long legs.]

   a. (R / L) (_____) _____ [_____]
   b. (R / L) (_____) _____ [_____]
   c. (R / L) (_____) _____ [_____]

   Word Bank [*nagasan, inchasan, gumasan, magisan, takasan, hikusan*]

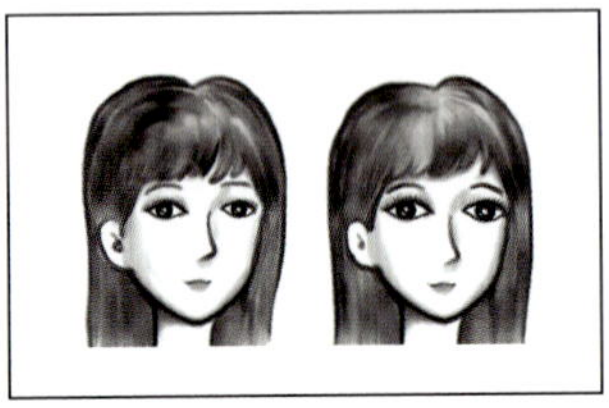

   (a) big eyes 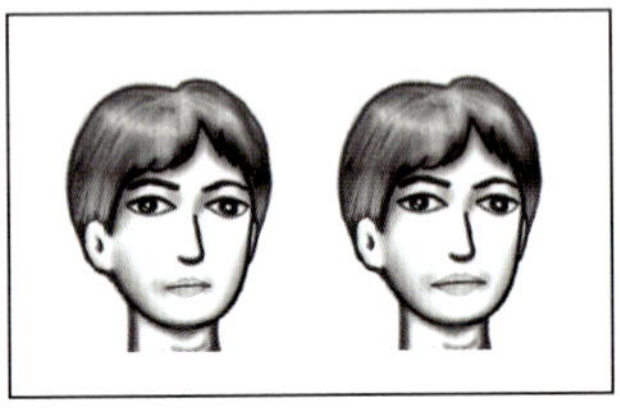   (b) small mouth 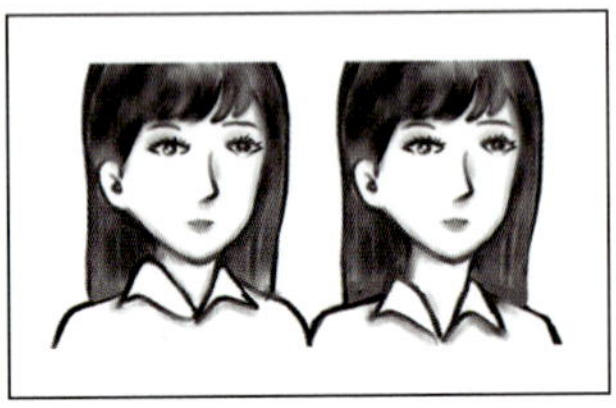   (c) long neck

2. Insert the appropriate word based on the picture to the right. Use the plain form for X, and the polite form for Y.

   a. X: (_____) nu (_____) ga?

      'Where does it hurt?'

      Y: (_____) nu (_____).

   b. X: (_____) nu (_____) ga?

      'Where does it *hurt*?'

      Y: (_____) nu (_____).

3. Rewrite the following sentences **in bold** into focus sentences with *du*.

   a. *Mimi ya aran.* ***Mii nu yamun.***   _____

   b. *Chinuu ya aran,* ***Chuu chukutan.*** _____

   c. *Taa ga su gayaa.* ***Shogo ga sumi?*** _____

LESSON 4   Do You Have Pain Somewhere?   77

   d. A: *Wata nu yamu ssaa. Kusui numu gayaa.* 'I wonder if I should take medicine.'

   B: **Numun.** _____

   e. **Achisami?** _____

4. Using the choices given to the right, match the correct interpretation of each of the following sentences. Write the correct letter in the [__].

   a. *Yin ya agai gayaa.*   [__]   (a) 'I wonder if (the value of) the yen will rise?'

   Yin ya agaimi?   [__]   (b) 'Will (the value of) the yen rise?'

   b. *Yin ya agatoon yaa.*   [__]   (a) 'You may not know yet, but (the value of) the yen has risen.'

   Yin ya agatoon doo.   [__]   (b) (After you checked the value of the yen with your friend, you say to your friend) '(The value of) the yen has risen, hasn't it?'

   c. *Maasan tee.*   [__]   (a) 'It must be good. (The children are eating a lot.)'

   Maasa ssaa.   [__]   (b) 'This is good. (Why don't you try it?)'

   Maasa sa.   [__]   (c) 'Yummy!'

DIALOGUE B

Niko:	*Sakkwii ya sabiran **shiga**, anmasa**nu**, daritooibiin.*	I don't cough, but I feel sick, and so I don't feel well.
Mother:	*Anshee chuu ya gakkoo yashimu **shee** mashi ya sa.*	Then you'd better skip school today.
Niko:	***Nuugana** kusui nu aibiimi?*	Do you have some medicine or something?
Mother:	***Nuu** nu ata gayaa.*	(Let me see.) What do I have?

(Mother goes to look for medicine in the medicine cabinet.)

(Niko takes the medicine and rests for a while.)

Niko: Kusui nuda **kutu**, nichi n sagati, mashi natooibiin. — Because I took the medicine, the fever has gone down and I feel better now.

Mother: Anshee, jootuu ya sa. — Then it's good! (I tell you!)

CORE VOCABULARY

sakkwii	'cough'
sabiran	← s 'do' + abi (POL.) + ran (NEG)
shiga	'however, but' [B1]
anmasanu	← anmasa 'sick' + nu [B2]
daritooibiin	← dari 'feel tired' + too (ASP) + ibiin (POL.)
yashimu (APO.FORM)	← yashimun 'rest, skip (school, etc.)'
shee	← shi + ya [B3]
mashi	'better'
nuugana	'something' [A2]
kusui	'medicine'
kutu/gutu	'so, because' [B1] [1]
sagati (G.FORM)	← sagain '(fever) goes down, and…' [L3(C3)]
jootuu	'great', 'fantastic'

[1] *kutu* and *gutu* are equally common. In this book, we only use *kutu*.

GRAMMAR B

1. Conjunctive Particles: [APO.FORM + *kutu*] 'so' vs. [APO.FORM + *shiga*] 'but'

Kutu and *shiga* are conjunctive particles which connect two clauses [Part II, Topic 6]. *Kutu* expresses causes as in 'A, so B', while *shiga* denotes contrasts, 'A, but B.' These two conjunctive particles attach to the Apocopated Form of verbs and adjectives as illustrated in the following examples:

- *numu-n* 'drink' → *numu* {kutu /shiga} (nonpast)
  nuda-n → *nuda* {kutu /shiga} (past)
- *maasa-n* 'delicious' → *maasa* {kutu /shiga} (nonpast)
  maasata-n → *maasa-ta* {kutu /shiga} (past)

However, for negatives, both *kutu* and *shiga* attach to the Negative Forms (*-(r)an*) **for nonpast**, and the Apocopated Form **for the past**.

- *numan* 'not drink' → ***numan*** {*kutu /shiga*} (nonpast)
  numan-tan → ***numan-ta*** (**tan*) {*kutu /shiga*} (past)

- *maakooneen* 'not delicious' → ***maakooneen*** {*kutu /shiga*} (nonpast)
  maakooneen-tan → ***maakooneen-ta*** (**tan*) {*kutu /shiga*} (past)

Here are some more examples. Notice 'A *kutu* B' can be translated as: 'A, so B', 'Because/since A, B', or 'B, because/since A'. Likewise, 'A *shiga* B' can be translated as: 'A, but B', '(Al)though A, B', or 'B (al)though A'. English has more flexibility in expressing these meanings, hence the multiple translations.

kutu

- *Ami nu fui **kutu** kasa kain.*
  'It will rain, so I will borrow an umbrella.'
  / 'I will borrow an umbrella because it will rain.'
- *Ami nu futa **kutu** kasa katan.*
  'It rained, so I borrowed an umbrella.' / 'I borrowed an umbrella because it rained.'

- *Kusui nuda **kutu**, nichi n sagati, mashi natooibiin.*
  'Since I took medicine, my fever went down and I've been feeling good.'
- *Muuchii ya maasa **kutu**, dateen kadan.*
  'The *muuchii* was good, so I ate a lot of them.'
- *Sakkwii ya sabiran **kutu**, hanafichee aibiran.*
  'Since I don't cough, I don't have a cold.'

shiga

- *Ami nu fui shiga kasaa karan.*
  'It'll rain, but I won't borrow an umbrella.' /
  'I won't borrow an umbrella although it will rain.'
- *Ami nu fuita shiga kasaa karantan.*
  'It was raining, but I didn't borrow an umbrella.' /
  'I didn't borrow an umbrella though it was raining.'
- *Wattaa yaaninjoo ikirasa **shiga**, unju naa taa ya ufusaibiin yaa.*
  'My family is small, but your family is big.'
- *Wattaa yaaninjoo ufukoonee(ya)biran **shiga**, unju naa taa ya ufusaibiin yaa.*
  'My family is not big, but your family is big.'

2. Expression of causes: [APO.FORM (Adj.) + *nu*] '(adj.) so ~'

Adjectives (not verbs) in their Apocopated Forms express **causes** when they are directly followed by the particle *nu*: 'A so B' / 'Because A, B' / 'B, because A.'

- *Anmasa**nu**, daritooibiin.* 'I feel sick, and so I am sluggish.'
- *Saataa nu ikirasa**nu**, naa ufee irii shee mashi yan.* '(The amount of) sugar is insufficient, so it is better to put some more in.'

3. Nominalization: [APO.FORM + *shi*]

Apocopated Forms are also used with the nominalizer *shi* to create abstract nouns for persons, things, places, times, acts, etc. When contracted with the topic particle *ya*, this particle appears as *shee*. This *shee* is different from the *shee* we studied in [L1(A3)] (e.g., *Uchinaaguchi shee* 'in Okinawan'). The *shee* in this earlier phrase is a contraction of *shi* (an instrumental particle, e.g., 'by, in') and *ya* (topic particle).

- *[Achaa gakkoo yashimu]* **shee** *Yuna yan.* 'The **one** [who will not go to school tomorrow] is Yuna.'
- *[Yuna {ga/*^x*ya} gakkoo yashimu]* **shee** *achaa yan.* 'The **day** [when Yuna will not go to school] is tomorrow.'

☞ The bracketed part in the Okinawan sentence modifies *shee*, and the subject (e.g. *Yuna*) appears within the modifying clause. In this case, *ya* (TOP) cannot be used, and *ga* (SUBJ) must be used.

- *Yuna ya [chuu gakkoo yashimu]* **shee** *mashi yan.* 'As for Yuna, it's best [that she skip school today].'
- *Shogo ga chinuu numuta* **shee** *Orion biiru yatan.* 'The **one** Shogo drank yesterday was Orion beer.'
- *Maasa* **shee** *chinkwaa yan.* 'The **one** that is tasty is pumpkin (flavor).'
- *Churasa* **shee** *Hanashiro Shinshii yan.* 'The **one** that is pretty is Prof. Hanashiro.'

Remember that when a concrete noun is used instead of the *shi* nominalizer, you must use the Adnominal Form. See [A3]. Compare these with the above examples.

- *Achaa gakkoo yashimu**ru** tchoo Yuna yan.* 'The **person** who will not go to school is Yuna.'
- *Maasa**ru** muuchii ya nankwaa yan.* 'The *muuchii* that is tasty is pumpkin (flavor).'

ADDITIONAL VOCABULARY

araimun 'laundry, something (to be) washed'
chuusan 'strong'
dateen 'a lot'
shikaraasan 'lonely'
madu 'window'
mandoon 'very strong'
kaagi / gutee nu mandoon 'very handsome, beautiful'
kain 'to borrow'
shima 'Okinawan-style sumo wrestling'
yaasan 'hungry'
yii kaagi 'handsome, beautiful'

EXERCISES B

1. Complete the *kutu* and *shiga* clauses below as in the example.

   Example:
   ʔwiijun: since I will swim → **ʔwiiju kutu**; although I swam → **ʔwiija shiga**

   a. *yuufuru nkai iin*: although I'll take a bath → _____

   b. *nichi nu an*: since I have a fever → _____

   c. *michiin*: since I didn't close the windows → _____

   d. *shikaraasan*: although I was lonely → _____

2. First, find the reasonable continuation for each sentence from the list on the right-hand side. Then, translate the whole sentence.

   a. (__) *Chinuu ya chiburu nu yamuta kutu,*   A. *gakkoo ya yashimantan.*

   b. (__) *Duu nu darusata shiga,*   B. *kumaa takasan.*

   c. (__) *Kuree maakooneenta kutu,*   C. *nintootan.*

   d. (__) *Amaa yassa shiga,*   D. *kamantan.*

   e. (__) *Chinuu nuda shee*   E. *kunu kusui du yarui?*

a. _____
b. _____
c. _____
d. _____
e. _____

3. Choose the correct form.

   a. A: *Yaasa ssaa!*   'Boy! Am I hungry!'

      B: *Muuchii { kamani / kamu ga}?*   'Want to eat *muuchii*?'

      A: *Ii.*

      B: *Ai, muuchii ya { neen / an } doo.*   '[After checking], Oh, no! There's NO *muuchii*.'

      A: *Anshee, { nuu / nuugana } kamu ga?*   'Then, what shall we eat?'

      B: *{ Nuu / Nuugana } neen gayaa.*   'I wonder if there's anything to eat.'

   b. A (to his friends): *{ Taagana / Taa ga} jin mutchoomi?*

      B: *Wannee { neen / a } shiga, {taagana / taa ga} mutchoo ga?*

      Tamanaha san ya chaa ya gayaa.

      A (to Tamanaha san): *ʔyaa jin mutchoom { i / ga}?*

      B: *Yii yii, { neen / an } doo.*

4. Follow the example, and report who is doing these activities.

| Ex |  | Edie

ATM kara jin ʔnjachoo shee (shi + ya) Edie yan. |

LESSON 4   Do You Have Pain Somewhere?   83

a.		Amy
b.		Lewis
c.		Leo
d.		Shogo
e.		Lina (dinner)

5. Insert Okinawan verbs in the blanks. Be sure to use the correct form (the Apocopated Form or Adnominal Form).

   a. *Chinuu (_____) munu ya isatuu yatan.* (caught)

      Chinuu (_____) shee aakeejuu yatan.

   b. *Sally ga (_____) munoo tako raisu yatan.* (cooked)

      Sally ga (_____) shee tako raisu yatan.

   c. *Ari ga (_____) geemu ya Final Fantasy yatan.* (did)

      Ari ga (_____) shee Final Fantasy yatan.

84 PART I Conversation

6. Answer the following questions negatively. Be sure to use **wuu wuu** (polite) or **yii yii** (plain) for the first blank and provide the appropriate information for the second blank (Cf. [L3(B4)]). Be sure also to think about the level of speech both for the 'no' part and the predicate.

   a. A: *ʔyaa n bideo geemu san-i?* (**A and B are friends**)

   B: (_____), *wannee achaa shiken nu a kutu,*

   chuu ya (_____).

   b. A: *Amaa takakoo neen-i?* (**A is older than B**)

   B: (_____), (_____) *doo. Baagen*

   'bargain' ya kutu yassa du aibiiru.

APPLICATIONS

1. Sing along with the Okinawan version of the 'head, shoulders, knees and toes…' song.

   https://www.youtube.com/watch?v=BIcnuPk83co

   ✍ The word *uppi* said at the end means 'that's all'. Another word with the same meaning is *ussa*.

2. Using adjectives you know in their Adnominal Form, create exchanges as in the example:

   A: *Hisa nu feesaru tchoo taa ya ga?* 'Who runs fast?'
   B: *Lewis yan yaa.* 'It is Lewis.'

3. Using the following example as a model, create your own short conversation by writing a sentence in the blanks.

   Example:

   A: *Chuu ya jun ni ʔwiirikisan.*
   B: **Nuugana ai du shii?** ('Is it that something (good) happened?')
   A: **Waa tesutu ya sa.** *Dateen agatan* doo.

   ✍ The past-tense focus pattern [*du…shi-i?* (verb) / *du…ati-i?* (adjective)] in question is not formally introduced in this lesson, but we recommend memorizing it as a formulaic expression as it is useful in conversations.

A: *Chuu ya junni ʔwiirikisan.*
B: **Nuugana ai du shii?**

A: _____ ('got an A').

A: *Chuu ya junni nachikasan.* ('sad')
B: **Nuugana ai du shii?**

A: *Bittocoin nu* _____ ('Bitcoin "cryptocurrency" has plummeted').

4. Referencing the example below, describe one of your family members.

   Example: *Wattaa yatchii ya ippee yii kaagi yaibiin. Hisa nu magisaibii kutu, duu n magisaibiin. Gutee n mandoo kutu, shima n ippee chuusaibiin. Yashiga, chiburoo magikooneebiran. Binchoo ya ansuka naibiran yaa.*

   _____

   _____

   _____

   _____

   _____

   _____

   _____

5. Your friend doesn't seem well. Make a dialogue between you and your friend similar to the one in this lesson.

   _____

   _____

   _____

   _____

   _____

   _____

   _____

CULTURAL NOTES

1. Spirits: *shii* and *mabui*

In Okinawa, we hear the expression *shii nugitoon* 'the spirit has escaped' when one is sick. Also related to this, some Okinawan people believe people lose their *mabui* 'spirit' when they fall down or get injured. When this happens, people would return to the location and perform a *mabui-gumi* 'regaining spirit' ritual. In the following, *saa* and *suu* also mean 'spirit' (Takara 2005a: 72–73).

saa-dakasan   'sensitive to spiritual things'
suu-juusan   'where sprits are strong (e.g. cemetery, location of frequent traffic accidents)'

- You may have read about phenomena in which spirits travel out of their bodies in comic book stories such as *Dragon Ball* and *Yuuyuu Hakusho*. Find out what they do in these comic book stories. Do you know any other comic book or anime stories that feature such spirit travels? Describe when that happens and what they do.
- Do you know any culture in which one's body and spirit are viewed as two different entities? Describe their practices and your own thoughts about it.

2. "God Bless You!" in Okinawan

Sneezing is often associated with an onset of catching a cold. In Okinawa, people say *kusu kwee hyaa* to someone who sneezes. When translated literally, it means 'Eat shit!'. You may think this is a terrible thing to say to someone, but it is actually directed at the evil spirit that causes sneezing. During the time of dialect suppression (cf. Shinzato 2003b), students could not use any words from their dialect and were expected to use Standard Japanese. If they broke this rule, they would be punished. One day, someone sneezed. One student was about to say *kusu kwee hyaa,* but changed his mind and instead translated it into Japanese as *unko meshiagare* 'Please eat your shit (in polite Japanese).' The entire class burst into laughter. (For etymologies of this Okinawan incantation originating in the Buddhist term *kusoku manmei* 'rest forever' and cross-cultural studies of related chants, see Onochi 2008.)

- In English, we say "God bless you!" Why do we say that? Do you know similar expressions in any other language(s)?
- We also have expressions to avoid bad luck. What does "Break a leg!" mean? Do you know any similar expressions in any other language(s)?

REVIEW EXERCISES

Lessons 3 and 4

1. Fill in the blanks.

DIC. FORM	Meaning	Neg.	Gerund	PAST-1 (S)	PAST-1 (Q)	PAST-2 (S)	PAST-2 (Q)
wakain	'to understand'		wakati	waka-tan	wakati-i?	wakai-tan	wakai-ti-i?
ʔwiijun				ʔwiij-an			
nnjun		nnd-an					
kunjun							
kachun		kak-an					
chichun			chichi				
muchun		mut-an				muchu-tan	
yubun		yub-an					
chichimun		chichim-an	chichid-an				
sun					sshi-i?		
iin	'to say'		ichi				
an						a-tan	a-ti-i?
wun	'to exist-ANIM'			wu-tan	wuti-i?	wu-tan	wu-ti-i?

88   PART I   Conversation

2. Fill in the blanks. You may use WB for the TR/INTR column. [s.o. = someone; s.t. = something]
   [G.ROOT—(t)oon]: Progressive ((s.o.) is doing (s.t.)) / Resultative ((s.t.) is done)

DIC.FORM	English	TR/INTR	Aspectual	Meaning
sagi-in	'to dangle from'	TR	*sagi-toon*	'(s.o.) is dangling x from y'
saga-in	'to be hung down'	INTR	*saga-toon*	'(s.t.) has been hung down'
iri-in				
i-in				
aga-in				
agi-in				

3. Choose the correct verb to match the given translation.

   a. *Araimun nu { sagitoon / sagatoon }.*   'The laundry is hung.'
   b. *Araimun { sagitoon / sagatoon }.*   'I'm hanging the laundry.'
   c. *Shiru nkai n(n)su { iriin / iin }.*   'I'll put miso in the soup.'
   d. *N(n)su ya { iritoon / itchoon }.*   'Miso is put in the soup.'
   e. *Tii { agiin / again }.*   'I raise my hands.'
   f. *Tii nu { agitoon / agatoon }.*   'A hand is raised.'

4. Fill in the blank to make a sentence that matches the given image or the cue. Be sure to use the appropriate particle in (__). If no particle is necessary, write 'X' in the (__).

   a. A: *Nuu soo ga?*
      B: *Saataa (_____) _____*

   b. A: *Saataa ya itchoo gayaa.*
      B: *Ii. Saataa ya _____* ('be put in').

   c. A: *Nuu soo ga?*
      B: *Taku (_____) _____* ('flying a kite')

   d. A: *Ama, Ama.* (A points to the kite in the sky.)
      B: *Ai, ai. Taku (_____) _____*

5. Match the following.

   a. (___) *Tinpura agiin.*   A. 'I deep fried (tempura ingredients).'

   (___) *Tinpuraa agatoon.*   B. 'I saw him deep frying it.'

   (___) *Tinpura agitan.*   C. 'It is deep fried.'

   (___) *Tinpura agiitan.*   D. 'Shall I deep fry it?'

   (___) *Tinpura agiimi?*   E. 'I am going to deep fry it.'

   b. (___) *Muuchii ya sagatoon.*   A. 'I hung up *muuchii*.'

   (___) *Muuchii sagiimi?*   B. 'I am hanging up *muuchii*.'

   (___) *Muuchii sagitoon.*   C. 'I saw him hanging up *muuchii*.'

   (___) *Muuchii sagitan.*   D. 'Shall (I) hang (your) *muuchii* up?'

   (___) *Muuchii sagiitan*   E. '*Muuchii* are hung up.'

6. Review the difference between PAST-1 and PAST-2 as below.

	Statement
PAST-1: G.ROOT + *an* (*yud-an*): PAST-2: APOCO + *tan* (*yumu-tan*):	Speaker's direct experience ('I did ~') Speaker's observation ('*I saw someone doing ~*')
	Question
PAST-1: GERUND + *i* (*yudi-i?*): PAST-2: change *-tan* (PAST-2) to *-ti-i*:	Hearer's experience ('Did *you* do ~?) Hearer's observation ('Did *you* see s.o. doing ~?')

Choose the correct form.

a. S: *?yaa ya chinuu muuchii { kadi-i / kamuti-i }?*

   H: *Ii, { kad-an / kamu-tan } doo.*

   S: *Ari n { kadi-i / kamuti-i }?*

   H: *Ari n { kad-an / kamu-tan } doo.*

b. S: *Wannee chinuu saafin { s-an / su-tan } doo. ?yaa n { shi-i? / su-tii? }*

   H: *Yii yii. Wannee santan.*

7. Review the focus sentences (*du* ... ADNOM.FORM).

   - [Hanako] ya chiburu nu yamun. → Hanako **ga du** chibu**ru** nu yamu**ru**.
     Hanako ya [chiburu] nu yamun. → Hanako ya chiburu **nu du** yamu**ru**.
     Hanako ya chiburu nu [yamun]. → Hanako ya chiburu nu **yami du suru**.

   - [UNIQLO] ya yassami? → UNIQLO **ga du** yassa**rui**? (not Gucci, for instance)
     UNIQLO ya [yassami]? → UNIQLO ya **yassa du arui**? (That's why you're buying?)

   Using the above patterns, rewrite the sentences below with the bracketed part as a focus.

   a. [Shogo] ya Uchinaaguchi narain. → _____

   b. Shogo ya [Uchinaaguchi] narain. → _____

   c. Shogo ya Uchinaaguchi [narain]. → _____

8. Here are the first parts of a few sentences. From the list below, choose the phrase that best finishes each sentence. Then translate each completed sentence into English.

   A. ari n magisan
   B. ari n ʔwiirikisan.
   C. gakkoo nkai ʔnjan.
   D. gakkoo yashidan.
   E. numantan.

   a. Chinuu ya anmasanu, (_____).

      English: _____

   b. Chiburu yamuta shiga, (_____).

      English: _____

   c. Wannee nuda shiga, aree (_____).

      English: _____

   d. Attaa taarrii ya magisa kutu, (_____).

      English: _____

9. Fill in the blanks using [ADNOM.FORM + CONCRETE NOUN] or [APO.FORM + *shi*].

   Example: *Higa sannoo Uchinaa shibai nnjun. Teruya sannoo Uchinaa nu uta chichun.*

   → *Shibai nnju**ru tchoo** Higa san yan. Uchinaa nu uta chichu**ru tchoo** Teruya san yan.*
   → *Shibai nnju **shee** (← shi + ya) Higa san yan. Uchinaa nu uta chichu **shee** Teruya san yan.*

   a. *Shikina san(n)oo (← san + ya) <u>chinkwaa</u> nu muuchii kamun.* (Note: ya → ga)

      → *Shikina san ga (_____) muuchii ya chinkwaa yan.*

      → *Shikina san ga (_____) chinkwaa yan.*

   b. *Yamashiro san ya <u>achaa</u> ʔwiijun.*

      → *Yamashiro san ga (_____) hii ya achaa yan.*

      → *Yamahiro san ga (_____) achaa yan.*

10. Choose the correct one.

    a. A: *Achaa nu tesutu ya muchikasa gayaa?*

       B: *Ii. Anu shinshii nu tesutu ya kutu, (muchikasan / muchikasa) tee.*

    b. A: *Maasaibiimi?*

       B: *Ii, (maasan / maasa) ssaa.*

    c. A: *Chuu ya toofu champuruu ya arani?*

       B: *(Yii yii / Ii) aran doo.* (Cf. [L3(GB4)])

    d. A: *Uree Yamatuguchee aran-i?* (A is B's grandmother, Cf. [L3(GB4)])

       B: *(Yii yii / Wuu wuu), (aran / aibiran / yan). Kuree Uchinaa-Yamatuguchi du yaibiiru.* [Note: *Uchinaa-Yamatuguchi* is a hybrid of Okinawan and Japanese.]

11. Select the correct words or forms for the conversations below.

    a. S: { *Maa / Maagana* } *yami du surui?*

       H: *Uu. Ufee* { *yamibiin / yamabiin* }.

       S: { *Maa / Maagana* } *nu yamu ga?*

       H: *Yamu* { *kutu / shiga / shee* } *wata yaibiin.*

       S: { *Nuu / Nuugana* } *kada ga?*

b. S: *Nuudii nu yamu { ssaa / tee }*. 'I have pain in my throat.'

   H: *Kusui { numu / numi / nuda } shee mashi ya sa. Uri uri.*

   — A few hours later —

   S: *Kusui nuda { kutu / shiga }, mashi natooibiin.*

LESSON 5

Riding in a Taxi / Grocery Shopping at the Market

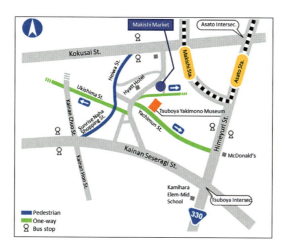

DIALOGUE A

Niko's host mother decided to take a taxi to the market to make Niko an Okinawan version of chicken soup.

(Mother is standing at a street corner near her house and is talking to herself.)

Mother: ***Basu tu takushii tu jiroo mashi ya** gayaa.* I wonder which is better, the bus or the
*Ai, ama kara takushii nu **chuu** sa.* taxi? Oh, I see a taxi is coming from
*Anshee takushii **kara ika**.* there. I will go by taxi.

(Mother gets into the taxi. The driver greets her.)

Driver:	Hai sai. Maa **madi menshee** ga?		Hello. Where are you going, ma'am?
Mother:	Machigwaa **nkai** yaa.		To the Makishi market, please.
Driver:	Kainan **kara** tuuibiimi?		Should I take the Kainan route?
Mother:	Yii yii, Asatu **karaa** mashee arani?		No, the Asato route might be better?
Driver:	Uu, yaibiin yaa sai. Kainanoo nama michi nu wassa nu, **tuuigurusa**ibii sa. Asatu nu du **ichiyassa**ibii sa.		Yes, that is right. As for Kainan, its road is bad, so it is difficult to go through. The Asato route is easy to go through.

CORE VOCABULARY

basu	'bus'
takushii	'taxi'
chuu (APO.FORM)	← *chuun* 'to come' [A1]
jiroo	← *jiru* 'which?' + *ya* (TOP)
kara	'by means of' (transportation)
ika (INT.FORM)	← *ichun* 'to go' [C2]
madi	'as far as' [A3]
menshee (APO.FORM)	← *mensheen* 'to go/come/stay (EXAL)' [C1]
Machigwaa	'Makishi Market'
gwaa	DIM (diminutive suffix) [A5]
nkai	'to' [A3]
kara	'through' [A4]
tuu-ibiim-i? or *tuu-yabiim-i?*	← *tuu* 'go through' + *ibiim* /*yabiim* (POL) + *i* (QP)
michi	'road'
wassa (APO.FORM)	← *wassan* 'bad'
tuui (ADV.FORM)	← *tuuin* 'to go through'
-gurisa-ibii (APO.FORM)	'hard to V' [A2]
ichi (ADV.FORM)	← *ichun* 'to go' [A1]

GRAMMAR A

1. Verbs of Motion: *ichun* 'to go' and *chuun* 'to come'

Basic verbs of motion are *ichun* 'to go' and *chuun* 'to come'. They are irregular verbs as shown below. Remember PAST-1 depicts directly experienced events (the speaker's experience) while the PAST-2 form is used for observed events (the speaker's observation of others' acts) (see [L3(B1)]).

[G.ROOT = GERUND ROOT, G.FORM = GERUND FORM, APO.FORM = APOCOPATED FORM]

Plain Forms

	DIC.FORM	APO. FORM	PAST-2	G.ROOT/ G.FORM	ASP	PAST-1	NEG. FORM	ADNOM. FORM
'to go'	ichu-n	ichu	ichu-tan	ʔnj/ʔnji	ʔnj-oon	ʔnj-an	ika-n	ichu-ru
'to come'	chuu-n	chuu	chuu-tan	tch/tchi	(t)ch-oon	ch-an	kuu-n	chuu-ru

Polite Forms

	POLITE	APO. FORM	PAST-2	ASP	PAST-1	NEG.FORM	ADNOM.FORM
'to go'	ich-abii-n	ich-abii	ich-abii-tan	ʔnj-oo-ibiin	ich-abi-tan	ich-abi-ran	ich-abii-ru
'to come'	cha-abii-n	cha-abii	cha-abii-tan	(t)ch-oo-ibiin	cha-abi-tan	cha-abi-ran	cha-abii-ru

Here are some examples of each of the forms from left to right in the tables above. Note that the motion verbs often occur with locational nouns (*Naafa, Hawai*) or locational demonstratives: *kuma* 'here', *uma* 'there', *ama* 'over there':

'To go'
- *Wannee achaa Naafa nkai **ichun**.* 'I will go to Naha tomorrow.'
- *Ama nkai **ichu** shee Jiibu san yan.* 'The one going there is Gibo.'
- *Aree chinuu Naafa nkai **ichutan**.* 'I saw him going to Naha yesterday.'
- *Wannee chinuu Naafa nkai **ʔnji**, chitu kootan.* 'I went to Naha yesterday, and I bought a gift.'
- *Aree nama Naafa nkai **njoon** doo.* 'He's gone to Naha (and is now there), you know.'

- *Wannee chinuu Naafa nkai ʔnjan doo.* — 'I went to Naha yesterday.'
- *Wannee achaa Naafa nkai ya ikan, Sui nkai du ichuru.* [focus pattern: *du…* ADNOM.FORM] — 'I won't go to Naha tomorrow, it is Shuri that I'm going to.'

'Come'

- *Nama shigu chuun.* — 'I am coming right away. / He will come here right away.'
- *Ama kara chuu shee Pensy yan.* — 'The one coming from there is Pensy.'
- *Aree ama kara chuutan doo.* — '(I saw him) coming from there, you know.'
- *Wannee chinuu kuma nkai tchi, chitu kootan.* — 'I came here yesterday, and bought a gift.'
- *Aree choon doo.* — 'He's come (and is now here), you know.'
- *Wannee chinuu kuma nkai chan doo.* — 'I came here yesterday (I tell you).'
- *Wannee achaa ya kuun, asati du chuuru.* — 'I won't be coming tomorrow, it is the day after tomorrow that I'm coming.'

2. Expressions of Ease and Difficulty: [ADV.FORM + *yassan*] 'easy to do (something)'; [ADV.FORM + *gurisan*] 'hard to do (something)'

The suffixes -*yassan* and -*gurisan* are used with the Adverbial Form (= B.ROOT + *i*) of verbs. The table below lists the Adverbial Forms and as a reference Gerund Forms. (Shaded areas show the differences in the consonants in the regular C-verbs.)

	Dictionary	ADV.FORM	Gerund Form	Form	Meaning
V	waka-in	waka-i	waka-ti	wakai-yassan	'easy to understand'
V	maga-in	maga-i	maga-ti	magai-gurisan	'difficult to turn'
1	ʔwiij-un	ʔwiij-i	ʔwiij-i	ʔwiiji-yassan	'easy to swim'
2	ninj-un	ninj-i	nint-i	ninji-gurisan	'difficult to sleep'
3	kunj-un	kunj-i	kunch-i	kunji-yassan	'easy to tie up'
4	kach-un	kach-i	kach-i	kachi-gurisan	'difficult to write'

LESSON 5 Riding in a Taxi / Grocery Shopping at the Market

	Dictionary	ADV.FORM	Gerund Form	Form	Meaning
5	*much*-un	*much-i*	*mutch-i*	*muchi-yassan*	'easy to hold'
6	*turas*-un	*turash-i*	*turach-i*	*turashi-gurisan*	'difficult to give'
7	*yub*-un	*yub-i*	*yud-i*	*yubi-yassan*	'easy to invite'
8	*yum*-un	*yum-i*	*yud-i*	*yumi-gurisan*	'difficult to read'
IRG	*ichun*	*ich-i*	*ʔnj-i*	*ichi-yassan*	'easy to go'
IRG	*chuun*	*chi-i*	*tch-i*	*chii-gurisan*	'difficult to come'
IRG	*sun*	*shi-i*	*ssh-i*	*shii-yassan*	'easy to do'

Here are some examples:

- *Kunu futonoo yafarasanu, **ninjiyassan**. Anu futonoo kufasanu **ninjigurisan**.*
  'This futon is soft, so it is easy to sleep. That futon is hard, so it's difficult to sleep.'

- *Kunu hunoo muchikasakooneen kutu, **yumiyassan**.*
  'Since this book is not difficult, it is easy to read.'

- *Uchinaa nu noojee **yumigurisaibii** ssa.*
  'Okinawan names are hard to read.' (inset)

- *Kainanoo nama michi nu wassanu, **tu-uigurisaibii** sa.*
  'As for the Kainan area, its road is bad, so it is difficult to go through.'

3. Particles: *nkai* 'to' and *madi* 'as far as (time/space)'

The following two particles are used to show the goal of a motion with a location noun. *Madi* can be also used with a temporal noun (e.g., 'until noon').

***nkai* 'to (goal)'**

✍ *nkai* has been introduced as an indirect object marker [Preliminary Lesson]; 'into' [L3(C2)]; 'at/in' [L2(B6)].

- *Machigwaa **nkai** ichun.*   'I will go to Makishi Market.'
- *Nijiri **nkai** magain.*   'I will turn right.'
- *Kuma **nkai** kuun naa?*   'Won't you come here?'

✍ This particle has two variants: *-unkai* if the preceding noun ends with *n* (e.g. *Kainan unkai* 'to Kainan'), and *-ninkai* if it follows *wan* (*wan ninkai* 'to me'). These variants parallel the variants of the additive topic marker *n* 'also': *hun-un* 'book, too' and *wan-nin* 'I, too'.]

madi 'as far as (time/space)'

- *Maa **madi** menshee ga?*   '(As far as) where are you going?'
- *Ama **madi** kuruma kara ichun.*   'I will go there by car.'
- *Achaa **madi** machu sa.*   'I will wait until tomorrow.'

4. Particle: *kara* 'by means of' and 'through'

This particle has two different meanings in addition to the one meaning 'from', which was already introduced in [L3(C2)].

Kara (1) 'by means of (transportation)'

- *Ama madi takushii **kara** ichun.*   'I will go there by taxi.'
- *Hawai **kara**$_a$ kuma nkai ya hikooki **kara**$_b$ chan.*   'I came from$_a$ Hawaii by$_b$ an airplane.'

Kara (2) 'through (path/route)'

- *Asatu **kara** tuuibiimi?*   'Shall I go through (a route through) Asato?'
- *Michi **kara** atchun.*   'Walk along the street.'

5. Diminutive Suffix: *gwaa*

The diminutive suffix, *gwaa*, normally attaches to a noun and emphasizes smallness, cuteness, and/or affection, but in some circumstances, smallness may exude a derogatory tone as in the last example given below.

- *machiya **gwaa***   'small shop'
- *kuuga **gwaa***   'eggs'
- *Taraa **gwaa***   'Taraa (who is dear to me)'
- *yatchii **gwaa***   'my elder brother (with a derogatory tone)'

☞ A derogatory tone is created because normally an older brother is treated as 'big', not 'small'.

6. Wh-Word: *jiru* 'which?'

When asking 'Which one is...?', *jiru* is used with the topic marking particle *ya*. The combination of *jiru* + *ya* often gets contracted as *jiroo*.

- A: ***Jiroo** mashi ya gayaa.*   'I wonder which one you like.'
  B: *Wannee kurujaataa ya mashi yaibii ssaa.*   'I like the brown sugar (flavor)!'
- A: *Aree **jiroo** mashi ya gayaa.*   'I wonder which one he likes better.'
  B: *Chinkwaa ya mashi yaibii sa.*   '(I guess) he likes pumpkin (flavor).'

ADDITIONAL VOCABULARY

atchun 'walk'
futon 'bedding'
hikooki 'airplane'
katasan 'hard'
machiya 'small shop'

machun 'to wait'
shigu 'right away'
shishi 'meat'
yafarasan 'soft'

EXERCISES A

1. Suppose you are translating the following English sentences with 'to come/go' into Okinawan. What verb form do you need to use? Put the correct Plain Form of the Okinawan verb of motion in (__) and the name of the form in [__].

   Example: I will *go*. (*ichun*) [Dictionary Form]

   a. It is Pensy who will *go*. (_____)[_____]
   b. The person (i.e., *tchu*) who will *come* is … (_____)[_____]
   c. The one (i.e., *shi*) who will *come* is … (_____)[_____]
   d. I *went* there yesterday… (_____)[_____]
   e. I saw him *going*… (_____)[_____]
   f. He has *gone* there (i.e., he is there)… (_____)[_____]
   g. I *won't go*… (_____)[_____]
   h. I *went*, and… (_____)[_____]

2. Fill in the blanks with the appropriate verbs of motion.

   a. *Kunu basu n Asatu nkai* (_____) *doo*.
      'This bus also goes to Asato.'

   b. *Wannee chinuu Naafa nkai* (_____), *gurukun kootan*.
      'I went to Naha yesterday, and bought *gurukun*.'

   c. *Wannee chinuu kuma nkai* (_____) *doo*.
      'I came here yesterday (I tell you).'

PART I   Conversation

   d. *Aree chinuu ya* (_____), *chuu du* (_____).
      'He didn't come yesterday, it is today that he is coming.'

   e. *Aree chinuu Naafa nkai* (_____) *shiga, ʔyaa ya* (_____) *tii?*
      'He was going to Naha, but you didn't go?'

3. Complete the sentence with ~*yassan* or ~*gurisan* to describe the pictures below.

   a. *Kunu kusuee,* _____.

   b. *kunu hanbaagaa ya* _____.

   c. *Ari ga jii ya churasanu* _____.

   d. *Wannee haa nu neen kutu,* _____.
      ('difficult to say')

LESSON 5 Riding in a Taxi / Grocery Shopping at the Market

DIALOGUE B

Mother: *Uma nu **kadu wuti nijiri nkai magati**, anshikara, ama nu **ajimaa wutooti fijai** nkai magati **kwimisooree**. Atoo **chichiatai** madi **chaa mattooba** yaa **tai**.

Turn right at the corner, and then go (as far as) to the intersection, then (turn) left. Then, go straight to the end, okay?

Driver: *Uu.*

Yes.

(The taxi arrives at the destination.)

Mother: ***Chassa** naibii ga?*

How much?

Driver: *happyaku-yin natooibiin. Nifee deebiru.*

It is 800 yen. Thank you.

CORE VOCABULARY

kadu	'corner'
wuti/wutooti	'at' [B1]
nijiri	'right'
magati (G.FORM)	← *magain* 'turn' [B4]
ajimaa	'intersection'
fijai	'left'
-kwimisooree	'please do ~' [B3]
atoo	← *atu* 'later' + *ya* (TOP)
chichiatai	'T-intersection (at the end of a road)'
chaa mattooba	'straight on'
chassa	'how much?' [B2]
na-too-ibiin	← *na* 'become' + *too* (ASP) + *ibiin* (POL)

GRAMMAR B

1. Particles: *wuti/wutooti* 'in, at'

These particles indicate a location of activity, corresponding to 'in', 'on', or 'at'. These should be distinguished from *nkai* 'to (a destination)'.

- *Chuu ya yaa* **wuti/wutooti** *binchoo sun.*   'Today, I will study at home.'
- *Ama* **wuti/wutooti** *hijai nkai magati kwimisooree.* 'Please turn left over there.'

2. Wh-Word: *chassa* 'how much?'

Chassa {yaibii ga? / ya ga?} 'How much is it?' and *Chassa {naibii ga? / nai ga?}* 'How much does it come to?' are common expressions to use when you ask for the price of an item at a store. Study the following mini conversations:

- A: **Chassa** *nai ga?* 'How much is it?'
  (lit. 'How much does it come to?')
  B: *Sen yin naibiin.* 'It's 1,000 yen.'
  A: *Yassan yaa.* 'Cheap, isn't it?'

- A: *Uree chassa ya ga?* 'How much is it?'
  B: *Ichi man yin naibiin.* 'It's 10,000 yen.'
  A: *ʔyaa munoo ippee takasan yaa.* 'Yours is so expensive!!'
  Ama wutee hassen yin shi utoon doo. 'Over there, (they sell it) for 8,000 yen.'

3. Request: [G.FORM + *kwimisooree*] 'Please do ~'

This construction expresses a request. You can make a request by other constructions (see [L8(A2/A3)]). In the table below, we used *kwimisooree* as a representative request suffix.

	Dictionary	GERUND.FORM	Request	Meaning
V	tumi-in	tumi-ti	**tumiti** kwimisooree	'Please stop it (TR)'
V	tuma-in	tuma-ti	**tumati** kwimisooree	'Please stop here (INTR)'
V	maga-in	maga-ti	**magati** kwimisooree	'Please turn (INTR)'
V	kee-in	kee-ti	**keeti** kwimisooree	'Please return (INTR)'
1	ʔwiij-un	ʔwiij-i	**ʔwiiji** kwimisooree	'Please swim'

	Dictionary	GERUND.FORM	Request	Meaning
2	*ninj-un*	*nint-i*	***ninti*** *kwimisooree*	'Please sleep'
3	*kunj-un*	*kunch-i*	***kunchi*** *kwimisooree*	'Please tie up'
4	*kach-un*	*kach-i*	***kachi*** *kwimisooree*	'Please write'
5	*mach-un*	*match-i*	***matchi*** *kwimisooree*	'Please wait'
6	*turas-un*	*turach-i*	***turachi*** *kwimisooree*	'Please give'
7	*yub-un*	*yud-i*	***yudi*** *kwimisooree*	'Please call'
8	*yum-un*	*yud-i*	***yudi*** *kwimisooree*	'Please read'
IRG	*ichun*	*ʔnj-i*	***ʔnji*** *kwimisooree*	'Please go'
IRG	*chuun*	*(t)ch-i*	***tchi*** *kwimisooree*	'Please come'
IRG	*sun*	*sshi*	***sshi*** *kwimisooree*	'Please do'

In the dialogue, the host mother made a request to the driver: *hijai nkai magati kwimisooree* 'Please turn to the left.' Here are a few other direction-giving expressions.

- *Nijiri nkai **magati kwimisooree**.*   'Please turn to the right.'
- *Chaa mattooba **ʔnji kwimisooree**.*   'Please go straight.'

4. Useful Expressions for Giving Directions

The essential words in giving directions are: **nijiri** 'right', **hijai** 'left', and **chaa mattooba** 'straight'. The basic verbs combined with these directional words are **magain** 'to turn', **ichun** 'to go', and **tumain** 'to stop'. When you combine sentences, you need to use the gerund such as *ʔnji* 'go and...' (← *ichun* 'to go').

- *Uma nu kadu **wuti nijiri nkai magati**, anshikara, ama wutooti **hijai nkai magati kwimisooree**.*   'Turn right at that corner, and then turn left there, please...'
- *Atoo, chichiatai madi **chaa mattooba ʔnji kwimisooree**.*   'Then go on straight to the end, please.'
- *Ama wuti **tumiti kwimisooree**.*   'Stop over there, please.'

[LOCATION (N + **ya / nkai ya**) **chaa sshi ichu/ichabii ga?**] is an expression often used to ask for directions. Literally, it means 'by means of how, do I go to LOCATION'.

- A: *Waikiki kara Hawai daigaku nkai ya chaa sshi ichu ga?*
  'How do I go to the University of Hawaii from Waikiki?'
  B: *Yon ban nu basu kara ichun doo.* 'We go by the #4 bus.'

- A: *Attaa yaa nkai ya chaa sshi ichabii ga?* 'How do we go to their house?'
  B: *Yuna ga wakai kutu, Yuna nu kuruma kara ichu shee mashi ya sa.*
   'Since Yuna knows (their house), it's better to go by Yuna's car.'

ADDITIONAL VOCABULARY

taachi mee 'the second one from here'
tumiin (TR) = 'to stop (something)'

tumain (INTR) '(something) stops'

EXERCISES B

1. Fill in the blanks with the appropriate words.

   a. A: *Gakkoo madi chaa sshi ichabii ga?*

   B: *Anu taachi mee nu kadu madi (_____) ʔnji, ama wuti*
                                              'straight'

   (_____) *magati, shigu yaibiin.*
     'to the left'

   b. A: *Suupaa ya maa yaibii ga?*

   B: *Anu (_____) madi ʔnji, ama wuti (_____) magati, shigu yaibiin.*
          'intersection'   'to the right'

   c. Amy: *Tanaka shinshii taa yaa ya maa nkai aibii ga?*

   Tanaka: *Gakkoo nu (_____) nkai an doo.*
                       'front'

2. Choose the most appropriate wh-word from the word bank and insert it in the parentheses.

   Word Bank [*chaa, chassa, jiroo, nuu, maa, taa, ichi*]

   a. A: *Hanbaagaa* 'hamburger' *n Kentakkii* 'Kentucky Fried Chicken' *n maasan yaa. ʔyaa ya (_____) mashi ya ga?*

   B: *Wannee Kentakii ga du maasan ndi umuyuru.*

   b. A: *Uri tu uri koora. (_____) ya ga?*

   (Note: *koora* ← *kooin* 'to buy' Dialogue [C])

   B: *1000 yin yaa, tai.*

LESSON 5 Riding in a Taxi / Grocery Shopping at the Market

c. A: *Naafa nkai ya* (_____) *ichu ga?*

   B: *Achaa ya* (_____) *ya gayaa.*

   A: *Anshee achaa ichu sa.*

d. A: *Anutchoo* (_____) *yaibii ga?*

   B: *?yaa wakarani? Wattaa gakkoo nu koochoo shinshii ya sa.*

e. A: *Kuree* (_____) *ndi ?yu ga?*

   B: *Kuree Uchinaaguchi shee nanachibushi ndi ?yu sa.*

f. A: *Kumaa* (_____) *ya ga?*

   B: *Kumaa Asatu nu ajimaa yan doo.*

DIALOGUE C

The host mother is talking to a female shopkeeper (SK) at the market.

SK:	***Mensooree.***	Welcome.
Mother:	***Warabi** nu nichi **wnjachi nintoo** kutu, chimushinji **chukura na** ndi **umutoo** shiga…*	My child has a fever and stays in bed, so I was thinking I should make *chimushinji*…
SK:	*Unu **chimu** gwaa ya chaa yaibii ga? **N(n)na** maasan ndi **imisheen** doo.*	How about this liver? Everyone says it is good.
Mother:	***Jootuu** yan yaa.* ***Chideekuni** n **hiru** n ami? Anshikara, kunu **boojishi** n **koora**.*	It looks excellent. Do you also have carrots and garlic? And I want this pork loin.
SK:	*Nifee deebiru. Chideekunee **yashiku natooibii** kutu, sen go hyaku sanjuu yin naibii sa tai.*	Thank you. Carrots are on sale, so (the total) is 1530 yen.
Mother:	*Ifee yashimiran **naa**? Uri, sen yon hyaku yin.*	Can you discount a little? Here, 1400 yen.

SK: *Ee tai, unjoo* **anshi chuubaa yamisheeru**[1]. *Wattaa mookee neen(ran) naibiin doo…*

Oh, you are such a good bargainer. I will not have any profit.

(Negotiation continues…)

[1] *unjoo anshi chuubaa yamisheeru*: The ending here is an Adnominal Form, but no focus particle is present. The Adnominal Form here is triggered by **anshi** 'very' (cf. Focus construction in [L4(A3)]), Part II, Topic 8.

CORE VOCABULARY

mensooree	'Welcome!'
nichi ʔnjasun	'to run a fever'
ʔnjachi (GERUND)	*ʔnjasun* 'to put out' (TR) ↔ *ʔnji-in* 'to leave, depart' (INTR)
nintoo (APO.FORM)	← *nint* 'sleep' + *oo* (ASP)
chimu shinji	'soup with pork liver' [Cul2]
chukura (INT.FORM)	← *chukuin* 'to make' [C2]
na	SFP [C4]
umutoo (APO.FORM)	← *umu* 'think' + *too* (ASP)
chimu	'liver'
n(n)na	'everyone'
imisheen (EXAL)	'to say (EXAL of *i-in*)' [C1]
chideekuni	'carrot'
hiru	'garlic'
boojishi	'pork loin'
koora (INT.FORM)	← *kooin* 'to buy' [C2]
yashiku (ADV.FORM)	← *yassan* 'cheap' [C3]
ifee	← *ifi* 'little' + *ya* (TOP)
yashimiran (NEG.FORM)	← *yashimiin* 'to reduce the price'
naa	SFP [C4]
anshi	'very'
chuubaa	'tough person'
mooki	'profit'
yamisheeru (ADNOM.FORM)	← *ya* (COP) *-misheen* (EXAL) [C1]

GRAMMAR C

1. Exalting Verbs

Exalting verbs express the speaker's respect to the referent person(s), which very often corresponds to the subject of the sentence. A more complete treatment will be given later in [L8(B1/B2)]. Here, a handful of common exalting verbs are introduced.

Meaning	DIC.FORM (Plain)	Polite	Exalting Form
'to go'	ichun	ich-abiin	} mensheen
'to come'	chuun	cha-abiin	
'to be (existence)'	wun	wu-ibiin	
'to eat'	kamun	kam-abiin	} usaga-in/usaga-misheen
'to drink'	numun	num-abiin	
'to be (COP)'	yan	ya-ibiin	ya-misheen
'to say to (someone)'	iin	i-(y)abiin	i-misheen

The polite suffix *-ibiin* can replace the final *n* of the exalting forms for added politeness: e.g. *menshee-n* → *misheebiin* (see the second example below).

- *Maa **madi menshee** ga?* 'Where are you going?'
- *Shinshii ya nama gakkoo nkai **mensheebiin**.* 'The teacher is at school now.'
- *Asatu-shinshii ya rafutee **usagamisheen**.* 'Teacher Asato will eat *rafutee*.'
- *Anu tchoo wattaa shinshii **yamisheen**.* 'That person is my teacher.'
- *Jiibu shinshii ya 'Chibari yoo!' ndi **imisheetan**.* 'Teacher Gibo said, "Do your best!"'

2. Intentional Form

The 'Intentional Form (INT.FORM)' expresses the speaker's intention or his/her invitation to others ('let's ~').

This form is the Negative Forms ([L2(C2/C4)]) without the final *n*.

- *kee-ran* (NEG.FORM) → minus *n* → *keera* 'I will go home/Let's go home.'
- *num-an* (NEG.FORM) → minus *n* → *numa* 'I will drink/Let's drink.'

Here is a more complete table. It is important to remember that only verbs that can express the speaker's will or agency can have the Intentional Form. Otherwise, intransitive verbs do NOT have this form: *agira* 'to raise/fry (TR)' vs. ˣ*agara* 'to be raised/fried (INTR)'.

	Dictionary	NEG.FORM	Intentional Form	Meaning
V	tu-in	tu-**ran**	tur**a**	'I'll take / Let's take'
V	maga-in	maga-**ran**	mag**a**r**a**	'I'll turn / Let's turn'
V	kee-in	kee-**ran**	kee**ra**	'I'll return / Let's return'
1	ʔwiij-un	ʔwiig-**an**	ʔwiig**a**	'I'll/Let's swim'
2	ninj-un	nind-**an**	nind**a**	'I'll/Let's sleep'
3	kunj-un	kund-**an**	kund**a**	'I'll/Let's tie up'
4	kach-un	kak-**an**	kak**a**	'I'll/Let's write'
5	much-un	mut-**an**	mut**a**	'I'll/Let's hold'
6	turas-un	turas-**an**	turas**a**	'I'll/Let's give'
7	yub-un	yub-**an**	yub**a**	'I'll/Let's invite'
8	num-un	num-**an**	num**a**	'I'll/Let's drink'
IRG	ichun	ikan	**ika**	'I'll/Let's go'
IRG	chuun	kuun	**kuu**	'I'll/Let's come'
IRG	sun	san	**sa**	'I'll/Let's do'

As noted above, this form is used in two related ways:

(a) Speaker's intention: *numa* 'I will drink it.'
(b) Speaker's invitation to the addressee: *numa* 'Let's drink.'

You can clarify the first meaning by adding SFP *huu* [polite] / *hii* [plain], which seeks confirmation, 'okay?' (the fourth and fifth examples below, respectively). The last example, *Kuri koora*, means 'I will buy this', and is often used as an expression, 'Please give me this' in a shopping context.

(a) Speaker's Intention

- **Ika.**   'I will go!'
- **Tuura.**   'I will pass (the route).'
- **Chukura** na.   'I'll make it!'
- Wannee **ika** huu?   'I will go, is it okay?'
- **Keera** hii?   'I'm gonna go home, okay?' [Note: *kee-in* is a motion verb like *ichun* and *chuun*.]
- Kuri **koora.**   'Let me have this.'

If the Intentional Form follows interjections such as *dii, dikka, ditcha* (or *rii, rikka, ritcha* in the Naha variety), it conveys the second meaning.

(b) Speaker's Invitation to the Addressee

- *Dii,* **ika.** 'Let's go!'
- *Dika, takushii kara* **ika.** 'Let's go by taxi.'
- *Dikka Naafa kara* **tuura na.** 'Let's go through Naha.'

Notice the Intentional Form can be also made into the polite style from Polite Negative Forms.

- V-verb: *-ibira-n* (POL.NEG) → *-ya(←i)bira* (INT.FORM)   e.g. *magayabira* 'Let's turn'
- C-verb: *-abira-n* (POL.NEG) → *-abira* (INT.FORM)   e.g. *ichabira* 'Let's go'

This form appears in the commonly used expressions below.

- **Chaabira** *sai/tai.* 'Hello, may I come in?' (at a doorstep) *chaabiran* → *chaabira*
- *Kwatchii* **sabira** *sai/tai.* 'Let me have some (delicious food).' *sabiran* → *sabira*

3. Change of State: [Adj. (*-ku* form) / Noun] + *nain* 'to become'

The construction with the adjective *-ku* form or a noun followed by *nain* expresses a change of state. *Nain* often takes the *-(t)oon* form as *natoon* [L3(A3)]. When the *neen/neeran* (the Negative Form of *an*) precedes *nain*, it means 'to become none', or 'to vanish, disappear' as in the last example.

- *Chideekunee* **takaku natoon.** 'Radishes have become expensive.'
- *Hiiku* **natoon.** 'It has become cold.'
- *Unu chimu gwaa ya* **yashiku natooibiin** *doo.* 'This liver has become cheap, you know.'
- *Wattaa mookee* **neen/neeran naibiin** *doo.* 'My profit will be gone.'

Nain can be combined with a noun or a nominal adjective instead of the *-ku* form of adjectives.

- *Kunu warabee tiichi* **naibiin.** 'This child has become one year old.'
- *Chimu shinji* **jooji natoon.** '(I have become) skillful making liver soup.'
- *Chinuu ya chiburu nu yamuta shiga, chuu ya* **mashi natoon.** 'Yesterday, I had a headache, but today, I have become better.'

Jooji 'skillful' and *mashi* 'better' are examples of so-called nominal adjectives (i.e., adjective-like in meaning, but follows a nominal pattern, not having a *-ku* form).

4. Sentence Final Particles: [INT.FORM + *na*] and [FINITE.FORM + *naa*]

The two sentence final particles, *na* and *naa*, are somewhat similar, but different in three respects: vowel length, preceding verb form, and meaning.

[INTENTION FORM + ***na***] = the speaker's intention/invitation ('will do', 'let's do')
[FINITE FORM + ***naa***] = a yes/no question marker

- *Chukura **na**.* 'I'll make it! / Let's make it.'
- *Ifee yashimiran **naa**?* 'Can you give me some discount?'
- *Yuubi nu sangoo-bin gwaa nukutoon **naa**?* 'Do you still have the small bottle of *sake* from last night?' (cf. Application [4])

ADDITIONAL VOCABULARY

dikka/ditcha 'Let's'
keein 'to return INTR'
kii chikiin 'pay attention, be careful'
kunchi 'stamina'
kushi 'back (vs. front)'
mee 'front'

nukuin 'to be left'
shokudoo 'cafeteria'
uin 'to sell'
usagain/usagamisheen 'to eat/drink (EXAL)'

EXERCISES C

1. Write the Intentional Forms.

    a. to eat _____

    b. to drink _____

    c. to ask _____

    d. to buy (cf. Cultural Note (3)) _____

    e. to have/hold _____

    f. to return, go home _____

2. Choose the most appropriate word.

    a. A: *Nuu (kamu / usagamishee / menshee) ga?* (B is older than A)

       B: *Toofu chanpruu yaa.*

LESSON 5   Riding in a Taxi / Grocery Shopping at the Market

b. A: *Maa nkai (chuu / imishee / menshee) ga?* (A = taxi driver)

   B: *Naafa nkai yaa.*

c. Niko: *Anu tchoo shinshii (yan / yamisheen / yamisheem)-i?*

   Katsuko: *Yii. Yamisheen doo.*

d. A: *Anu tchu nu naa ya nuu yaibii ga?* (B is older than A)

   B: *Asatu shinshii ndi (yan / iin / imisheen).*

3. Change the parts in bold using the appropriate exalting verbs.

   a. *Asatu Shinshii ya wattaa gakkoo nu Uchinaaguchi nu shinshii* **yaibiin**.
      (_____)

   b. *Nama gakkoo nu shokudoo nkai* **wuibiin**. (_____)

   c. *Asatu Shinshii ya chuu n toofu-chanpuruu* **kamabiin**. (_____) or
      (_____)

   d. *"Toofu-chanpuruu ya ippee maasan" ndi* **iyabiin**. (_____)

   e. *Asatu Shinnshii ya achaa Uchinaa nkai* **ichabii** <u>kutu</u>, *shikaraashiku naibiin*. (miss him) (_____)

4. Make negative questions as shown in the example.

   Example: A: *Tatsuya ya shukudai suti-i?*   (B shook his head)   A: **San-tan naa?**

   a. A: *Chuu ya sushi kamun doo yaa.*   (B shook his head.)

      A: (_____)?

   b. A: *Anshi ʔwiirikisaru. 100 ten doo.*   (B says it's not A's test, but C's test.)

      A: *Kuree* (_____)? 'It's not my test?'

   c. A: *Wattaa warabee ama nkai wu sa.*   (B says he's not A's child.)

      A: *Ama nkai* (_____)? 'He's not there?'

      Aree wattaa warabee (_____)? 'He's not my child?'

5. Choose the correct word in [ ]. Translate the whole passage.

   Warabaa nu nichi ʔnjach-oo kutu, achaa ya Naafa nu Machigwaa madi ikana **[ndi / nkai]** *umutoon. Machigwaa* **[nkai / wuti]**, *chimu gwaa tu boojishi kooti, chimu shinji* *chukura* **[na / naa]** *ndi umutoon. Chimu shinji nu naaka* **[wuti / nkai]** *ya hiru tu chideekuni n irii kutu, uri n kooin. Chimu shinji ya ansuka maakooneen shiga, Uchinaa wutee (← wuti + ya), kunchi nu chichi, hanafichee shigu nooin* **[ndi / nji]** *iin doo.*

✍ *ʔnja-ch-oon* ← *ʔnjachi* (GERUND FORM of *ʔnjasun*) + *oo* (ASP)]

_____
_____
_____
_____
_____
_____
_____
_____
_____

APPLICATIONS

1. **Role Play.** Draw a simple map of a city. Student A (a passenger) explains to Student B (a taxicab driver) how to get to the destination.

2. **Role Play.** Student A is a shopper. Prepare a shopping list. Use WB to find out the names of items you want to buy at the shop. Student B is a shopkeeper. Create a conversation at the shop.

3. We have already learned *kara* 'from'. Here is a joke. Can you guess what *kushi* and *mee* mean? Check WB.

    A: *Unjoo maa* **kara** *mensoocha-ga?*   'Where did you come from?'

    B: *Kushi* **kara**.   'I came from the _____.'

    A: *Maa* **nkai** *menshee ga?*   'Where are you going to?'

    B: *Mee* **nkai**   'I'm going _____.'

    A: *Anshee naa, kii chikiti mensoori yoo.* 'Then take care of yourself going (forward).'

4. Listen to a contemporary popular song, *Haisai Ojisan*.

    https://www.youtube.com/watch?v=D6FVgUoCTW0

    The following are some phrases from this song. Check the meanings of all words you are not familiar with. Can you identify the grammatical patterns (e.g. SFP) used in this song?

    Ichi-goo 180ml / san-goo 300ml / yon-goo 720ml / isshoo 1800ml

    Hai *sai*. **(polite Sentence-Final Particle for male speakers)**

    Sangoo-bin-***gwa(a)*** (inset) (_____)

    Nukutoon **naa** (_____)

    Wakiran **naa** (_____)

    ʔyun **na** (due to the metrical structure, *na* appears short, but is long)

    (_____)

    fusuku ya-***mishee***... (_____)

    kwi-***miseem***-i? (_____)

    Study the lyrics below and sing along. The song is a conversation between Ojisan (Mister) and a young adult. Ojisan's lines are marked with **. We translated *sangoo-bin* (600 ml) as 'a small bottle' and *ishoo-bin* (1800 ml) as 'a large bottle'. See the sizes of bottles (inset above).

Okinawan	English
Hai-sai Ojisan, Hai-sai Ojisan	Hi, Mister. Hi, Mister.
Yuubi nu sangoo-bin gwa nukuto(o)n naa	Do you still have a small bottle of sake from last night?
Nukutoora, wan ni wakiran naa	If you have it, can you share some with me?
**Ari ari warabaa, ee, warabaa.	Hey, hey, kid, hey, kid.
**Sangoo bin nu atai shi wan ni nkai	Such a small bottle! Are you asking me ...
**Nukutoo ndi ʔyun na, ee warabaa.	if I still have it left, hey, kid.
Anshee ojisan, sangoo-bin shi Fusuku ya-mishee-raa,	Then, Mister, if a small bottle is not appropriate,
Issu bin wan ni kwi-miseem-i?	Please give me a big bottle.

CULTURAL NOTES

1. *Ishigantoo*

In Okinawa, you will see many *Ishigantoo* signs (inset) at a street corner or in front of a house. This sign is to divert an evil spirit called Majimun so that it will not enter the house.

- Do you know any superstitions to protect yourselves from an evil spirit?
- Shiisaa is a tutelary deity found ubiquitously in Okinawa. Do some research on Shiisaa, such as its history and cultural significance. Any resemblance to the Sphinx in Egypt?

2. Liver and Heart

Chimushinji (*chimu* = liver, *shinji* = decocted soup) used in the dialog in this lesson is soup with pork liver, believed to be very nutritious. It used to be a common staple for people who got sick with a cold (cf. chicken soup in the American culture). *Chimu* also means 'heart', as in a phrase *chimu gukuru* (← *kukuru* 'heart'). *Chimu* also appears in some common expressions as follows:

chimu jurasan	('liver/heart' + 'beautified' = 'kind-hearted')
	(*jurasan* ← *churasan*)
chimu ganasan	('liver/heart' + 'lovely' = 'darling', 'sweet', 'charming')
	(*ganasan* ← *kanasan* 'dear')
chimu gurisan/gurusan	('liver/heart' + 'hard' = 'pitiful')

There are many other related expressions with onomatopoeic words. (Takara 2005a:156–157).

chimu dondon soon	'feel happy'
chimu futufutuu soon	'feel scared'
chimu wasawasa soon	'feel uneasy'
chimu saazaatu natan	'feel relieved'

English also uses internal organs in expressions such as 'She broke my *heart*' or 'She has *guts*.' Do you know any other similar expressions in English, or any other languages? Professor James Matisoff of UC Berkeley (1986) reports that many Asian languages use body parts such as the heart, liver, or belly to express emotions. Japanese has the following expressions:

kimo-ttama	(liver ball)	['courage']
hara ga suwaru	(stomach sits)	['undisturbed', 'calm']
hara ga tatsu	(stomach stands)	['get angry']

- Do you know any similar expressions in any other language(s)?

3. Okinawan Humor

Below is a humorous exchange between a boy (customer) and an old lady *obaa* (a shop owner) (from Takara 2005a:96). Here, *koora* serves as a homophone.

Boy: *Obaa, koora.* [C2]
Old woman: *Obaa ya ui shee aran.* (*shee* ← *shi + ya* [L2(C2/C4)])
Boy: *Kooraa, koora.*
Old woman: *Koori, koori.*
Boy: *Koori ya aran. Kooraa, koora.*

LESSON 6

Cherry Blossom Festival

DIALOGUE A

An international student (Niko) is talking to his host mother and her daughter, Yuna.

Niko:	*Chimu shinji nuda kutu, shigu nootooibiin doo. Unju nu ukaji yaibii sa.*	I got better as I drank *chimushinji*. Thank you very much.
Mother:	*Yami? Anshee kundu nu doyoobee Nachijin (n)kai sakura **nnjii ga** ika yaa.*	Oh. Then let's go see cherry blossoms in Nakijin this Saturday.
Yuna:	*Wan nin ichi**busa** ssaa.*	I want to go, too.
Mother:	*Anshee, n(n)na **saani** ʔnj**aani**, sakura nnch**ai**, maasa mun kad**ai** sa yaa.*	We should all go there together, and let's do things like seeing the flowers and eating delicious food.

117

CORE VOCABULARY

nuda (APO.FORM)	← *nud* 'drink (G.ROOT)' + *a* (PAST-1)
nootooibiin	← *noo* 'recover (INTR)' + *too* (ASP) + *ibiin* (POL); *noosun* (TR)
ukaji	'help'
yam-i?	← *yan* (COP) + *i* (QP)
kundu	'this coming'
doyoobi	'Saturday' (Jp. loan)
Nachijin	place in the North [Cul1]
sakura	'cherry blossoms'
nnjii ga	'in order to see' [A2]
ichi-busa	← *ichi* 'go' + *busa* 'want' [A1]
saani	'by' [A5]
nj-aani	'going there and' [A3]
nnch-ai	'seeing and…' [A4]

GRAMMAR A

1. **Desire Expressions: [ADV.FORM + *busan*] 'want to do'; [Noun {*nu* / ∅} *fu(u)san*] 'I want (something)'**

    a. **Desire for an Action: [ADV.FORM + *busan*] 'want to do'**

This construction expresses the speaker's desire to do something in a statement. In a question, *-busan* refers to the hearer's desire. You can make the Adverbial Form simply by adding *-i* to the B.ROOT (i.e., dictionary form minus *in/un*). A table listing Adverbial Forms is available in [A2] below. The only irregular form is *shi* for *sun* 'do'. The first person subjects *wan/wannee* are often left out in a statement. In a question, it is the second person subjects *ʔyaa/ittaa* that are optional. Thus, the subject *ʔyaa* is missing in the second example. In expressing the desire of a third person, this pattern cannot be used by itself. Instead *-busa-s-oon* 'want-do-ASP' (lit. doing the gesture of wanting/showing the sign of wanting) is used.

- (*Wannee*) *uttu yubibusan*.   'I want to invite my (younger) sister.'
- A: *Miji numibusami?*   'Do you want to drink water?'
  B: *Ii, numibusa ssaa.*   'Yes, I do.'

- *Anu warabaa ya kamibusa-s-oon.*   'That child looks like he wants to eat (this).'
- *Ooshiro sanoo Hawai nkai ichibusa-s-oon.*   'Mr. Oshiro wants to go to Hawaii.'

The second element in this construction *-busan* comes from the independent verb *fu(u)san*, meaning 'to want'. This verb can be used in the following construction.

b. Desire for an Object: [Noun {*nu* / Ø} *fu(u)san*] 'I want (something).'

The 'Noun' here is a desired object which is marked by *nu* or left unmarked (Ø). The subject is often unexpressed, but when expressed, it often takes the subject particle *nu*.

- *(Wannee) Uchinaaguchi nu jiten* {*nu* / Ø} *fusan*.   'I want an Okinawan dictionary.'
- *Tamaki sanoo kubushimi fusasoon.*   'Mr. Tamaki wants cuttlefish sashimi.'
- A: *Nuu nu fusa ga?*   'What do you want?'
  B: *Magi yaa fusan.*   'A big house.'

2. Purposive: [ADV.FORM+ (*i*) + *ga* + *ichun/chuun*] 'go/come in order to do V'

This is a purposive construction. With a verb of motion ('to go', 'to come', 'to return', etc.), it means 'go/come/return (to a location) in order to do something'. The purpose is expressed by the Adverbial Form (= B.ROOT + *i*) of a verb (Part II, Topic 6). An extra *i* will be added before the particle *ga* for C-verbs (cf. C-1 to C-8). V-verbs do not have the extra *i* (e.g., *tu-i*, *na-i*, not ˣ*tu-i-i*, ˣ*na-i-i*).

	DIC.FORM	ADV.FORM	'go to do'	Meaning
V	*tu-in*	*tu-i*	*tui ga ichun*	'go to take'
V	*agi-in*	*agi-i*	*agii ga ichun*	'go to fly (a kite)'
C-1	*ʔwiij-un*	*ʔwiij-i*	*ʔwiiji-i ga ichun*	'go to swim'
C-2	*ninj-un*	*ninj-i*	*ninji-i ga ichun*	'go to sleep'
C-3	*kunj-un*	*kunj-i*	*kunji-i ga ichun*	'go to tie up'
C-4	*kach-un*	*kach-i*	*kachi-i ga ichun*	'go to write'
C-5	*much-un*	*much-i*	*muchi-i ga ichun*	'go to hold (something)'
C-6	*noos-un*	*noosh-i*	*nooshi-i ga ichun*	'go to fix (a car)'
C-7	*yub-un*	*yub-i*	*yubi-i ga ichun*	'go to call'
C-8	*yum-un*	*yum-i*	*yumi-i ga ichun*	'go to read'

	DIC.FORM	ADV.FORM	'go to do'	Meaning
IRG	ichun	ich-i	—	—
IRG	chuun	ch-ii	—	—
IRG	sun	shi-i	shi-i ga ichun	'go to do'

A location phrase (~ nkai) can appear at the beginning of the sentence.

- *Machigwaa **nkai** nakami **kooi ga** ichun.*   'I go to the Makishi market to buy nakami.'
- *Nachijin **(n)kai** sakura **nnjii ga** ika yaa.*   'I go to Nachijin to see the cherry blossoms.'

3. The *aani* Clause: [B.ROOT + *(y)aani*] 'doing ~ and/then ~'

The -(y)aani form of a verb works like a gerund that connects two clauses. The two clauses represent two actions that happen either sequentially (i.e., 'and then') or concurrently (i.e., 'doing ~ and ~'). The -(y)aani is attached to the Basic Root (B.ROOT). -y appears with V-verbs but not with C-verbs.

- *na-in:*   na +yaani → *na-yaani*   'become and…'
- *ninj-un:*   ninj +aani → *ninj-aani*   'go to bed and…'

Notice some irregular patterns for the verbs marked with * in the table.

	DIC.FORM	B.ROOT	-*aani* Form	Meaning (-*aani*)
V	noo-in	noo-	noo-**yaani**	'be recovered and…'
V	maga-in	maga-	maga-**yaani**	'turn and…'
C-1	ʔwiij-un	ʔwiij-	ʔwiij-**aani**	'swim and…'
C-2	ninj-un	ninj-	ninj-**aani**	'sleep and…'
C-3	kunj-un	kunj-	kunj-**aani**	'tie up and…'
C-4	kach-un	kach-	kach-**aani**	'write and…'
C-5	much-un	much-	much-**aani**	'hold and…'
C-6	noos-un	noos-	noos-**aani**	'fix and…'
C-7	yub-un	yub-	yub-**aani**	'invite and…'
C-8	yum-un	yum-	yum-**aani**	'read and…'

	DIC.FORM	B.ROOT	*-aani* Form	Meaning (*-aani*)
IRG	*ich-un*	*ich-*	**ʔnj-aani***	'go and…'
IRG	*chu-un*	*ch-*	**ch-aani***	'come and…'
IRG	*s-un*	*s-*	**s-aani***	'do and…'
IRG	*ʔy-un / i-in / i-yun*	*ʔy-**	**ʔy-aani***	'say and…'

- N(n)na (s)shi **ʔnjaani**, sakura nnjun. 'We should all go there together and see the cherry blossoms.'
- Ama wutooti sakura **nnjaani**, maasa mun kamu shee tanushimi yan. 'I look forward to eating delicious food while viewing the cherry blossoms.'
- "Maasan, maasan" ndi **ʔy-aani**, muru kamu sa. 'Saying "Tasty, tasty," they eat everything!'

4. Representative Actions: [[G.ROOT + *(t)ai*] + [G.ROOT + *(t)ai*] + sun] 'doing X…doing Y…'

This pattern lists (usually) two representative actions with the meaning of 'doing X and doing Y, among other things'. Note that the V-verbs take *-tai* while the C-verb takes *-ai*. The formation of this pattern may remind you of the PAST-1 forms. The only difference is in the final elements: *-i* vs. *-n* as in *uta-tai* (-(t)ai pattern) vs. *uta-tan* (PAST-1).

- *uta-in, moo-in*   (V-verb) → *uta-tai, moo-tai* 'singing and dancing and things like that'
- *kam-un, num-un*   (C-verb) → *kad-ai, nud-ai* 'eating and drinking and things like that'
- *kach-un, yum-un*   (C-verb) → *kach-ai, yud-ai* 'writing and reading and things like that'

	Dictionary	G.ROOT	-(t)ai Form	Meaning
V	*tu-in*	*tu*	*tu-tai*	'taking, etc.'
V	*maga-in*	*maga*	*maga-tai*	'turning, etc.'
C-1	*ʔwiij-un*	*ʔwiij*	*ʔwiij-ai*	'swimming, etc.'
C-2	*ninj-un*	*nint*	*nint-ai*	'sleeping, etc.'
C-3	*kunj-un*	*kunch*	*kunch-ai*	'tying up, etc.'
C-4	*kach-un*	*kach*	*kach-ai*	'writing, etc.'
C-5	*much-un*	*mutch*	*mutch-ai*	'holding, etc.'
C-6	*ʔnbus-un*	*ʔnbuch*	*ʔnbuch-ai*	'steam, etc.'
C-7	*yub-un*	*yud*	*yud-ai*	'inviting, etc.'
C-8	*yum-un*	*yud*	*yud-ai*	'reading, etc.'
IRG	*ichun*	*ʔnj*	*ʔnj-ai*	'going, etc.'
IRG	*chuun*	*tch*	*tch-ai*	'coming, etc.'
IRG	*sun*	*s*	*s-ai*	'doing, etc.'
IRG	*ʔyun*	*ich*	*ich-ai*	'saying, etc.'

After representative actions with *-(t)ai*, very often the gerund of *sun* 'do' follows as *sshi* as seen in the examples below:

- *Chinuu ya* **nudai, kadai sshi**, *ippee ʔwiirikisatan.* 'Yesterday, we had fun eating and drinking, etc.'
- *Nichiyoobee, yaa nu sooji* **sai**, *binchoo* **sai sshi** *ichunasatan.* 'I was busy on Sunday, cleaning up the house and studying.'

5. Particles: *saani* (a) 'by (means of)', (b) 'with (everyone/everything)'

(a) This particle and *(s)shi* (cf. [L1(A3)]) indicate a tool you use when doing some action. In most circumstances, they are interchangeable. Remember, however, the meaning of 'by (means of transportation)' is usually marked by *kara*, e.g., *basu kara* 'by bus' [L5(A4)].

- *Chimu shinjee nuu **saani/(s)shi** chukui-bii ga?* 'With what (ingredients), do you make *chimu shinji*?'
- *Sannin **saani/(s)shi** muuchii chichimun.* 'Wrap it with *sannin* leaves.'

(b) These two particles also appear in the expression *muru saani/(s)shi*, which means 'by everyone/everything' or 'with everyone/everything (included)'.

- *Yaa ninju muru **saani/(s)shi** Nachijin (n) kai sakura **nnjii ga** ika yaa.* 'Together with the family, let's go to Nakijin to see cherry blossoms.'
- *Uree muru **saani/(s)shi** chassa ga?* 'All together, how much is it?'

ADDITIONAL VOCABULARY

afasan 'bland'
fu(u)san 'bland'
ichunasan 'busy'
hashiru 'sliding door'
miji 'water'

noosun 'fix (TR)'
shimiin 'close'
tanushimi 'fun'
yagamasan 'noisy'

EXERCISES A

1. Choose the most appropriate word from the word bank for each (__).

   Word bank: [ga, nkai, wuti, kara, kutu, saani, shi, ya] Use each item only **once**.

   A: *?yaa (_____) maa (_____) ichu ga?* 'Where are you going?'

   B: *Naafa madi, doo.* 'To Naha.'

   A: *Nuu shii (_____) ichu ga?* 'To do what?'

   B: *Machigwaa (_____), kooi (_____) nu an.* 'I have something to buy at the market.'

   A: *Wattaa n ichu (_____), wattaa kuruma (_____) n(n)na (_____) ikani?* 'We are going, so let's go together with my car.'

2. Using the ~ *busan* form as in the examples, write the sentences below in Okinawan. For the second pattern, review [L4(B3)].

   Example: *Wannee NYC nkai* **ichi-busan**. 'I want to go to NYC.'

   Wan ga **ichi-busa** *shee* (← *shi* + *ya*) *NYC yaibiin*. 'The place I want to go is NYC.'

   a. *Wannee NYC wuti shibai* (_____). 'I want to see a play in NYC.'

      Wan ga NYC wuti (_____) *shee* (_____).
      'The one I want to see in NYC is a play.'

   b. *Wannee iPhone* (_____). 'I want to buy an iPhone.'

      Wan ga (_____) *shee* (_____). 'The one I want to buy is an iPhone.'

   c. *Wannee* _____
      (Make your own sentence.)

      Wan ga _____ *shee* _____.

3. Fill in the blanks with -*ai* form, paying attention to the cues provided below the parentheses.

   a. *Doyoo, Nichiyoo ya,* (_____) *kuruma* (_____) *sshi ichunasan*.
                            'clean up the house'   'wash'

   b. *Chinuu nu yuroo,* (_____), (_____) *sshi ʔwiirikisatan*.
                          'drink'   'eat'

   c. *Chuu ya dushi gwaa tu* (_____), *eega* (_____) *sa ndi umutoon*.
                                 'study'   'see'

   d. *Anu warabaa ya hashiru* (_____), (_____) *sshi yagamasan*.
                                'open'   'close'

4. Translate the following into Okinawan, paying special attention to the words in boldface.

   a. I went **to see** cherry blossoms in *Nakijin* with my family.

   _____

   b. I went **to see** fish at *Churaumi Suizokukan* with my friends.

   _____

   c. I had a good time **singing, dancing and things like that**.

   _____

   d. A: **With** what do you make *tofu chanpuruu?*

   _____

   B: You make it **with** tofu and vegetables.

   _____

DIALOGUE B

(Yuna and Niko are talking to Yuna's mother)

Yuna: N(n)na ik**ee**, wiirikisaibii sa.
If everyone goes, it would be fun.

Niko: Yuru na**ree**, **akaa**, **ooruu**, **chiiruu** nu akagai nu kii nkai chichi, ippee churasan ndi chichabitan doo.
I heard that when the night falls it is beautiful with red, blue/green, and yellow lights illuminated on the trees.

Mother: Un **gutu** churasa**ree**, jifi **ika(n) nee naran** yaa. ʔwaachichee chaa ya gayaa. Ami ya**ree** naran shiga…
If it is that beautiful, we must go. I wonder what the weather is like. If it rains, we can't do it…

Niko: Yaibiin yaa. Ami nu furan**daree** nai shiga, fu**ree**, muchikasaibiin yaa.
Right. If it's not rainy, it's possible; if it rains, it is difficult.

(On the day of the outing)

Yuna: Ami nu **fuin nee sun** yaa. Yii ʔwaachichi nairu **gutu** unigee sabira.
I have a feeling that it's going to rain. May we have good weather!

CORE VOCABULARY

ik-ee	← *ik* 'go' + *ee* (COND) [B2]
yuru	'evening'
na-ree	← *na* 'become' + *ree* (COND) [B2]
akaa	'red (Noun)', *akasan* (Adj.)
ooruu	'blue/green'
chiiruu	'yellow' (also *kiiruu*)
akagai	'light'
kii	'tree'
chichi (G.FORM)	← *chichun* 'turn on' (INTR) *chikiin* (TR)
gutu	'like' [B3]
churasa-ree	*churasa* 'beautiful' + *ree* (COND) [B2]
jifi	'by all means'
ika(n) nee naran	← *ika* 'go (NEG)' + *neenaran* 'must' [B1]
ʔwaachichee	← *ʔwaachichi* 'weather' + *ya* (TOP)
ami	'rain'
ya-ree	← *ya* (COP) + *ree* (COND) [B2]
fu-ran-daree	← *fu* 'rain (N.ROOT)' + *ran* (NEG) + *daree* (COND) [B2]
fu-ree	← *fu* 'rain' + *ree* (COND) [B2]
nee sun	'to have a feeling that' [B4]

GRAMMAR B

1. Obligation: [N.FORM + {*daree* / *nee*} *naran*] 'must'

This obligation construction is formed by adding *neenaran* to the Negative Form as below:

- V-verb: *iriran* (NEG) + {*daree* / *nee*} *naran* = *iriran daree / nee naran* 'should put in'
- C-verb: *numan* (NEG) + {*daree* / *nee*} *naran* = *numan daree / nee naran* 'should drink'
- Irregular: *ikan* (NEG) + {*daree* / *nee*} *naran* = *ikan daree / nee naran* 'should go'

Here are some examples.

- *Chimu shinji nkai ya, chideekuni **iriran nee naran** yaa.*   'We have to put carrots into *chimu shinji*, you know.'
- *Chiburu nu yamu kutu, kusui **numan daree naran**.*   'I have a headache, so I have to take medicine.'
- *Jifi **ika neenaran** yaa.*[1]   'I have to go by all means.'

[1] The double *nn* in the original *ikan nee* often becomes simplified as *ika nee* to avoid the double *nn*.

2. The *(r)ee* Conditional: 'If/when S₁, then S₂'

The conditional sentence consists of S_1 (condition) and S_2 (consequence): '**If** S_1, then S_2.' In this structure, the conditional clause *-(r)ee* comes at the end of S_1. Okinawan conditionals can also mean '**When** S_1, S_2' in some cases. [Part II, Topic 6]

a. Verbs

The *(r)ee* conditional is formed by adding *(r)ee* to the Negative Root. Since N.ROOT is also used for forming Negative Forms, one can say the conditional forms can be made by changing *(r)an* of the Negative Form to *(r)ee*: *(r)an* (NEG) → *(r)ee* (COND). The consonant *r* appears in V-verbs but not in C-verbs.

V-verbs

tu-ran	→ *tu-ree*	'if you/he/she (etc.) take(s)…'
na-ran	→ *na-ree*	'if you/he/she (etc.) become(s)…'
fu-ran	→ *fu-ree*	'if it rains,…'
i-ran	→ *i-ree*	'if you/he/she (etc.) say(s)…'

C-verbs

nnd-an	→ *nnd-ee*	'if you/he/she (etc.) see(s)…'
num-an	→ *num-ee*	'if you/he/she (etc.) drink(s)…'

- *Yuru **naree**, akagai n kii nkai chichun doo.*   'When it becomes nighttime, (even) lights on the trees will be turned on, you know.'
- *Uree uchinaaguchi sshi **iree**, nuu nai ga?*   'What would it be if you were to say this in Okinawan?'
- *Ami nu **furee**, naran yaa.*   'If it rains, it is not possible.'
- ***Nndee**, wakai sa. Ippee churasan doo.*   'If you see it, you will know. It's very beautiful.'
- *Takushii kara **ikee**, feesa sa.*   'If we go by taxi, it's faster.'

b. Irregular Verbs

Some irregular verbs (**an** 'to exist', **sun** 'to do', **chuun** 'to come', **yan** 'to be (copula)', and **iin** 'to say') have the following conditional forms. Note also the expression *shiga yaa* 'would do / be ~' often appears in the second part of the conditional sentence (S₂) to express a wish contrary to the fact.

- *an:* **aree**
  *Jin nu **aree**, amirika nkai ichu shiga yaa.*   'If I had money, I would go to America, you know.'

- *sun:* **shee**
  *Kuri sshi **shee**, nai sa.*   'If you do it with this, you can do it.'

- *chuun:* **ku(u)ree**
  *Ari ga **ku(u)ree**, ʔwiirikisa shiga yaa.*   'If he would come, it would be fun.'

- *yan:* **yaree**
  *Ami **yaree**, muchikasan yaa.*   'If it rains, it will be difficult.'

- *iin:* **iree**
  *Ari ga **iree**, attaa n chuusa.*   'If he says, they will come.'

If a predicate is negative, add *daree* directly to the Negative Form.

- *Ami nu fran**daree** nai shiga, furee, muchikasan yaa.*   'If it doesn't rain, we can do it, but if it rains, it's a bit difficult, you know.'
- *ʔyaa ga san**daree**, taa ga su ga?*   'If you don't do it, who will?'
- *Warabi-n-chaa ga Uchinaaguchi naraan**daree** (← nararan daree), Uchinaaguchee neen nain doo.*   'If children don't learn Okinawan, Okinawan will be lost.'

c. Adjectives

For adjectives, the final *n* is replaced by *-ree*: *churasa-**n*** → *churasa-**ree***.

- *Churasa-**ree**, Jifi nnjibusan.*   'If it is beautiful, I would like to see it by all means.'
- *Achisa**ree**, chuu ya ikan shee mashi yaa.*   'If it is hot, it is best not to go today.'
- *Hiisa**ree**, naa ufee chin chii shee mashi doo.*   'If you are cold, it is best to wear a bit more clothes.'
- *Afasa**ree**, naa ufee maasu irii sa.*   'If it's bland, I will put in some more salt.'

3. Use of *gutu*

The word *gutu* can be used in the following formulaic expressions. The preceding forms are either Adnominal Forms or Negative Forms.

a. Better alternative action: [(S₁ N.FORM-*gutu*), S₂] 'It's better to do (S₂), rather than doing S₁'

This construction indicates speaker's preference of one action over another, e.g., 'it's better to do A rather than B.' The Negative Form is used before *gutu*.

- *Anu tchu nkai wakaran **gutu** wan ninkai kwimisooree.*   'Please give it to me without letting him know.'
- *Kainan karaa tuuran **gutu**, Asatu kara ichu shee mashi ya sa.*   'It is better to go through Asato and not go through Kainan.'
- *Chuu ya nichi nu a kutu, gakkoo nkai ya ikan **gutu** yaa wuti yashimu shee mashiyan.*   'Since you have a fever today, it is best to stay home and rest and not go to school.'

b. Outcome: [S₁ *gutu nain*] 'It has come to be like S₁'

When the S₁ ends with the verb in Adnominal Form plus *gutu*, it can be followed by *nain* (non-past) or *natan* (past). This construction expresses a change (See [L5(C3)], [L3 (Cul3)]).

- *Kuji atata kutu, wattaa ya Hawai nkai **ichuru gutu** natan.*   'We won the lottery, so (it has come to be like) we are going to Hawaii.'
- *Chuu ya ami nu agata kutu, Nachijin nkai **ichuru gutu** natan.*   'Today the rain stopped, so (it has come to be like) we are going to Nakijin.'
- *Meenachi renshuu sa kutu, Uchinaaguchi n ufee **wakairu gutu** natoon.*   'Since I practiced every day, I have come to understand Okinawan a little.'

c. Praying expression: : [S₁ *gutu u-nigeesabira*] 'I pray for...'

Praying expressions can be made with the affirmative form preceding *gutu* (e.g., 'I pray for...')

- *Yii ʔwaachichi nairu* **gutu** *u-nigeesabira.*
  'I pray for good weather' (or 'May tomorrow be a nice day!')
- *Yii daigaku nkai iiru* **gutu** *u-nigeesabira.*
  'I pray for entering a good university' (or 'May you please help me get into a good university!')
- *Yutasaru* **gutu** *u-nigeesabira.*
  'I pray for your kindness.' (See Preliminary Lesson.)

4. Conjecture: [Finite Form + *nee sun*] 'I have a feeling that ~'

This construction expresses the speaker's conjecture based on what he/she has felt with or without any hard evidence. What comes before *nee* can be a verb, an adjective, or a noun + *yan*.

- *Ami* **fuin nee sun.**
  'It appears that it will rain.' (the speaker may have felt a raindrop)
- *Nama madi kuun kutu, chuu ya* **kuun nee sun.**
  'Since he still has not come, my gut feeling tells me that he's not going to come.'
- *Chinuu yakaa chuu ya* **hiisan nee sun.**
  'It seems today is colder than yesterday.'
- *Chiburu nu yamu shiga, hanafichi* **yan nee sun.**
  'My head hurts; it seems that I have a cold.'

5. Color Words

Here is a list of basic color words. They are nouns, and their adjectival forms are added in parentheses if they are available.

'black'	*kuruu (kurusan)*	'red'	*akaa (akasan)*	'pink'	*bin* (cf. *bingata*)
'white'	*shiruu (shirusan)*	'blue'	*ooruu / mijiiru*	'brown'	*chaairuu*
		'yellow'	*chiiruu / kiiruu*	'green'	*miduri*

ADDITIONAL VOCABULARY

amasan 'sweet'
agin 'rain stops'
atain 'to be hit, win'
chaain '(lights) be turned off (INTR)'
chaasun 'to turn off (TR)'
karasan 'spicy'
kuji 'lottery'
kumu 'clouds'
maasu 'salt'
madu 'time'
majun 'together'

narain 'to learn'
nengajoo 'New Year's greeting card (Jp. loan)'
shiisan 'sour'
shiwaashi 'December'
suujuusan 'salty'
taki 'height'
usaji 'rabbit'
yaku (ni) tachun 'to contribute, be of use'

EXERCISES B

1. Write the color terms in Okinawan.

   a. black   (_____)   c. yellow (_____)

   b. blue   (_____)   d. red   (_____)

   Write two sentences, using color(s) of your choice from the choices above [e.g., *shirusa shee (shi+ya) usaji / kumu*]

   Example: *Shirusa shee usaji yan.*   *Shirusa shee kumu yan.*

   _____
   _____

2. Insert the *-(r)ee* conditional form of a verb or an adjective for each blank. Use the word suggested in the parentheses.

   a. *Waa ga mutchooru doru* 'dollars' *nu* (**agin**) [_____], *wannee yaa kooi shiga yaa.*

   b. *Wannin jin nu* (**an**)[_____], *kuruma kooi shiga.*

   c. *Ari ga* (NEG **ichun**) [_____], *wannin ikan.*

132   PART I   Conversation

   d. A: *Kuree nuu ya ga?* (inset)

      B: (**akiin**) [_____], *wakai sa.*

   e. A: *Afasam-i?* (**afasan**) [_____], *maasu irii sa.*

      B: *Maasu* (**iriin**) [_____], *ii saku nain yaa.*

   f. *Kunu kanjee (kanji + ya) muchikasa shiga, anu tchu* (**yan**) [_____], *wakai sa.*

   g. *Saki* (**numun**) [_____], *kurumaa mutaran doo.*
      'If you drink sake, you can't drive (lit. you can't hold the car).'

   h. *?yaa ga* (**chuun**) [_____], *umusa shiga.*

   i. (**achisan**) [_____], *fuka karaa akkan*[1] *gutu, yaa nkai wushee mashi ya sa.*

[1] The form *akkan* is the Negative Form of *atchun* 'walk'. This is an irregular form.

3. Using the verb in the parentheses, write an obligation sentence with *-nee naran*.

   a. *Kanji sshi* _____. ('to write')

   b. *Shukudai ya achaa* _____. ('to submit', use *?njasun*)

   c. *Jifi UCLA nkai* _____. ('to enter, get in')

   d. *Basu kara* _____. ('to go')

   e. *Meenachi Uchinaaguchi renshuu* _____. ('to do')

4. Match the following:

   a. (___) *Denki nu chaa-toon.*   A. 'I'm turning on the lights.'

   b. (___) *Denki chiki-toon.*   B. 'I turned on the lights.'

   c. (___) *Denki chiki-tan.*   C. 'The lights are on.'

   d. (___) *Denki nu chich-oon.*   D. 'The lights turned off (and I saw it).'

   e. (___) *Denki nu chaai-tan.*   E. 'The lights are off.'

5. Translate the following sentences into Okinawan. Pay special attention to the part in bold.

   a. (Praying) **May I become** taller a little more. (← 'May my height be higher' ('height' = *taki*) [B(3-a)])

b. **I have a feeling** that Mr. Higa will not come today. (See [B4].)

APPLICATIONS

1. You come by your friends who are making something. The following is one possible scenario. Make your own script with your partners, and use the conditional pattern as in bold below. Useful expressions related to taste are provided in the word bank.

   Word Bank [*amasan* 'sweet' *karasan* 'spicy hot' *shiisan* 'sour' *suujuusan* 'salty']

   Niko: *Nuu soo ga?*
   Yuna: *Nama kwaashi chukutoon.*
   Chaa ya ga? (Yuna let Niko taste.)
   Amakooneendaree saataa irii shiga.
   Niko: *Ufee iriishee mashi yaa.*

   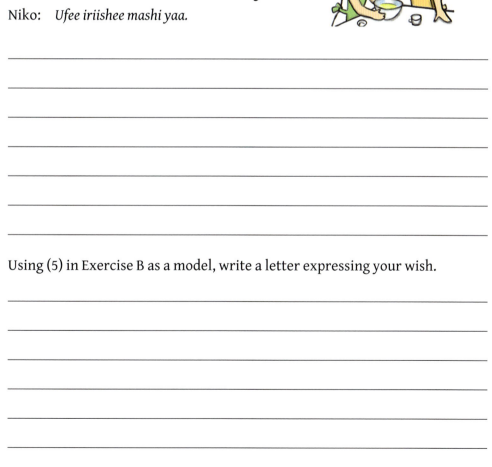

2. Using (5) in Exercise B as a model, write a letter expressing your wish.

3. You are a student / teacher / businessman/woman, and it is the busiest time of the year. You run into your acquaintance on the street and start chatting, as in below. Create your own script with a list of things you have to do.

   A: *Shiwaashi nati ichunasan yaa.*

   B: *Ii, **yaa nu soojee san nee naran**. Niwa nu kusa n **karan nee naran**, Nengajoo n **kakan nee naran**. Ninjuru madu n neen sa.*

   A: *Junni yaa.*

   _____
   _____
   _____
   _____

4. Translate the following sentences. Pay special attention to the part in bold.

   UCLA ʔnjiti atu 'after I graduate from UCLA', *wannee isa nkai nai**busa**ibiin. Isa nkai nati, tchu nu yaku **tata na** ndi umutooibiin. Yashiga, isa gakkoo nkai ii shee ippee muchikasaibii kutu, iiru **gutu unigee sabira**.*

   _____
   _____
   _____
   _____
   _____

5. Using the above passage as a model, write a letter expressing your wish.

   _____
   _____
   _____
   _____
   _____

CULTURE NOTES

1. Northern Dynasty, Central Dynasty, Southern Dynasty

Okinawa was divided into three polities in the 14th and 15th centuries. They were called *Hokuzan* (Northern Dynasty), *Chuuzan* (Central Dynasty), and *Nanzan* (Southern Dynasty). The *Hokuzan* King had his castle in *Nachijin* (= *Nakijin*), which was conquered by King Sho Hashi of the Central Dynasty in 1416. The Central Dynasty also conquered the Southern Dynasty, and Okinawa was unified in 1429.

- Do you know of the history of another country which they used to be divided?
- What do you think are the merits and demerits of divisions and unifications? Tell us about your thoughts.

2. *Churasan* and Okinawan poetry (*Ryūka*)

The dialogues in this lesson are filled with the adjective *churasan* 'beautiful' describing cherry blossoms. *Churasan* reminds many people in Japan of the NHK drama *Churasan*, which made the Okinawan word *churasan* 'beautiful' a household name throughout Japan. *Churasan* means 'beautiful', but its original meaning was more like 'pure' (Nakasone 1987 [1979]: 285–288). This word is abundant in the oldest Okinawan text *Omoro Sōshi* and *Ryūka* poems. It also appeared with the word cherry blossoms in one of the *Ryūka* poems depicted in the traditional Okinawan theater (*Uchinaa shibai*). In this scene, a woman read the first two verses, and male suitors continued the second lines. The poem by the suitor that impressed the woman the most is shown below after the woman's first verse. Note the syllable structure of *Ryūka* must follow the 8-8-8-6 pattern. For more on this type of courtship (e.g., *moo ashibi*), see Takara (2005b: 32–33) and Gillan (2015: 689).

First verses by a woman (8–8):
Nagariyuru miji-ni   sakurabana ukiti
'Placing cherry blossom flowers on the stream of a river…'

Second verses by a man (8–6):
Iru churasa ati du   sukuti ncharu
'It is for the beauty of the flower that I scooped it up.'

- Read about Ryūka and famous female poets described in Hijirida and Oshiro (2011: Lesson 4), also in http://manoa.hawaii.edu/okinawa/wordpress/wp-content/uploads/2010/12/Handbook_L4_Songs-and-Dances.pdf.

- Does this type of courtship remind you of any literary work? Explain.
- What are differences between Japanese short poems (*waka*) and Okinawan short poems?
- Compose your own *waka* or *ryūka*.
- [For your curiosity] Smallpox in Okinawan is called *churagasa* 'lit. beautiful scab'. Obviously, *chura-* is not appropriate but nonetheless used based on the belief that calling smallpox by such a complimentary name would soothe the bad spirit to leave (Sanada and Tomosada 2007: 299).

REVIEW EXERCISES

Lessons 5 and 6

1. Fill in the blanks.

Plain	Meaning	NEG.FORM	COND	INT.FORM	ADV.FORM	ADNOM.FORM	*aani*
tuu-in	'to go through'	tuu-ran				tuui-ru	
chiki-in	'to turn on' (TR)			chiki-ra			
ʔnji-in			ʔnji-ree				ʔnji-yaani
yum-un			yum-ee				
chich-un		chik-an				chichu-ru	
ʔnjas-un	'to put out'				ʔnjash-i		ʔnjas-aani
ichun		ik-an				ʔnja-ru	ʔnj-aani
sun				sa			
i-in				i-i	ii-ru		
an					a-ru		
wun							wu-yaani
Yan	(copula)	aran			ya-i		

2. The following patterns use one of the forms in the chart above. Fill in the blanks in the chart. The first row has been completed for you.

Form	Elements to follow	Meaning
ADV.FORM	+ yassan / gurisan	'easy /difficult to …'
	+ busan	'to want to …'
	+ (i) + ga ichun / chuun	'to go /come to (location) to …'
	+ nee sun	
	+ naa	
	+ na	
	+ nee naran	
	+ (t)ai sun	'doing X … doing Y'
B.ROOT	+ (y)aani	
	+ gutu V	'V so as to …'

3. Select the correct forms.

   a. A: *Chuu ya ami nu { fui / fuin / fute } nee sun yaa.*

   B: *Yan yaa. Anshee, chuu ya { ikan / ichun / ichu } gutu achaa ichumi?*

   A: *Ii,. Dii! achaa { ika / ichu / ichu } na.*

   b. A: *Achaa majun eeqa { nnju / nnjii / nnjun } ga ikani?*

   B: *(Ichu / Ichi /Nji) busa shiga, binchoo { san / shi / sun } nee naran kutu, ikaran saa.*

   c. A: *ʔyaa jii ya gumasa nu { yumu / yudi / yumi } gurisan yaa.*

   Naa chukeen { kachun / kakan / kachi } naa?

   B: *(B writes again) Namaa chaa ya ga?*

   A: *Namaa { waka / wakati / wakai } yashiku natoo sa.*

   d. A: *Kundu nu doyoobi ya nna shi karaoke nkai { ich / ik / ʔnj } -aani,*

   { utattai / utatai }, { moottai / mootai } { kamutai / kadai } sa yaa.

   B: *Yii kangee ya sa.*

4. Fill in the blanks with the appropriate form of *ichun* or *chuun*.

   a. A: *Tashikiti kwiree!* 'Help!'

      B: *Nama (_____) sa.*

   b. A: *Chuu Naafa nkai (_____)-i?* ['…not go? (invitation)']

      B: *Ii, (_____).* ['Let's go!']

      C: *Yii yi, wannee chuu ya ichunasa kutu (_____).*

         Achaa (_____) sa.

5. Fill in the blanks with the appropriate conditional form of the predicate in the parentheses.

   a. *Denki nu (_____), churasan doo.* ('turn on')

   b. *Naa chukeen (_____), wakai sa.* ('read')

   c. *Achaa (_____) asati ichun.* ('cold')

   d. *Saki (_____), kurumaa mutan shee mashi doo.* ('to drink')

   e. *Aree teefa na* 'humorous' *mun yakutu, ari ga (_____), ʔwiirikisan.* ('to come')

   f. *Jin nu (_____), kuruma kooi shiga yaa.* ('to exist', 'to have')

6. Change the following forms in bold into their exalting forms as in the example:
   Ex. *Anu tchoo Asatu shinshii* **yan** → *Anu tchoo Asatu shinshii* **yamisheen**.

   a. *Asatu Shinshii nu naa ya Susumu ndi* **i-in**.

      → *Asatu Shinshii nu naa ya Susumu ndi (_____).*

   b. *Asatu Shinshii ya heya nkai* **wun**

      → *Asatu Shinshii ya heya nkai (_____).*

   c. *Asatu Shinshii ya achaa kuma nkai* **chuum**-*i?*

      → *Asatu Shinshii ya achaa kuma nkai (_____)?*

7. Fill in the blanks with the exalting form to match the English meaning in the parentheses.

   a. Waitress: (_____). ('welcome')

      Nuu (_____) *ga?* ('eat')

      Customer: *Toofu chanpuruu yaa.*

b. Student A: *Ama nkai shinshii ga (_____)*.

   Student B: *Shinshii, maa nkai (_____) ga?*

   Teacher: *Naafa madi ya sa.*

   Student B: *Wattaa n Naafa nkai ichabii kutu, majun (_____)-i?* ('invitation')

8. Change the following sentences to express the change of state meaning of 'become.'

   - Adjective: *~ku nain* (affirmative) [*hii-**ku nain*** 'become cold']
     ~koo (= *ku ya*) ***neen nain*** (negative) [*hii-**koo neen nain*** 'become not cold']

   a. *Achaa ya achikooneen* → _____

   b. *Jin ya neen* → _____

   c. *Hana ya…* (see pictures—Right → Left) → _____

   _____

9. Fill in the blanks with the appropriate particle (*ga, nkai, madi, kara1* 'means', *kara2* 'path', *saani/(s)shi, na, naa*). **Use each item only once.**

   a. *Achaa ya Naafa (_____) irichii kooi (_____) ichun.*

   b. *Asatu (_____) tuuti, Machigwaa (_____) ichun.*

   c. *Takushii ya takasa kutu, basu (_____) ichun.*

   d. *Sannin (_____) muuchii chichimun.* 'wrap up *muuchii* **with** *sannin*.'

   e. *Yuubi nu kwatchii nukutoon (_____)?*

   f. *Nukutooraa, dii, kama (_____).*

10. Give the English equivalents for the following wh-words.

    nuu (_____), *taa* (_____), *maa* (_____), *ichi* (_____), *chaa* (_____), *chassa* (_____)

11. Using one of the wh-words given above, fill in the blanks in the X-Y dialogues:

    a. X: *Uri tu uri koora. (_____) ya ga?*   Y: *1000 yin naibiin.*

    b. X: *Naafa nkai ya (_____) ichu ga?*   Y: *Chuu ya naran. Achaa ya nai shiga…*

c. X: *Anu tchoo (_____) yamishee ga?* Y: *Wattaa gakkoo nu shinshii yamisheen doo.*

d. X: *(_____) ya ga?* Y: *Ippee maasan doo. ?yaa n kamani?*

e. X: *Kuree (_____) ndi ii ga?* Y: *Kuree Uchinaaguchi shee isatuu ya sa.*

12. You are a customer. Based on the prompt, give the taxi driver directions.

    a. 'Turn right':   (_____)_*kwimisooree.*
    b. 'Turn left':   (_____)_*kwimisooree.*
    c. 'Go straight':   (_____)_*kwimisooree.*
    d. 'Go until the intersection': (_____)_*kwimisooree.*
    e. 'Go to the T-section': (_____)_*kwimisooree.*

LESSON 7

Beach Outing

DIALOGUE A

Yuna is inviting Niko to go to the beach tomorrow as it is a special day for *hamauri* 'clam-digging'.

Yuna:	*Achaa ya hama nkai ʔnjaani, chinbooraa gwaa tuti kuuni? Sangwachi sannichii, hamauri ya sa.*	Why don't we go to the beach and get some sea snails? It's March 3rd and is the day for *hamauri*.
Niko:	*Ii, ii.*	Yes, yes.

Mother:	Iina urijin natoo sa yaa. Chichi nu hai ya ʔnma nu hai ya sa yaa.	Oh, it's already the *urijin* season. Time flies (lit. 'time runs like a horse runs'), doesn't it?
	(To Yuna) *Aashi nkai du ichurui? Oojima-nkai du ichurui?*	(To Yuna) Are you going to Awashi? or Ojima?
Yuna:	Maa **nu/ga ga** mashi **yara**. (*Aashi tu Oojima tu,*) maa ga chichasaibii ga?	I wonder which place is better? Which one is closer, Awase or Ojima?
Mother:	*Aashi* **yaka** *Oojima* **ga** *du chichasaru.*	Ojima is closer than Awase.

CORE VOCABULARY

hama	'beach'
chinbooraa	'sea snail'
kuun-i	← *kuun* 'to come' (NEG) + *i* (QP) [L3(B4)], [L5(A1)]
sangwachi	'March'
sannichi	'third day of the month'
hamauri	'digging for clams' [Cul1][1]
iina	'already'
urijin	'spring-like season' [Cul1]
hai (NOUN)	← *hain* 'to run'
chichi	'time'
ʔnma	'horse'
Aashi	'place name, Awase (see the inset)'
Oojima	'place name (see the inset)'
ichuru (ADNOM.FORM)	← *ichun* 'to go' (Focus Construction (1) [L4(A4)]
ga...yara	Focus (2): *ga...*RA.FORM [A2]
chichasaibii (APO.FORM)	← *chichasa* 'close' + *ibii* (POL)
yaka	'rather than'

[1] *Hamauri* is called by various names such as *hama urii* and *sangwachi sannichii* 'the third day of the third month (according to the lunar calendar)'. This started as a day for the women's purification rite (more on this, see Hijirida and Oshiro 2010: Chapter 6). At the time of *Tumai Aakaa* (see Cul3), this was one of the few days when daughters from upper class families were allowed to go to a beach with their attendant lady alone. Nowadays, people go to the beach to dig clams, sea snails, get seaweed, etc.

GRAMMAR A

1. Directional Motion: [G.FORM + *ichun/chuun*] 'do something and go/come'

The verbs of motion, *ichun* 'to go' and *chuun* 'to come' can be used as auxiliary verbs (AUX) after the Gerund Forms of the main verb. Together, the combined structures express directional motions (i.e., 'do V~ and go/come').

- *Kuri **mutchi ichun**.*   'I will take it.' (lit. 'hold and go')
- A: *Maa nkai ʔnja ga?*   'Where did you go?'
  B: *Umi wuti **ʔwiiji chan** doo.*   'I came back from swimming in the ocean.'
- *Aashi nkai ʔnji, chinbooraa gwaa **tuti kuuni**?*   'Shall we go to Awase to get sea snails?'
- A: *Wannee chuu ya ichunasanu machigwaa nkai ichibusa shiga, naran saa.*   'I'm busy so I can't, although I want to go to the market today.'
  B: *Anshee wan ga ʔnji shishi **kooti chuu** sa.*   'Then I will go and buy meat and come back.'

2. Focus Construction (2): [...*(nu/ga) ga*...RA.FORM] 'I wonder...'

In Lesson 4 [L4(A4)], we learned Focus Construction (1), [X *du*...ADNOM.FORM], 'it is X that ~' where X represents a focused element marked by *du*. Focus Construction (2) introduced here forms **a self-addressed question** (i.e., "I wonder if JOHN is the one who does...") (Part II, Topic 8). It uses *ga* to mark a focused element and the *Ra* Form to conclude the sentence. You can make the RA.FORM by adding *ra* to the Apocopated Form (see a full explanation below). Here is a comparison of the two types of focus construction.

Focus Construction (1) : [...X ***du***...ADNOM.FORM]   'It is X that...'
(focused statement)

Focus Construction (2) : [...X ***ga***...RA.FORM]   'I wonder if it is X that...'
(self-addressed question)

Note that it is possible for two *ga*'s to appear in sequence as in the first example below. In this case, the first *ga* is the subject marker and the second *ga* is the focus particle. The *nu ga* combination is also possible as shown by the second example:

- *Yuna **ga**_{SUBJ} **ga**_{FOCUS} chuura.*   'I wonder if (it is) Yuna (who) is coming.'
- *Tui **nu**_{SUBJ} **ga**_{FOCUS} nachoora.*   'I wonder if (it is) the bird (that) is chirping.'

As noted earlier, the *Ra* Form is made by adding *ra* to the Apocopated Form for both V- and C-verbs:

- V-verb: *tui* + *ra* → *tui-ra*
- C-verb: *ʔwiiju* + *ra* → *ʔwiiju-ra*

For V-verbs, the RA Form resembles the Intentional Form we learned earlier as both forms end in *ra*. The table below has these two forms side by side for a comparison. These two forms appear similar for V-verbs, but be sure to distinguish the Intentional Form and the *Ra* Form, as the latter has *-i* before *ra*.

	DIC.FORM	INT.FORM	RA.FORM	Meaning of RA.FORM
V	tu-in	tu-**ra**	tui-**ra**	'I wonder if he'll take…'
V	maga-in	maga-**ra**	magai-**ra**	'I wonder if he'll turn'
V	na-in	na-**ra**	nai-**ra**	'I wonder if he'll become…'
1	ʔwiij-un	ʔwiig-**a**	ʔwiiju-**ra**	'I wonder if he'll swim'
2	ninj-un	nind-**a**	ninju-**ra**	'I wonder if he'll sleep'
3	kunj-un	kund-**a**	kunju-**ra**	'I wonder if he'll tie up…'
4	nach-un	nak-**a**	nachu-**ra**	'I wonder if it'll chirp'
5	much-un	mut-**a**	muchu-**ra**	'I wonder if he'll hold…'
6	turas-un	turas-**a**	turasu-**ra**	'I wonder if he'll give…'
7	yub-un	yub-**a**	yubu-**ra**	'I wonder if he'll invite…'
8	yum-un	yum-**a**	yumu-**ra**	'I wonder if he'll read…'
IRG	ichun	ika	ichu-**ra**	'I wonder if he'll go'
IRG	chuun	kuu	chuu-**ra**	'I wonder if he'll come'
IRG	sun	sa	su-**ra**	'I wonder if he'll do…'

For adjectives and copulas, you can make the *Ra* Form by changing the final *-n* of Finite Forms to *-ra* as below:

- Adjectives: *achisa-n* → *achisa-ra* 'I wonder if it is hot…'
- Copulas: *ya-n* → *ya-ra* 'I wonder if it is…'

In the construction below, the focus is on the question word.

Focus Construction (2) : [… wh **ga** …] RA.FORM 'I wonder it is wh that…'
  (self-addressed)

A wh-word is in focus in the first sentence. The second sentence is a variant of the first sentence.

- *Maa [**nu/ga**] **ga** mashi **yara**.*   'I wonder (it is) WHERE (that) is better.'
- *Nuu **nu ga** mashi **yara**.*   'I wonder (it is) WHICH ONE (that) is better.'

When the focused noun is a wh-word, the subject marker may be *ga* even if it is an inanimate subject, as in *maa **ga** ga*.

Here are some more examples of all three predicate types:

- Verbs: *kamun* → *nuu **ga** kamura*   'I wonder what he is going to eat…'
- Adjectives: *churasan* → *taa **ga ga** churasara* 'I wonder who is beautiful…'
- Copulas: *Niko yan* → *taa **ga ga** Niko **yara*** 'I wonder who is Niko…'

We have learned a listener-oriented question pattern with the sentence-final question particle *ga* [L1(B4)] as in the first question below. In contrast, the second and third questions are self-addressed questions to which the listener is not expected to respond. Note that in the second example, the sentence-final particle *gayaa* is used for 'I wonder', but it does not focus *maa* 'where' as in the third sentence.

- Listener-oriented question: *Maa {nu/ga} mashi ya **ga**?*   'Which place would be better?'
- Self-addressed question: *Maa {nu/ga} mashi ya **gayaa**.*   'I wonder which place would be better.'
- Self-addressed focus question: *Maa {nu/ga} **ga** mashi **yara**.* 'I wonder WHICH place would be better.'

3. Comparison of Items

a. Adjective Comparison

Q: [X **tu** Y **tu/too** (← tu + ya) **jiroo** Adj.]   'Between X and Y, which is more Adj.?'
A: [X **yaka** Y **ga** (**du**) Adj.]   'Y is more Adj. than X.'

The wh-word *jiroo* (← *jiru* + *ya*) in self-addressed questions was already introduced in [L5(A6)]. Here its answer pattern is added. This Q-A pattern is used for comparing two objects (e.g., 'X is better/cheaper/faster…than Y').

- Q: *Gooyaa chanpuruu **tu** toofu champuruu **tu** jiroo maasa ga?*   'Which is more delicious, *gooyaa chanpuruu* or *toofu chanpuruu*?'
- A: *Toofu chanpuru **yaka** Gooyaachanpuruu **ga du** maasaru.*   '*Gooyaa chanpuruu* is more delicious than *toofu chanpuruu*.'

Jiroo cannot be used in a comparison of people, places. Use *taa* 'who' and *maa* 'where' instead.

- *Niko tu Amy tu {ˣjiroo / ᵒtaa ga} Uchinaaguchee jooji ya ga?*   'Between Niko and Amy, who is better at Okinawan?'
- Q: *Aashi tu Oojima tu, {ˣjiroo / ᵒmaa ga} chichasaibii ga?*   'Between Awase and Ojima, which is closer?'
  A: *Aashi **yaka** Oojima **ga** du chichasaru.*   'Ojima is closer than Awase.'

b. [Adj.-*ku* + Verb] Comparison

Q: [X *tu* Y *tu/too* (← *tu* + *ya*)   *jiroo* Adj.-*ku* + V]
A: [X *yaka* Y *ga* (*du*) Adj.-*ku* + V]

An adjective's *-ku* form works as an adverb, which appears before a verb. Compare how adjectives and their derived adverbs are used in the following sentences.

- Q: *Kunu in tu anu in tu/too, jiroo fee**ku** hai ga?*   'Between this dog and that dog, which one runs faster?'
  A: *Kunu in **yaka** anu in **ga** du fee**ku** hairu.*   'Rather than this dog, that dog runs faster.'

c. Comparison of Three or More Items

[wh-word *nu/ga* + *ichiban* Adj. *ga*]   'Who/What/Where is the most Adj.?'

[wh-word *nu/ga* + *ichiban* Adj. -*ku* Verb *ga*]   'Who/What/Where does...most Adv.?'

For comparisons of more than three items, regular *wh*-question words such as *taa* 'who' and *maa* 'where' are used by adding *ichiban* as below:

- *Uchinaa wutee, **maa** nu/ga **ichiban** churasa ga?*   'In Okinawa, where is the most beautiful place?'
- ***Taa** ga **ichiban** ufooku tut-ee ga?*   'Who has gotten the most?'

'*Ichiban* Adj.'/'*ichiban* Adj. -*ku* V' can be used in a statement as well.

- *Aree **ichiban dikiyaa** ya kutu, muchikasaru kanji n wakain.*   'He is the smartest student, so he can understand even difficult kanji.'
- *Dushi gwaa nu naaka wutee Niko ga **ichiban takee takasan**.*   'Among my friends, Niko is tallest.'

ADDITIONAL VOCABULARY

dikiyaa 'smart person/student'
ichiban 'best'
ichunasan 'busy'
kanji 'Chinese character (Jp. loan)'
maasu 'salt'

gohan 'rice'
nachun 'to chirp', 'to cry'
suba 'noodles'
tii 'karate'
ufooku (Adv. Form of *ufusan* 'a lot')

EXERCISES A

1. Translate the following in English.

   a. *Kuri **mutchi ichun**.* (_____)

   b. *Yamashiro sanoo gooyaa chanpuruu **chukuti choon**.* (_____
   _____)

2. Using the word in [ ] as a FOCUS, rewrite the following into focus sentences.

   Example: [*Ari*] *ya Orion numun*   [*Nuu*] *chukui ga?*
   → [*Ari*] *ga ga* (ˣ*ya ga*) *Orion <u>numura</u>.* → [*Nuu*] *ga chukuira.*

   a. *Anu tchoo* [*Yamatu n tchu*] *yan.* → _____

   b. [*Taa*] *ga ichiban jooji ya ga?* → _____

   c. [*Pensy*] *ya ichunasan.* → _____

   d. *Higa sanoo* [*kunu muuchii*] *kunjun.* → _____

   e. [*Shikina san*] *ga Teruya san yubun.* → _____

   f. [*Shogo*] *ya ichiban dikiyaa yan.* → _____

3. Use the example sentences as references, and respond to the questions in (a–f).

   Example: A: *Akaa tu ooruu tu, **jiroo** mashi ya ga?*
   B: *Wannee ooruu ga mashi ya ssaa.*
   A: *Anu shiitu nu naaka wutee, **taa ga** saafin ichiban jooji ya ga?*
   B: *Kanoa ga **ichiban** jooji yan.*

   a. Among Okinawan dishes, which one do you like the most?
      Fill in (_____) with the particle.

      Uchinaa nu kwatchii nu naaka (_____) _____ ga ichiban mashi yan.

   b. As for *karate* (*tii*), who is stronger than Kiyuna Ryoji?

      Tii ya Kiyuuna Ryooji (_____) _____ shee _____.
      [Kiyuna Ryoji is the gold medalist in karate at the Tokyo 2020 Olympics]

   c. In Okinawa, where would you like to go most? (Translate into Okinawan.)

      _____
      _____

   d. In Okinawa, what would you like to do most? (Translate into Okinawan.)

      _____
      _____

   e. Which one is more delicious, Japanese noodles (*Yamatu suba*) or Okinawan noodles (*Uchinaa suba*)? (Translate into Okinawan.)

      _____
      _____

   f. Between X and Y, which one is more Z? (Fill in X, Y and Z with the words of your choice). _____
      _____

4. Answer the following questions, using the A *yaka* B *ga/nu* Adjective pattern.

   a. *?yaa ya gohan tu pan tu, jiroo mashi ya ga?* (_____
      _____)

   b. *?yaa ya chukui shi tu kamu shi tu, jiroo mashi ya ga?* (_____
      _____)

DIALOGUE B

Niko:	*Ama wutee chinbooraa bikeen du tura**riiru**i?*	You can only get sea snails over there?
Yuna:	*Afakee n wun doo. Anshikara, sunui n tura**riin** doo.*	There are also clams. And you can get seaweed.
Niko:	*Waa ga **yati n** tu**yuusu** gayaa.*	I wonder if even (a novice like) I can get any?
Mother:	*Ii, **taa yatin** nain doo. Kuri mutchi-ichu kutu, warabi **ga n** nain.*	Yes, anyone can do it. We will take this (i.e., rake), so even a child can do it.
(Showing the raking motions)		
	*Un-gutu(u) (s)shi. Shigu chika-**yuusuru** gutu nai sa.*	Like this. You will be able to use it soon.

CORE VOCABULARY

bikeen/bikaan	'only'
-rariiru (ADNOM.FORM)	potential AUX [B1]
afakee	'clam'
sunui	'*mozuku* seaweed'
yati n	'even if it's ~' [B2]
-yuusun	'can' [B1]
taa yati n	'anyone'
nain	[L6(B3)]
~ ga n	'even for ~' [B2]
un gutu (s)shi	'doing this way' [L6(B3)]
chikai (ADV.FORM)	← *chikain* 'to use'
-yuusuru gutu	'come to be able to ~'

GRAMMAR B

1. Potentials: Situational Possibility vs. Agent's Ability

Potentials are often divided into two types: **situational possibility** and the **agent's ability**. For instance, it is possible to interpret the English phrase, "**can** play the piano" in the following two ways:

a. **Situational Possibility 'be allowed to ~':**
I'm not allowed to play the piano before 9:00 a.m. here. But it's 10:00 a.m., so I'm allowed to play the piano now. That is, 'I can play the piano!'

b. **Agent's Ability 'have the ability to ~':**
I'm good at playing the piano (I have been taking lessons for ten years.). That is, 'I can play the piano!'

Although the English *can* denote both types of potentials, Okinawan uses two distinct potential suffixes for each potential:

- **Situational Possibility:** [INT.FORM + **riin**]   'can do'
- **Agent's Ability:**   [ADV. FORM + **yuusun**]   'can do'   (ADV.FORM = B.ROOT + *i*)

Here are some examples:

- *Sunui n **tu-rariin** doo.*   '*Sunui* (seaweed) can also be harvested.' (possibility)
- *Wan nin **tu-yuusun**. {ˣ tui-yuusun} gayaa.*   'I wonder if I can get them, too.' (ability)
- *Uma wuti **kama-riim**-i?*   'Is it possible to eat here?' (possibility)
- *Wattaa warabee duu chui (s)shi **ka-mi-yuusun** doo.*   'Our kid (e.g., a toddler) can eat by herself.' (ability)

If the Adverbial Form ends in *-ai /-ui*, the last vowel *-i* often drops when combined with *-yuusun*. Thus, *tu-yuusun* is used instead of *tui-yuusun*. Similarly, *chika-yuusun* is used instead of *chikai-yuusun*.

2. Concessive Conditionals

a. [**Wh** + **yati** + **n**] 'no matter *wh~*'

b. [**Noun** + **yati** + **n**] 'even if Noun ~'

Yati is the Gerund Form of the copula *yan* and *n* is the additive topic particle.

 The gerund copulas can also be replaced by a verbal or adjectival gerund, which will be introduced later.

Here are some examples with Pattern (a) above:

- **Taa yati n** *nain doo.* 'Whoever it is, (s)he can do it.' (i.e., 'Anyone can do it.')
- *Aree* **nuu yati n** *kamun.* 'He can eat no matter what.' (i.e., 'He can eat anything.')
- **Maa yati n** *ichun.* 'I will go anywhere.'
- **Ichi yati n** *shimun doo.* 'I can do it any time.'

 Shimun means 'finish, end' and 'sufficient.' In a sentence with *yatin*, it means 'whatever/whenever/whoever etc. (is sufficient, good, or works).'

Further examples with Pattern (b):

- *Waa ga* **yati n** *shii-***yuusu** *gayaa.* 'I wonder if even I can do it.'
- *Warabi (ga)* **yati n** *na-in doo.* 'Even a child can do it.'
- *Ufutchu (ga)* **yati n** *wakaran sa.* 'Even an adult can't understand.'

3. Double Particle: [Subject particle {*nu/ga*} + Topic particles {*ya/n*}]

The topic particle **ya** and the additive topic particle **n** can combine with the subject particle *nu* or *ga* to form a double-particle construction. When that happens, it expresses distinct shades of meanings as follows (Part II, Topic 2):

- Subject X *nu/ga* + *ya* → *noo/gaa* 'As for X (compared to others)'
- Subject X *nu/ga* + *n* → *nu n/ga n* 'Even X'

Here are some examples:

- *Warabi* **gaa** *nain.* 'Children (as compared to adults) can do it' (e.g., children, but not adults, can squat because they are flexible—see the pictures above.)
- *Warabi* **ga n** *nain.* 'Even a child can do it (even though they are less skillful)' (implying 'Why can't you—an adult—do it?' (e.g., doing something simple, like making instant ramen.)

ADDITIONAL VOCABULARY

ashibun 'to play'
duu chui 'by oneself'
fudi 'brush'

munu wakain 'to become reasonable (after coming of age)'
tu 'with, as' (compare with *tu* 'and' [L2(C6)])

EXERCISES B

1. Change the following sentences into sentences of Situational Possibility (= SP) or Ability.

    a. *Anu warabee kanji [yumun].* (Ability) → _____

    b. *Toshokwan wuti hoogen shinbun [yumun].* (SP) → _____

    c. *21 nata kutu saki n [numun].* (SP) → _____

    d. *Wannee fudi sshi jii [kachun].* (Ability) → _____

    e. *Wannee uchinaaguchi [chichun].* (Ability) → _____

2. Fill in the blanks using the Concessive Conditional patterns [B2].

    a. A: *Ichee mashi ya ga?*
       B: (_____) *shimu sa.* 'No matter when it is, it's okay.'

    b. A: (_____) *nkai ichu ga?*
       B: (_____) *shimu sa.* 'No matter where it is, it's okay.'

c. A: (_____)? 'Who should we go with?'

   B: (_____) shimu sa. 'No matter whom it is, it's okay.'

d. A: *Higa sanoo amasa shee kaman doo.*

   B: *Kuree ansuka amakooneen kutu,* (_____) *kamu sa.*

   'Even Higa-san…'

3. Choose the most likely item you would use in the given situations.

   a. The cake you made is very sweet. You feel it would only appeal to the kids, not to the adults.

   (   ) *Warabee kamun.*

   (   ) *Warabi n kamun.*

   b. The cake you made is not too sweet. You are confident it would also appeal to the adults.

   (   ) *Ufutchoo kaman.*

   (   ) *Ufutchu n kamun.*

4. Match the following Okinawan phrases with their English meanings.

   a. (___) *Nuun naran.*   A. 'X can do nothing.'
      (___) *Nuu yati n nain.*   B. 'X can do anything.'

   b. (___) *ʔwiiji-yuusun.*   A. 'He can swim.'
      (___) *ʔwiiga-riin.*   B. 'Swimming allowed.'

   c. (___) *Shishee kamun.*   A. 'I'm a vegetarian, so…'
      (___) *Shishee kaman.*   B. 'I don't like to eat vegetables…'

   d. (___) *Ufutchu nu n umusan ndi umuyuru haji.* A. 'simple storyline…'
      (___) *Ufutchunoo umusan ndi umuran haji.*   B. 'several plots…'

DIALOGUE C

The first scene below shows Niko and Yuna digging *chinbooraa* 'sea snails' on the beach. The second scene shows them eating their catch at home.

(At the beach)

Yuna: *Ichi jikan shi anshi dateen **tuteeru**!*
In just one hour, you got so many of them (sea snails)!

Niko: *ʔyaa tu yinu saku ya sa. Ama wutee **tiichi n** turaranta kutu, waa **gaa** naran (n)di umuta shiga. Firumasa ssaa yaa.*
It's the same as you. I could not get even one over there, so I thought I could not do it, but… Never expected this many!

Yuna: *Uri usu nkai **chikitoochu** shee mashi doo.*
It's better to soak them in salt water.

(At dinner)

Yuna: *Duu shi **tuticheeru** chinbooraa ya yuku maasan yaa. Ai, **nuu n neen** natoo sa.*
The *chinbooraa*s that we got and brought ourselves are even better. Oh, all gone.

Niko: (To Host Mother) *N(n)na joogu yaibiin yaa. Chuu ya ippee ʔwiirikisaibiitan yaa.*
(To Host Mother) Everyone likes it! Today was so enjoyable.

CORE VOCABULARY

ichi jikan shi	'in one hour'[1]
tu-teeru (ADNOM.FORM)	← *tu* 'catch' + *teeru* (RES) [C1][2]
yinu (yunu) saku	'same amount'[3]
tiichi n	'not even one' [B3]
tu-ra-ran	← *tu* 'get' + *ra* (POT) + *ran* (NEG) [B1]
gaa	← *ga* + *ya* [B3]

firumasa (APO.FORM)	← *firumasan* 'surprising'
usu	'salt water'
chiki-toochu (APO.FORM)	← *chiki* 'soak' + *toochun* (preparatory aspect) [C1]
duu shi	'by oneself'
tuti-ch-eeru (ADNOM.FORM)	← *tuti* 'get' + *ch* 'come' + *eeru* (RES) [C1]
yuku	'even'
nuu n neen	'there is nothing' [C3]
joogu	'like'

[1] *Ichi-jikan shi* is a 'quantity + *shi*' construction where *shi* delimits the quantity to which the predicate is applicable. *Ussa shi shimun* 'This is enough' (lit. *this* is the delimited quantity that the predicate *enough* applies to).

[2] The Adnominal Form here is triggered by the adverb *anshi* 'unexpectedly' (see [L5(DialC)].

[3] The adjective *yinu* (*yunu*) must be followed by a noun like *saku* 'amount' here.

GRAMMAR C

1. Resultative: [G.ROOT + *(t)een*] 'have done'

a. 'have done'

This **Resultative** construction denotes the result of an action: 'have done'. This construction should not be confused with the **Simple Past** construction [L3(B1)]. For example, compare 'I lost my key (but I found it now)' and 'I have lost my key (so I cannot go into my office).' The former is the Simple Past and the latter the Resultative. In the Resultative, the effect of the past action still lingers on to the present. The Resultative is made by attaching -*(t)een* to the Gerund Root: *tu* + *teen* → *tu-teen* 'have taken', *yud* + *een* → *yud-een* 'have read'. (Remember the Gerund Root is used in the aspectual form [G.ROOT +*(t)oon*] (e.g., *yud-oon* 'is reading' ([L3(A3)]) as shown in the chart in [C2] below.)

V-verb
- G.ROOT + *teen*: **tu-teen** (e.g., 'She has taken it.')
- G.ROOT + *teen*: **fu-teen** (e.g., 'It has rained.')

C-verb
- G.ROOT + *een*: **yud-een** (e.g., 'They have read it.')
- G.ROOT + *een*: **nint-een** (e.g., 'The kids have slept.')
- G.ROOT + *een*: **kach-een** (e.g., 'They have written it.')
- G.ROOT + *een*: **tuti-ch-een** (e.g., 'They took them and have come back.')

b. *(t)een* form

The *(t)een* form also indicates **surprise** as in the second example below.

- *Duu shi **tuti-ch-eeru** chinbooraa ya yuku maasan yaa.* (Result) — 'The sea snails we got ourselves taste even better.'
- *Anshi dateen **tu-teeru**!* — 'You've got so much!' (Surprise)

c. Conjecture

This construction may also describe the speaker's **conjecture**. He/she assumes something happened based on the evidence from his/her physical senses (seeing, hearing, smelling etc.), such as in the statement 'It must have rained' (because the leaves on the tree are wet—visual evidence). This **evidential** sense contrasts with that of the extended past (PAST-2), which indicates what the speaker **directly witnessed**, e.g., '(I saw) Taro reading a *manga* book' [L3(B1)]. Here the three types of *past* sentences are compared.

- *Wannee kunu manga **yud-an**.* — 'I read this comic book.' (PAST-1)
- *Aree kunu manga **yumu-tan**.* — '(I saw) he read this comic book.' (PAST-2)
- *Aree kunu manga **yudeen**.* — 'He has read this comic book.' (Resultative); or '(I think) he read this comic book (because it is left open).' (Evidential)

These evidential sentences often end in the sentence-final particles *tee* or *sa* [L4(A5)].

- *Ami nu fu-**teen** tee. Jii nu ndit-oo kutu.* — 'It **must've** rained. The ground is wet.'
- *Kunu sunui ya attaa ga tuti ch-**ee** sa. Chuu Aashi nkai ichu ndi iita kutu.* — 'They **must've** harvested this seaweed. Because they said they were going to Awase.'

2. Preparatory aspect: [G.ROOT + *(t)oochun*] 'do it for future use'

This -*(t)oochun* construction indicates the meaning of 'doing something in anticipation for future use'. We call this the '**preparatory aspect**.' This means you don't need to do it now, but it may become necessary in the future, so you do it now. For example, I am not hungry and don't need to eat now, but I will be busy and have no time to eat lunch at noon, so I will go ahead and eat an early lunch now at 11 a.m. (*kad-oochun* 'I eat now'). The form is similar to the *(t)oon* aspectual form. Add *chun* after -*oo*- (e.g., *kad-oon* → *kad-oochun*).

	DIC.FORM	G.ROOT	Aspectual	Preparatory Aspect	Meaning
V	tu-in	tu	tu-**toon**	tu-**toochun**	'to take for now/future'
V	sagi-in	sagi	sagi-**toon**	sagi-**toochun**	'to hang for now/future'
C-1	ʔwiij-un	ʔwiij	ʔwiij-**oon**	ʔwiij-**oochun**	'to swim for now/future'
C-2	ninj-un	nint	nint-**oon**	nint-**oochun**	'to sleep for now/future'
C-3	kunj-un	kunch	kunch-**oon**	kunch-**oochun**	'to tie up for now/future'
C-4	kach-un	kach	kach-**oon**	kach-**oochun**	'to write for now/future'
C-5	much-un	mutch	mutch-**oon**	mutch-**oochun**	'to hold for now/future'
C-6	ʔnbus-un	ʔnbuch	ʔnbuch-**oon**	ʔnbuch-**oochun**	'to steam for now/future'
C-7	yub-un	yud	yud-**oon**	yud-**oochun**	'to invite for now/future'
C-8	yum-un	yud	yud-**oon**	yud-**oochun**	'to read for now/future'

- *Muuchii tinjoo kara **sagi-toochun**.*   'I will hang *muuchii* from the ceiling **(for future use)**.'
- *Uri, usu nkai **chiki-toochu** shee mashi doo.*   'It is better to soak them in salt water **(for future use)**.'

Here are the verb forms of various tenses and aspects introduced thus far:

- *Chinbooraa tu-**in***   'I **will pick** sea snails.'
- *Chinbooraa tu-**toon***   'I **am picking** sea snails.'
- *Chinbooraa tu-**toochun*** 'I will pick sea snails **for future use**.'
- *Chinbooraa tu-**tan***   'I **picked** sea snails.'
- *Chinbooraa tu-**teen***   'I **have picked** sea snails.'
- *Chinbooraa tui-**tan***   'He picked sea snails and **I witnessed it**.'
- *Chinbooraa tuti-**ichun*** 'I will pick sea snails and **go**.'
- *Chinbooraa tuti-**chuun*** 'I will pick sea snails and **come back**.'

3. Total Negation: [Numeral (one) + *n* + NEG] 'not even one'/ [Wh + *n* + NEG] 'no one, nothing…'

The phrases 'number (one) + *n*', and 'wh-word + *n*' followed by NEG indicates **total negation** as in 'not even one exists', or 'no one does it.' Here are some examples:

- ***Tiichi n neen** natoon.*   'It became none.' (lit. Not even one left.)
- ***Chui n kuun** tan.*   'Not even one came.'
- ***Muru neen** natoon.*   'It became none.' (lit. Everything is gone.)

- A: *Kuree taa ga nai ga?*   'As for this, who can do it?'
  B: **Taa n naran.**   'No one can do it.'
- A: *Nuugana kamu shi ami?*   'Isn't there anything I can eat?'
  B: *Yii yii,* **nuu n neen.**   'No, there is nothing.'

ADDITIONAL VOCABULARY

diigu 'Erythrina (prefectural flower of Okinawa)'
duu humii 'self-praise'
ji 'o'clock'
ndiin 'to get wet'
tuji 'wife'
wutu 'husband'

EXERCISES C

1. Give the English meaning for the verbs below, and write the -(t)een and -(t)oochun forms.

	Meaning	-(t)een	-(t)oochun
a. *chichun*	( )	[ ]	[ ]
b. *chikiin*	( )	[ ]	[ ]
c. *chikain*	( )	[ ]	[ ]
d. *akiin*	( )	[ ]	[ ]
e. *michiin*	( )	[ ]	[ ]
f. *yumun*	( )	[ ]	[ ]
g. *noosun*	( )	[ ]	[ ]
h. *ichun*	( )	[ ]	[ ]

2. Translate the following into English.

   a. *Naafa nkai ʔnji, mangoo* **kooti kuun**-*i?* (_____)

   b. *Anshi dateen* **chukuteeru!** (_____)

   c. *Muuchii tinjoo kara* **sagitoochun.** (_____).

3. Match each sentence on the left to its appropriate follow-up sentence on the right to complete the speaker's utterance. Write the corresponding letter (A–F) in the parentheses.

   a. (___) X n yutasan. Y n yutasan,   A. *anu warabaa ya wakai ssaa.*

   b. (___) 1 + 1 = 2 ya muchikashikoo neen.   B. *taa yati n shii-busan tee.*

   c. (___) Aree gooyaa chanpuruu kamu gayaa.   C. *jiru yati n jootuu yan.*

   d. (___) Aree gooyaa chanpuruu chuku-yuusu gayaa. D. *Aree nuu yati n nai sa.*

   e. (___) Ufutchu yati n wakaran shiga,   E. *warabi yati n nain doo.*

   f. (___) Kunu geemu ya umusan. Taa ga san ga? F. *Aree nuu yati n kamu sa.*

4. Answer the following questions using the appropriate total negation pattern (Numeral (one) + *n* + NEG 'not even one' or Wh + *n* + NEG 'no one, nothing…').

   a. *Kunu eegoo taa ga yumi-yuu su ga yaa.* → _____

   b. *Jinoo maa nkai a ga?* → _____

   c. *Chinuu kadaru anu u-kwaashee ikuchi a ga?* → _____

APPLICATIONS

1. Construct a conversation between A and B. A has his/her opinion, but B does not agree. For example, A is considering to apply for a big company, but B thinks it is not a good idea. An example is given below. You can use any other situations with two opposing views. You must use *-neenti n* in B's response. Use WB for help.

   A: *Magi kaishaa kyuuryoo nu 'salary' takasa kutu, wannee magi kaisha nkai iibusan.*

   B: *Kyuuryoo ga takasaree, shikuchi ga umukoo**neenti n** shimum-i?*

2. Referencing the dialogue between Nobita and Doraemon, make your own conversation.

   Example ideas: run a hundred meters in eleven seconds (*byoo*); swim from here to there; etc.

162   PART I   Conversation

Nobita:	*?yaa ya kuri wakaim-i?* $e^{i\pi} + 1 = ?$[1]
Doraemon:	*Wannee mayaa du yaru, tchu ya aran.*
	Wan **gaa** *(ga + ya) wakaran sa.*
Nobita:	*Anshee, taa ga ga wakaira?*
Doraemon:	*Dekisugi yar-ee, wakai sa.*[2]
	Ari ga wakaran-ree, **taa ga n** *wakaran sa.*

[1] This is the famous Euler's Equation, which is arguably called "the most beautiful equation."
[2] *Dekisugi* is a last name of a boy who is extremely smart in the *Doraemon* comic. There is a play on words, as *Dekisugi* is composed of *deki* 'able' + *sugi* 'excessively'.

CULTURAL NOTES

1. *Urijin* and *Wakanachi*

Though there are no real four seasons in Okinawa, *urijin* and *wakanachi* are two words that bring special seasonal feelings to Okinawan people. *Urijin* begins in the second or the third month of the lunar calendar when the earth gets damp with light rain. Following *urijin* a few months later, *wakanachi* arrives when the sun gradually gets stronger (Hokama 1976: 256–257).

- Do you have any special seasonal words you like in any language (besides the names of the four seasons)? Please explain why.
- In Okinawan, there are many words related to rain. *Suuman-boosuu,* for example, refers to two periods of the rainy season; *suuman* is around May 21 and *boosuu* around June 6 according to the new calendar (OGJ2, p. 140). Check WB for the meanings of *tiidaami, katabui, uchiami, yugafuu ami*, etc. Do you know any cultures that have many words relating to rain or any aspects of weather? Please explain.

2. *Diigu (Deigo)* 'Erythrina'

Diigu (*Deigo*) is the prefectural flower of Okinawa. It blooms at the beginning of summer (*wakanachi*) around March and April of the solar calendar. Okinawan people believe that a year when *diigu* (*deigo*) flowers bloom in abundance is a year when there will be many typhoons. Based on this belief, some people interpret the song "Shimauta" as depicting a year with many typhoons, and further a year with many falling bombs during the Battle of Okinawa.

https://www.youtube.com/watch?v=-Dkxq9uSNQ4
   (Performance by The Boom)
https://www.youtube.com/watch?v=8foQlu_yW70
   (Performance by Natsukawa Rimi)

- (If you are musically oriented, try to answer this question.) Within the song, there is one place, where the Okinawan scale changes to the Japanese scale. If you could identify that, further research why the artist didn't continue with the Okinawan scale.

3. The Musical *Tumai Aakaa*

The famous musical *Tumai Aakaa,* one of the four famous tragic stories, begins with a scene of *hamauri.* A son from a prestigious family happened to see a girl who came to the beach with her chaperone. In no time, the two fell in love. The son could not concentrate on his work because he missed her so much. Having begun to worry about his son, the father sent him to a faraway island. The girl fell ill during the many months she could not see him. The son finally came back, but learned that the girl had passed away. In sorrow, the son committed suicide.

- Several Okinawan operettas are tragic like this one. Compare *Tumai Aakaa* with a tragic story you know in any culture.
- If you were to write a romantic tragedy, how would your story develop? How did the two first meet? What caused the two to be separated? How would the story end?

LESSON 8

Visit to an Ancestral Grave in Celebration

DIALOGUE A

Next Sunday is *U-shiimii*, the day to visit the family grave to pray for one's ancestors [Cul1]. Yuna has asked Niko to clean the grave with her before the family gathers in front of it.

Yuna: *Taarii nkai u-haka nu kusa kati **kuu** ndi **irattoo** kutu, ʔyaa n tiganee **sshi kwiran** gayaa.*

I was told by my father to clear the weeds near the grave, so can you help me, too?

Niko: *Ii, shimun doo.*

Yes, sure.

CORE VOCABULARY

u-shiimii	[Cul1 & 2]
u-haka	← pol. prefix + 'grave'
kusa	'grass'
kati (G.FORM)	← kain 'to cut'
kuu (IMP)	← chuun 'to come' [A3]
irattoon	← i 'say' + rari (PASS) + toon (ASP)[1]
sshi kwiran	← sshi (G.FORM) 'do' + kwiran [A1]
shimun	'complete (without a problem)'; shimun doo is often used to agree to do something, 'OK, sure'

[1] ira-ri-toon → (i dropping) ira-r[ ]toon → (assimilation) irattoon

GRAMMAR A

1. Verbs of Giving

- **kwi-in**   'give' (Neutral),   1st   → 2nd/3rd ; 2nd/3rd → 1st
- **kwi-misheen**   'give' (Exalting), 2nd/3rd → 1st
- **usagi-in**   'give' (Humble),   1st   → 2nd/3rd

The neutral verb of 'giving' is **kwi-in**. The speaker can be either the giver or a recipient [Diagram A; the circle represents the location of the speaker and the arrow shows the direction of giving]. However, if an honorable person gives something to the speaker, the verb is **kwi-misheen** (exalting verb) [Diagram B]. If the speaker gives something to an honorable person (e.g., a teacher), the verb must be **usagi-in** (humble verb) [Diagram C]. (see [B1]).

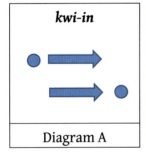
Diagram A

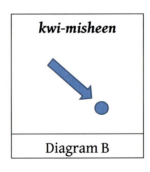
Diagram B

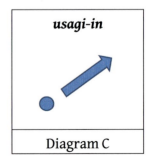
Diagram C

- *kwi-in*
  Wannee kuri **ari** nkai kwi-in. '**I** will **give** this to **him**.'
  Aree uri **wan** ninkai kwi-in. '**He** will **give** that to **me**.'
- *kwi-misheen*
  Anu tchoo kuri **wan** ninkai kwi-misheen. '**He** will **give** this to **me**.'
- *usagi-in*
  Wannee kuri **anu tchu** nkai usagi-in. '**I** will **give** this to **him**.'

Though not included for a full exposition, there are some more verbs of giving such as *turasun* 'give' [DialogueB] and *utabimisheen* 'give (EXAL)' [DialogueC], etc.

2. Benefactive: [G.FORM + verbs of giving] 'do something for someone'

The three giving verbs introduced above can appear after the Gerund Form of a verb to express a benefactive action performed for someone, i.e.. 'A father **buys** something **for** his child.'

	DIC.FORM	G.FORM	Benefactive	Meaning
V	koo-in	koo-ti	koo**ti kwiin**	'…buy something for me'
V	wara-in	wara-ti	wara**ti kwiin**	'…smile for me'
C-1	ʔwiij-un	ʔwiij-i	ʔwiij**i kwiin**	'…swim for me'
C-2	ninj-un	nint-i	ninti **kwiin**	'…sleep for me (e.g., to a baby)'
C-3	kunj-un	kunch-i	kun**chi kwiin**	'…tie up…for me'
C-4	kach-un	kach-i	ka**chi kwiin**	'…write…for me'
C-5	much-un	mutch-i	mut**chi kwiin**	'…hold…for me'
C-6	noos-un	nooch-i	noo**chi kwiin**	'…fix…for me'
C-7	yub-un	yud-i	yu**di kwiin**	'…invite…for me'
C-8	yum-un	yud-i	yu**di kwiin**	'…read…for me'
IRG	sun	**sshi**	**sshi** kwiin	'…do…for me'
IRG	chuun	tchi	t**chi** kwiin	'…come for me'
IRG	ichun	ʔnji	ʔnji **kwiin**	'…go for me'

Here are some examples.

- *Wan ga kooti **kwii** sa.* 'I will buy it for you.'
- *Shinshii ga shiitu nkai hun yudi **kwimisheen**.* 'The teacher read a book (for us, the students).'
- *Ari ga wattaa warabi Churaumi nkai sooti ʔnji **kwiitan**.* (*****kwitan** [PAST-1]) 'He took my children to the Churaumi Aquarium (for me).'
- *Yukiko sanoo warabi nkai meenachi yaasee juusu chukuti **kwiitan**.* 'Yukiko made vegetable juice for her children every day (for their benefit).'
- *Wannee taarii nkai chimushinji chukuti **usagitan**.* 'I made the soup for my father.'

Below the three forms of *kwi-in* are added after *chichi* (G.FORM of *chichun* 'listen') in order of increasing politeness (*kwi-in, kwi-misheen, kwimiishee-biin*) from top to bottom.

(Talking *about* a third person) 'If it's that person, he'll listen to what you say.'

- *Anu tchu ya-ree, ʔyaa ga ii shi* *chichi* **kwiin** (Nonexalting, plain)
- *Anu tchu ya-misheeree,…* *chichi* **kwimisheen** (Exalting, plain)
- *Anu tchu ya-misheeree,…* *chichi* **kwimisheebiin** (Exalting, polite [L5(C1)])

3. Imperative Forms: [NEG.ROOT + *(r)ee*] and [N.ROOT + *(r)i*] + *yoo*[1] 'Do it!'

Imperative forms are used when you make an order or request to someone to do something (e.g., 'Come here!', 'Take this medicine!'). There are two ways to say, 'Do something!'

a. [NEG.ROOT + *(r)ee*] 'Do (something!)'

This form consists of the Negative Root with *(r)ee*. Since the Negative Form is [NEG.ROOT + -*(r)an*], you can make the imperative form simply by replacing -*an* with -*ee*. Here are some examples. We added * for irregular forms which require your special attention.

V-verbs
- *iri-ran*   'not put in'   → *iri-ree*   'Put it in!'
- *i-ran*   'not go in'   → *i-ree*   'Go in!'
- *aki-ran*   'not open'   → *aki-ree*   'Open it!'

C-verbs
- *kam-an*   'not eat'   → *kam-ee*   'Eat it!' (from a mother to her child)
- *ʔnjas-an* 'not put (take) it out' → *ʔnjash-ee** 'Put (Take) it out!' [also *ʔnjas-ee*]
- *kak-an*   'not write it'   → *kak-ee*   'Write it!'
- *mut-an*   'not hold it'   → *mut-ee*   'Hold it!'
- *ʔwiig-an* 'not swim'   → *ʔwiig-ee* 'Swim!'
- *kund-an*   'not tie up'   → *kunde-e*   'Tie them up!'

Irregular verbs
- *kuun*   'not come'   → *kuu**   'Come!'
- *ik-an*   'not go'   → *ikee*   'Go!'
- *s-an*   'not go'   → *shee**   'Do it!'

b. [N.ROOT + *(r)i*] + *yoo*¹ 'Do (something)'

Another way to make imperatives is to add the Sentence Final Particle *yoo*¹ to the [N.ROOT + *(r)i*]. (See Dialogue [B]) in Lesson 9 for different types of *yoo*.) The two imperative forms are compared below. This form alone may be also used as an imperative.

	Imperative (a)	**Imperative (b)**
'Put it in!'	*iri-ree*	[ˣ*iri* (ADV.FORM) + *i-yoo*]
'Go in!'	*i-ree*	*i-ri yoo*
'Come (exalting)'	*mensoo-ree*	*mensoo-ri yoo*
'Eat!'	*kam-ee*	*kam-i yoo*
'Put (Take) it out!'	*ʔnjash-ee*	*ʔnjash-i yoo*
'Come!'	*kuu*	*kuu-yoo*
'Go!'	*ikee*	*ik-i yoo*
'Do it!'	*shee*	*sh-i yoo*

The difference between the two imperative patterns is that the first form (e.g., *ik-ee*) sounds more blunt than the second form (*iki yoo*). The latter form also sounds more personal. Thus, you may hear a friend asking a very close friend with *karashee* as shown below, which is acceptable.

- *Ifee jin karashi* (yoo). 'Lend me some money (to someone not too close).'
- *Ifee jin karashee.*   'Lend me some money (to someone very close).'

You may have seen or heard the expression *Mensooree* 'Welcome!' at a storefront (see the picture) or at the airport to welcome customers and tourists. Although it is widely used in signs and posters, many native speakers feel the expression is unnatural to be used for nonspecific majorities like tourists at the airport. On the other hand, the use of *mensooree* is natural in talking to older people within a close circle.

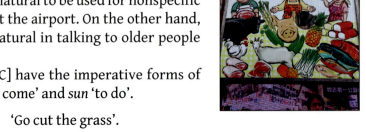

Dialogues [A] and [C] have the imperative forms of irregular verbs *chuun* 'to come' and *sun* 'to do'.

- *Kusa kati* **kuu.**   'Go cut the grass'.
- *Usandee* **shee.**   'Do *usandee* (= Take the offerings from the alter and eat).'

 In Okinawan culture, people first offer food to their ancestors' altar and pray. After the prayer, they enjoy sharing the food among themselves [Cul1].

4. Negative Imperative: [NEG.FORM + *kee*] and [NEG.FORM + *ki yoo*] 'Don't do it!'

Negative Imperative forms are used when you make an order or request to someone NOT to do something (e.g., 'Don't come here!', 'Don't eat this!'). You can make the Negative Imperative forms by adding **kee** or **ki yoo** to the Negative Forms.

a. [NEG.FORM + **kee**] 'Don't do (something)!'
b. [NEG.FORM + **ki yoo**] 'Don't do (something)!'

V-verbs
- iri-ran → iriran-**kee** → iriran-**ki yoo**   'Don't put it in!'
- i-ran   → iran-**kee**   → iran-**ki yoo**   'Don't enter!'
- ʔnji-ran → ʔnjiran-**kee** → ʔnjiran-**ki yoo** 'Don't go out!'

C-verbs
- kam-an   kaman-**kee**   → kaman-**ki yoo**   'Don't eat it!' (from a mother to her child)
- kak-an   → kakan-**kee** → kakan-**ki yoo**   'Don't write!'
- ʔnjas-an → ʔnjasan-**kee** → ʔnjasan-**ki yoo** 'Don't take it out!'

Irregular verbs
- kuun → kuun-**kee** → kuun-**ki yoo**   'Don't come!'
- ikan → ikan-**kee** → ikan-**ki yoo**   'Don't go!'
- san → san-**kee** → san-**ki yoo**   'Don't do it!'

- *Kusa {**karan kee** / **karan ki yoo**}*   'Don't cut the grass!'
- *Namaa usandee {**san kee** / **san ki yoo**}*   'Don't get the offerings now!'
- *Shiwaa **san kee**. Makutu sookee, nankuru naisa.*[1]   'Don't worry. If you lead an honest life, things will turn out all right!'

[1] This is a common saying in Okinawan. The first word, *shiwaa*, is the topic form of *shiwa* which means 'worries.' *Makutu sookee* means 'If you keep doing things honestly'—see [L3(Cul3)].

5. Passive Constructions

The passive sentence (e.g., 'The mouse was chased by the cat') is related to the active sentence (e.g., 'The cat chased the mouse').

a. The Passive Form: [INT.FORM + *riin*]

In English passive sentences, the BE verb with the past participle ('be eaten', 'be chased', 'be brought', 'be seen', etc.) is used. In Okinawan, you need to use passive forms. They are identical to the potential forms of situational possibility [L7(B1)], which is [INT.FORM + *riin*]. Remember the Intentional Form is the Negative Form without the final *-n*.

	Negative		INT.FORM-PASS	
V-verbs				
•	*agira-**n***	→ *agira*	→ *agira-**riin***	'be raised'
•	*sagira-**n***	→ *sagira*	→ *sagira-**riin***	'be lowered'
•	*tura-**n***	→ *tura*	→ *tura-**riin***	'be taken'
C-verbs				
•	*nnda-**n***	→ *nnda*	→ *nnda-**riin**.*	'be seen'
•	*kama-**n***	→ *kama*	→ *kama-**riin***	'be eaten'
Irregular verbs				
•	*sa-**n***	→ *sa*	→ *sa-**riin***	'be done'
•	*kuu-**n***	→ *kuu*	→ *ku(u)ra-**riin***	'be come'*[1]
•	*ira-**n***	→ *ira*	→ *ira-**riin***	'be said' (as in 'something bad was said about me')
•	*warara-**n***	→ *warara*	→ *wara-**ariin***	(← [r-deletion] *wara-**rariin***)

[1] This is not possible in English. However, it is possible in Okinawan and also in Japanese with the connotation that the event expressed is not favorable to the speaker. See the adversity passive below.)

As discussed in [L3(B1)], there are two past tense forms. To make a passive sentence with PAST-1 ('[What happened to me was] I was done…'), change *-riin* to *-ttan*. To make a passive sentence with PAST-2 ('I saw someone being done…'), change the *-n* to *-tan*.

- *tura-**riin*** → *tura-**ttan***   'was taken (my experience)'
             → *turarii-**tan***   'was taken (my observation)'
- *kama-**riin*** → *kama-**ttan***   'was eaten (my experience)'
              → *kamarii-**tan***   'was eaten (my observation)'
- *sa-**riin*** → *sa-**ttan***   'was done (my experience)'
             → *sarii-**tan***   'was done (my observation)'

b. The Regular Passive Sentence: [Y *ga/ya* X *nkai* INT.FORM + *riin*]
'X is V-ed by Y'

Below is the structural relationship of the active (e.g., 'My little brother ate that cake') and the regular passive (e.g., 'The cake was eaten by my little brother') sentences. In a nutshell, the subject and the object swap their positions in the two types of sentences. The **agent** (X), i.e., someone who acts on someone or something else, is the subject and marked by the particle **ga** or **ya** in the active sentence, but it is marked by **nkai** in the passive sentence. The **patient** (Y), i.e., someone/something that receives an action, is the object in the active sentence, but is a subject marked by *ga/ya* in the passive sentence.

- **Regular Passive**

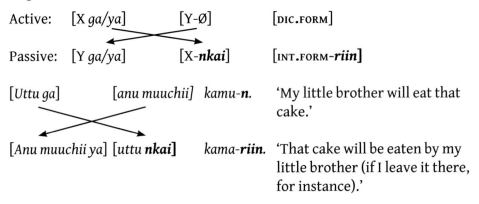

c. The Adversity Passive Sentence: [Z *ya* X-*nkai* Y-Ø INT.FORM-*riin*]
'Z is negatively affected by X's doing of something to Y'

There is another type of passive called the **adversity** passive in Okinawan. In the adversity passive, a victim or an affected party (Z) is included as a topic of the sentence. As in the regular passive, the original subject (X) in the active sentence will be marked with *nkai*. The original object stays as an object. The victim phrase (Z) is now marked with *ga/ya*.

- **Adversity Passive**

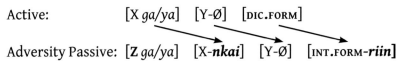

LESSON 8   Visit to an Ancestral Grave in Celebration   173

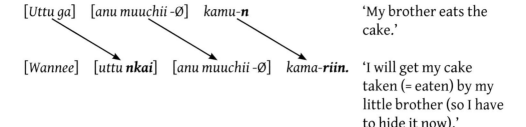

[Uttu ga] [anu muuchii -Ø] kamu-**n**   'My brother eats the cake.'

[Wannee] [uttu **nkai**] [anu muuchii -Ø] kama-**riin**.   'I will get my cake taken (= eaten) by my little brother (so I have to hide it now).'

Here are some more examples of regular and adversity passives.

- *Aashi wuti maasu chukuin.* → *Maasu ya Aashi wuti chukurariin.*
  'Salt is made in Awase.'
- *Oojima wuti sumui tuin.* → *Sunui ya Oojima wuti turariin.*
  'Sunui is harvested in Ojima.'
- *Shiija ga yuu uttu nurain* → *Uttu ya yuu shiija nkai nuraariin.*
  (← nurara-riin) 'The little brother is often yelled at by his big brother.'
- *Momotaroo ga uni suguitan.* → *Unee Momotaroo nkai suguraiitan.* (PAST-2)
  'The ogre was hit by Momotaro.'
- *Uttu ga waa muuchii kamutan.* → *Wannee uttu nkai waa muuchii kama-ttan.* (PAST-1)
  'I got my *muuchii* taken (= eaten by my brother.' (Adversity)

In addition, there is another type of passive that is rarely seen in other languages. This is a 'warning' passive, which is uttered only in sending warnings. For instance, instead of the expected active *suguin doo* 'I will hit you!', it is more common in Okinawan to use the 'warning' passive, *sugu-rariin doo* 'You'll be hit'.

ADDITIONAL VOCABULARY

gani 'crab'
kaki 'persimmon'
karasun 'to lend'
nagiin 'to throw'
nurain 'to scold'
saaru 'monkey'
shiwa 'worry'

sooti ichun/chuun 'to take/bring someone'
suguin 'to hit'
tami (ni) 'for the sake of, in order to'
uni 'ogre'
warain 'to laugh'
yoo (SFP) 'Do something!'

EXERCISES A

1. Fill in the blanks with the appropriate verbs of giving.

   a. A: *Kuri fusam-i?*

      (B nods)

      A: *Anshee (_____) sa.*

   b. A: *Uri kooim-i?*

      B: *Yii yii. Uree, atu kara Tamashiro shinshii ga (_____) ndi imisheetan.*

      'No. As for this, as Mr. Tamashiro said he will give it to us.'

   c. A: *U-cha deebiru. Usagati-(_____).* 'Please have some.'

   d. A: *?yaa tiganee shi (_____) yoo.* 'Will you help me?'

      B: *Ii, dushi gwaa nu tami ya kutu.*

2. Give two imperative forms for each of the following:

   a. *kunjun*   [_____ / _____]

   b. *iin* 'to get in'   [_____ / _____]

   c. *numun*   [_____ / _____]

   d. *agiin*   [_____ / _____]

   e. *ninjun*   [_____ / _____]

3. Give passive forms for the following:

   a. *yumun*   [_____]

   b. *nnjun*   [_____]

   c. *numun*   [_____]

   d. *iin* 'to say' [_____]

   e. *warain*   [_____]

LESSON 8   Visit to an Ancestral Grave in Celebration   175

4. Change the following active sentences to passive sentences. For (f) and (g), fill in the (__) with the appropriate particle. If no particle is necessary, write X. Add the passive verb in [__]. Keep in mind that some sentences may have two *nkai*: 'into, to' and 'by an agent'.

   a. *Sannin nu faa nkai muuchii chichimun.*

      → _____

   b. *Uya ga warabi byooin nkai sooti ichun.*

      → _____

   c. *Aashi wuti kunu maasu chukuin.*

      → _____

   d. (If you leave your bag here,) *Nusudu ga kaban tuin doo.*

      → _____

   e. *(Wannee) warabi nkai "Naa ufee matee" ndi ichan.* (PAST-1)

      → _____

   f. *Saaru ga gani nkai kaki nagiitan.* (PAST-2) 'The monkey throws a persimmon at the crab.' → *Gani* (_____) *saaru* (_____) *kaki* (_____) [_____].

   g. *Mayaa ga iyu tutan.* 'The cat took my fish.' → *Wannee mayaa* (_____) *iyu* (_____) [_____] (PAST-1) (adversity passive, challenging)

DIALOGUE B

(On the day of u-shiimii)

Father: *Ufugushiku nu tanmee n **mensheeru haji** ya shiga, tanmee ya hisa nu kana(i)**misooran** kutu, ʔyaa **unchikee sshi** kuu yoo.*

Grandfather Ufugushiku is also expected to come, but his legs are weak. So can you go bring him over?

Yuna: *Uu.*

Yes.

(Ufugushiku's house)

Yuna: *Chaabira tai. Tanmee tai, u-haka nkai unchikee sabira.*

Hello. Grandfather, I will take you to the family grave.

Grandfather: *An **suraa**, sooti ʔnji **turashi** yoo.*

In that case, take me there.

CORE VOCABULARY

Ufugushiku	family name
mensheeru (ADNOM.FORM)	← *mensheen* 'to come, EXAL' [L5(C1)]
haji	'It is expected that ~' [B4]
kanai (ADV.FORM)	← *kanain* 'to be able to ~'
-misooran (NEG)	← *-misheen* [B1]
unchikee sshi (G.FORM)	← *unchikee sun* 'to bring someone EXAL' [B2]
chaabira tai	'I am here (a greeting at the door when visiting someone)'
sabira (INT.FORM)	'let me ~'
an suraa	'in that case' [B3]
sooti nji (G.FORM)	← *sooti ichun* 'to take someone'
turashi (IMP)	← *turasun* 'to give'

GRAMMAR B

1. Exalting Expressions: [ADV.FORM + *misheen*] / [ADV.FORM + *misooran*]

In [L5(C1)], we introduced a handful of mostly idiosyncratic exalting verbs including 'to go/come', 'to be (copula)', 'to exist', 'to say', and 'to eat/drink'. Here we expand the list by introducing the exalting suffix -*misheen*. By adding this suffix to the Adverbial Form, you can make exalting forms out of regular plain verbs. The negative counterpart of -*misheen* is -*misooran* (Part II, Topic 3).

- *chuku-in* (V-verb): *chukui* + ***misheen*** → *chuku(i)misheen*   'to make' (EXAL)
                      chukui + ***misooran*** → *chuku(i)misooran*   'not to make' (EXAL)
  (Note: The final *i* of the Adverbial Form of V-verbs often drops.)

- *kach-un* (C-verb): *kachi* + ***misheen*** → *kachimisheen*   'to write' (EXAL)
                     kachi + ***misooran*** → *kachimisooran*   'not to write' (EXAL)

- *sun* (irregular): *shi* + ***misheen*** → *shimisheen*   'to do' (EXAL)
                   shi + ***misooran*** → *shimisooran*   'not to do' (EXAL)

2. Exalting and Humble Forms

In addition to exalting forms, Okinawan also has humble forms. Humble expressions are conceptual counterparts of exalting expressions. However, both exalting and humble forms ultimately **express respect to the referent** (i.e., the person you are talking about) by putting the referent (R in the insets) in a higher position than the speaker (S) in their *relative* status. The difference can be shown by the illustration on the right.

Exalting form—Raises the referent's (R) status higher than the speaker (S) (see ↑).

Humble form—Lowers the speaker's (S) status below that of the referent (R) (see ↓).

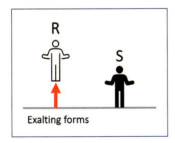
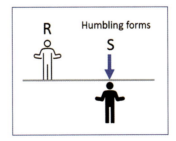

Okinawan exalting forms may be used in speaking about one's own elderly family members, even when speaking to people outside the family. For instance, speaking about one's own father, *taarii ya yuu saki* ***usagamisheen*** 'My father drinks *sake* often' is appropriate, but the same sentence would not be appropriate with the plain *numun* 'drink'.

The table below shows some important exalting and humble verbs.

Meaning	Plain Form (= DIC.FORM)	Humble Form	Exalting Form
'to go/come'	*ichun/chuun*	(*ichabiin/chaabiin*)	*mensheen*
'to be' (existence)	*wun*	(*wuibiin*)[1]	*mensheen*
'to be' (copula)	*yan*	(*yaibiin*)	*yamisheen*
'to say to (someone)'	*iin*	*unnukiin*	*imisheen*
'eat/drink'	*kamun/numun*	*kwatchii sabiin*	*usagain*[2]
'to bring (someone)'	*sooti-ichun/ sooti-chuun*	*unchikee sun*	*sooti mensheen*
'to give to me'	*kwiin*	—	*kwimisheen* *utabimisheen*
'to do'	*sun*	*sabiin*	*shimisheen*

[1] This is the polite form of *wun*, but can be also used as a humble verb.
[2] The expression *usagati utabimisheebiri* 'please have some' is an honorific form one rank higher than *usagati kwimisoori*. The former is used regularly in Shuri, but it is uncommon in the peripheral dialects.

Here are some examples from the above dialogue. Notice the first three sentences use exalting verbs while the last two use humble verbs.

- *Kana(i)***misooran**. '(Grandpa) cannot do it.'
- *Tanmee n* **mensheen**. 'Grandpa is also coming.'
- *Kuri n uri n ari n* **usagamisooree**. 'Have this, that (close to you), and that one over there as well.'

- *ʔyaa* **unchikee sshi** *kuu yo*. 'You go politely bring him here.' (Showing respect to the grandfather by using the humble verb *unchikee sun*.)
- *Kuree wan ga* **sabii** *sa tai*. 'I will do this one.'

3. Provisional Conditionals: [APOCO.FORM + *raa*] 'if that is the case,...'

Provisional Forms express the idea 'if that is the case (as you said).' It is often prompted by what another person has just said, as in the following exchange:

- A: Tomorrow will be a fine day.
  B: <u>If it is going to be a fine day tomorrow (as you just said)</u>, then let's go to the beach to dig clams.

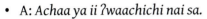

The above exchange in Okinawan would be:

- A: *Achaa ya ii ʔwaachichi nai sa.*
  B: <u>*Yii ʔwaachichi **nai-raa**,*</u> *hama nkai afakee tui ga ikan-i?*

Provisional forms are made by adding *-raa* to the Apocopated Form.

	DIC.FORM	APO.FORM	PROVISIONAL.COND	Meaning
V	tuin	tui	tui-**raa**	'if...get...'
V	michiin	michii	michii-**raa**	'if...close...'
C-1	ʔwiijun	ʔwiiju	ʔwiiju-**raa**	'if...swim...'
C-2	ninjun	ninju	ninju-**raa**	'if...sleep...'
C-3	kunjun	kunju	kunju-**raa**	'if...tie up...'
C-4	kachun	kachu	kachu-**raa**	'if...write...'
C-5	muchun	muchu	muchu-**raa**	'if...hold...'
C-6	turasun	turasu	turasu-**raa**	'if...give...'
C-7	ashibun	ashibu	ashibu-**raa**	'if...play...'
C-8	numun	numu	numu-**raa**	'if...drink...'
IRG	chuun	chuu	chuu-**raa**	'if...come...'
IRG	ichun	ichu	ichu-**raa**	'if...go...'
IRG	sun	su	su-**raa**	'if...do...'

Here is an example from the dialogue:

- A: *U-haka nkai unchikee sabira.*   'Let me take you to the (ancestral) grave.'
  B: *An **suraa**, sooti nji turashi yoo.*   'If that is the case, take me there (I'd be grateful for it).'

Here are some additional examples:

- A: *Nama kara Machigwaa nkai ichu shiga...*
  'I'm going to the (Makishi) market, but...'

  B: *Machigwaa nkai **ichuraa**, boojishi kooti tchi kwiri yoo.*
  'If you are going to the market (as you said), please get pork loin for me.'

- A: *Achaa ya kaji fuchun ndi ii shiga...*
  'I hear it will storm tomorrow, but...'

  B: *Kaji **fuchuraa**, nama kara kamu shee kootookan nee naran.*
  'If it will storm (as you said), I have to buy something to eat now (in preparation).'

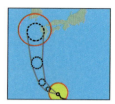

4. Speaker Conjecture: [ADNOM.FORM + *haji*] '(something) is expected (to happen / have happened)'

This structure expresses the speaker's conjecture by logical reasoning: '(something) should happen', '(something) is expected to happen', '(something) is supposed to happen', or '(something) should be/should have been the case'. What comes before *haji* is the Adnominal Form. Here is an example from the dialogue. The speaker may assume Mr. Ufugushiku is coming based on what he said, what he always does (on this occasion), etc.

- *Ufugushiku nu tanmee n **mensheeru** **haji** ya shiga...*
  'I expect Grandfather Ufugushiku will come, but...'

The Adnominal Form of adjectives and the Negative Forms of verbs can also appear before *haji*:

- *Achaa ya **achisaru haji**.* 'It should be hot tomorrow.'
- *Tchu nu mandooru munnu, ama nu suba yaa ya **maasaru haji**.* 'That noodle shop must be good since it is crowded with customers.'
- *Ufugushiku nu tanmee ya **mensooran haji** ya shiga...* 'I expect Grandfather Ufugushiku will not come, but...'

If a noun comes before *haji*, *nu* is added before it.

- *Anu tchoo yamatu n chu **nu haji** ya shiga, anshi Uchinaaguchi jooji yamisheeru.* 'I believe that person is from the mainland, but he speaks Okinawan so well!'
- *Chuu ya shima kutuba nu hii **nu haji** ya kutu, dikka shimakutuba chikara na.* 'Today should be a local language day, so let's use the language.'

 September 18 has been designated as *Shima Kutuba nu Hi* 'the day of the local language'

by the Okinawa prefectural government. The day, September 18, was selected based on a play on words: 9 is read as **ku** in Japanese (*kukunuchi* in Okinawan), 10 is **tuu** in Okinawan, and 8 is *hachi* (= **ba**) in Japanese; 9–10–8 is thus read as **ku-tu-ba** 'language'. Establishing such a day demonstrates the Okinawan people's effort to preserve and promote local languages on the Ryukyu Islands.

ADDITIONAL VOCABULARY

haarii 'boat race'
kaji 'wind'
munii 'local dialect'
tinchi yohoo 'weather forecast (Jp. loan)'
uturusan 'scary'
yuu 'often'

EXERCISES B

1. Fill in the blanks.

Meaning	Plain (= DIC.FORM)	Exalting Form	Humble Form
	chuun		
	yan		—————
	wun	mensheen	
		imisheen	
		usagamisheen	
	sooti ichun	sooti mensheen	
'to give to me'		kwimisheen/utabimisheen	—————
'to do'	sun		

2. Rewrite the verbs in bold using either the humble or exalting form as appropriate.

   a. *Shinshii ya achaa Yamatu nkai* **ichun**. → _____

   b. *Unjoo ichi* **ichu** *ga?* → _____

   c. *Anshee,* **kama**. → _____

   d. *Ama nkai ya Shoogo taa taarii ga du* **wuibiiru** → _____

182   PART I   Conversation

3. Write in the appropriate provisional conditional forms for the following conversations.

   a. A: *Achaa ya maa nkai ichu ga?*

      B: *Haarii* (see inset) *nnjii ga Naafa nkai ichun doo.*

      A: *?yaa ga Naafa nkai (_____), wan nin ichu sa.*

   b. A: *Anu tchoo ippee uturusa kutu, wannee achaa anu tchu taa yaa nkai ya ikan.*

      B: *?yaa ga (_____), wannin ikan sa.*

   c. A: *Wannin hanafichi yata shiga, kunu kusui nuda kutu, shigu nootan doo.*

      B: *Yami? ?yaa ga kunu kusui sshi (_____), wannin numu sa.*

   d. A: *Achaa ya ami ndi, tinchi yohoo (s)shi iitan doo.*

      B: *Tinchi yohoo (s)shi (_____), ami ya sa.*

   e. A: *Achaa nu u-shiimii ya Tamagushiku nu tanmee n mensheemi?*

      B: *Uu, menshee ndi imisheebiitan doo.*

      A: *Tanmee ga (_____), tibichi (Okinawan dish) chukuti usagii sa.*

4. Change the following sentences to express your guesses using *haji*.

   a. *Achaa ya ami nu (_____) doo.* (should rain)

   b. *Taarii n ayaa n chura kaagii ya kutu, Hanakoo n chura kaagii (_____).* ('should become a pretty person')

   c. *Attaa ya u-haka nkai kusa kai ga ichuta kutu, nama yaa nkai ya (_____).* ('shouldn't be home')

   d. *Anu tchu ga chukuteemishee kutu, kuree (_____).* ('should be tasty')

DIALOGUE C

(At the grave)

Mother: *U-juu n narabiteeibiin doo.*

The lunch boxes are laid out.

Father: (TO EVERYONE) *Anshiinee, nna, haka nu mee nkai chaani, tii usaashee…*

(TO EVERYONE) Then, everyone, come to the front of the grave and put your hands together to pray.

Father: (TO THE ANCESTORS) *Ayaa sai, Taarii sai, u-jaki n usagai**gachii**, kwatchii n dateen usagati utabimisheebiri.*

(TO THE ANCESTORS) Our father, our mother, while drinking sake, have lots of delicious food.

Father: (TO EVERYONE) *Too too, warabi-n-chaa kara naradi, usandee shee.*

(TO EVERYONE) OK, children line up first and get the offerings.

Guest: (TO MOTHER) *Dateen tideeti kwimisoochi, nifee deebiru.*
Kwatchii sabira.

(TO MOTHER) You prepared a lot. Thank you very much.
Thank you for the food.

CORE VOCABULARY

juu	'to stack up bento boxes'
narabi-tee-ibiin	← *nababi* 'to line ~ up, arrange ~ (TR)' + *tee* (ASP) + *ibiin* (POL)
u-jaki	← *u-* 'polite' + *saki* 'sake'
usaashee (IMP)	← *usaasun* 'to press, pray'
-gachii	'while doing A, do B' [C1]
-utabimisheebiri (IMP)	← *-utabimisheebiin* 'to give' (EXAL SUFFIX)
too too	interjection, 'OK, come on'
naradi (G.FORM)	← *narabun* 'to line up (INTR)'
usandee	food offering to the ancestors later to be consumed by the family (WB: 197)
usandee sun	'to have some offerings'
tideeti (G.FORM)	← *tideein* 'to prepare food for a special occasion'
-kwimisoochi (G.FORM)	← *-kwimisheen* 'to give' (EXAL SUFFIX)

GRAMMAR C

1. Simultaneous Actions: [V₁ (ADV.FORM) *gachii*, V₂] 'While doing V₁, do V₂'

This structure, [V₁ *gachii*, V₂], indicates that one is doing V₁ and V₂ at the same time. V₁ before *gachii* is in the Adverbial Form. The final vowel of this form *-i* frequently changes to *-a*, resulting in variations such as *atcha-gachii* (← *atchi-gachii* 'while walking') and *sa-gachii* (← *shii-gachii* 'while doing').

	DIC.FORM	ADV.FORM	*-gachii*	Meaning
V	*tu-in*	*tu-i*	*tui gachii*	'while taking…'
V	*aki-in*	*aki-i*	*akii gachii*	'while opening…'
C-1	*ʔwiij-un*	*ʔwiij-i*	*ʔwiiji gachii*	'while swimming'
C-2	*ninj-un*	*ninj-i*	*ninji gachii*	'while sleeping'
C-3	*kunj-un*	*kunj-i*	*kunji gachii*	'while tying up…'
C-4	*atch-un*	*atch-i*	*atchi gachii*	'while walking'
C-5	*much-un*	*much-i*	*muchi gachii*	'while holding…'
C-6	*ʔnbus-un*	*ʔnbush-i*	*ʔnbushi gachii*	'while steaming…'
C-7	*yub-un*	*yub-i*	*yubi gachii*	'while calling…'
C-8	*num-un*	*num-i*	*numi gachii*	'while drinking…'
IRG	*chuun*	**chii**	**chii** *gachii*	'while coming'
IRG	*ichun*	**ichi**	**ichi** *gachii*	'while going'
IRG	*sun*	**shii**	**shii** *gachii*	'while doing…'

Here is an example from the dialogue:

- *U-jaki n usagai* **gachii**, *kwatchii n dateen usagati-utabimisheebiri.* — 'Please have a lot of the delicious food while drinking sake.'

More examples…

- *Gooyaa chanpuruu* **kami gachii**, *saki gwaa* **numun.** — 'I will drink *sake* while eating the sautéed bitter melon dish.'

- *Wattaa n yuntaku **shii gachii, kwatchii** sabira.* (Note: *sa-gachii* is very common.) 'Let's have the delicious food while chatting with each other.'

- *Sakee, **atcha gachii,** kooi sa.* 'As for *sake*, we will buy it on the way (lit. 'while walking').'

- *U-koo ya neen kutu, u-haka nkai **ichi gachii,** koora yaa.* 'Since we don't have incense, let's buy it on the way to the grave.'

The *gachii* form also expresses a concessive meaning 'although'.

- *Maakoo neen ndi ii **gachii,** dateen kadoon.* 'Although he says it's not good, he's eating a lot.'

- *Sooji sun ndi ʔya-**gachii,** san sa.* [Note: *ʔya-gachii* is a variant of *ii-gachii*] 'Although he says he would clean up, he doesn't clean up.'

ADDITIONAL VOCABULARY

bingata 'textile with Ryukyuan motifs and designs' (inset in Lesson 1 Dial [A])

heein /feein 'spread widely', 'to be in fashion'

huka 'outside'

ichunasan 'busy'

naahin 'more'

shikuchi 'work'

u-koo 'incense'

ufu tanmee 'great-grandfather'

yuntaku 'chitchat'

EXERCISES C

1. Select the most appropriate item (some of the form options are from [A]).

   a. *Wattaa yaa wuti shiija ga karaoke su kutu, ʔyaa achaa jihi { kuu / kii / kuun } yoo.*

   b. *Namaa hanafichi nu heetoo kutu, huka nkai { ʔnjiran / ʔnjiin } ki yoo.*

   c. *Tamagushiku nu ʔnmee ga { chan / mensoochan } ndi wannee taarii nkai { imisheetan / unnukitan } doo.*

   d. Shogo: *Arakaki shinshii maa nkai { chuu / menshee } ga? Naafa nkai yaree, wattaa tu majun { ikan / yushiran / mensooran } -i?*

   Arakaki: *An su-raa, wannin { sooti iki / sooti mensoori } yoo.*

2. Study the example and make sentences using *gachii*, using the pictures and suggested words as cues.

186 PART I Conversation

Ex	(shikuchi sun; yaa nu kutu san nee naran) Shikuchi **shii gachii**, yaa nu kutu san nee naran.
a.	(ninjun; uta chichun) → _____
b.	(yuufuru nkai iin; sumafo chikain) → _____
c.	(munu kamun; tiribi nnjun) → _____
d.	(pianu hichun; uta utain) → _____
e.	(sumafo nnjun; jitensha nuin) → _____

LESSON 8   Visit to an Ancestral Grave in Celebration   187

APPLICATIONS

1. Form a group of four or five people and designate one person who will act as a teacher. The rest of the group will act as students. One of the students is organizing a potluck graduation party for the class. Assign your classmates food dishes/drinks they should bring to the party. The teacher should offer to bring something, but the students should kindly decline the offer.

    - (Student 1 to Student 2 and so on): *ʔyaa ya [_____] mutchi tchi kwiri yoo.*
    - (Student 2 and so on to Student 1): *Ii, wakatan.*
    - (Teacher to Student 1): *Wannee nuu mutchi-chuu ga? / mutchi chuushee mashi gayaa?*
    - (Student 1 to Teacher): *Shinshii ya nuun mutch mensooranti n shimabiin doo.*

2. You and your classmates are talking about multitasking. Tell your classmate what activities you do simultaneously.

    A: *Kunu guroo ichunasan yaa.*

    B: *Yan yaa. Wannee chinuu _____ gachii, _____ sa.*

    A: *Yami? Wan nin _____ gachii, _____ sa.*

    B: *Kunu doyoo, nichiyoo ya chaa su ga?*

    A: ...

    B: ...

3. Using the provisional conditional form as in the examples below, create your own dialogue.

    A: *Maasai biin yaa.*
    B: *Maasa raa, naahin kamee.*

    A: *Wannee chuu ya ichunasanu, ikaran ssaa!*
    B: *ʔyaa ga ikaran raa, wan nin ikan sa.*

CULTURAL NOTES

1. The Day to Pay Respect to One's Ancestors: *Shiimii / U-shiimii* (*Seimei sai*)

Shiimii / U-shiimii held in March of the lunar calendar is a cultural event that originated in China. In China, this day is called Tomb Sweeping Day and is still celebrated as a national holiday. In Okinawa, families bring *u-juu* (food in multilayered lacquered lunch boxes) and place food and drinks in front of their ancestral grave. They first offer food and drink to their ancestors and then they eat together (*usandee sun*). This is an important cultural activity in Okinawa where ancestors are treated with utmost respect.

- Do you have any specific activities dedicated to honor your ancestors?
- Are you interested in finding out your family history by using a DNA database? Why or why not?

2. *Shiimii* vs. *U-shiimii*

Depending on the region in Okinawa, this festival is called *shiimii* or *u-shiimii* with the polite prefix *u-*. *Shiimii* is a homophone of *shiimii* 'cicada' (see notes on homophones [L3(Cul4)]). People who typically call the festival *u-shiimii* think of cicadas upon hearing someone calling the event *shiimii.*

- In the previous lessons, you have encountered several words with the polite prefix *u-*. List those words. Why are they marked by *u-*? Some people criticize others for using *u-* too much. What are your opinions on the use of *u-*?
- Can you think of a case in your native language where polite prefixes, suffixes, or other elements figure significantly?

3. *Kamekoo-baka* 'turtleback tombs'

Kamekoo-baka refers to traditional Okinawan tombs. The name faithfully depicts the shape of the tomb. According to Bhowmik (2008: 93), the novel *Kamekoo-baka* written by Oshiro Tatsuhiro, the winner of the prestigious Akutagawa Prize, "is an account of one Okinawan family's escape from the ravages of war to the precarious safety of their ancestral tomb…built with a protective cowl that looks like the shell of a tortoise." Bhowmik continues on to say that the family in the story

"[f]ervently believ[es] that the spirits (*mabui*) of their ancestors will keep them from harm[.]" (For more information especially concerning the concept of rebirth, see Bhowmik 2008.)

- Do you and your family regularly visit your ancestors' graves? Give your thoughts about the difference between your customs and the Okinawan custom you learned about in this lesson.
- From a Western perspective, graveyards usually feel dark or deserted. What is your impression of the Okinawan custom of having a "picnic" in front of the grave?
- Write your thoughts about Okinawans' beliefs about *kamekoo-baka*.

REVIEW EXERCISES

Lessons 7 and 8

1. Fill in the verb conjugation chart.

DIC.FORM	Meaning	NEG.FORM	IMP	INT.FORM	Passive	RA.FORM	G.FORM
chiki-in	'to turn on'	chiki-ran	chiki-ri/ chiki-ree			chikii-ra	
ka-in				ka-ra	kara-riin		
	'to see'		nnd-i/nnd-ee			nnju-ra	
much-un					muta-riin		mutchi
chich-un	'to listen'	chik-an				chichu-ra	
ʔnjas-un		ʔnjas-an		ʔnjas-a			
sun	'to do'						
i-in	'to say'						ichi
						ara	
wun			wu-ri	wu-ra			
yan	'to be'						

192 PART I Conversation

2. The following constructions and patterns use the forms from the chart above. Fill in the chart. The first row has been completed for you as an example.

Form	Elements to follow	Meaning
G.FORM	+ ichun/chuun	'~ and go / ~ and come'
G.ROOT	+ (t)oochun	
	+ n	'even if ~'
	+ kwiin	
		'can ~'
		'while ~, do ~'
	+ riin	
APO.FORM		'if it is the case that ~ (as you said)'
		'it is expected that ~'
ga ... _____	_____ (= RA.FORM)	

3. Select the correct forms to complete the sentences below.

   a. A: *Kunu toofoo ippee maasaibiin yaa.*

      B: *Yami? Kuree ama wuti { koora / kooyu / kooti } cha sa.*

   b. A: *Yuroo ichunashiku nai kutu, nama yuuban { chukura / chukui / chuku } toochu sa.*

      B: *Ai, { chukuteen / chukuran / chukuin } doo.* 'I have already made dinner.'

   c. A: *ʔnbusanu, majuun { muchi / mutchi / muta } kwiran naa.*

      B: *Ii. Shimun doo.*

   d. A: *Sakee ama nkai { ichu / ika / ichi } gachii kooi sa.*

      B: *Anu suupaa wuti { koo / koora / kooyura } rariin doo.*

   e. A: *Wannee achaa Naafa nkai ichun.*

      B: *ʔyaa ga { ichu / ikan / iki } raa wannin ichu sa.*

      Higa-san (n)un { ika / ichu / ichuru } haji doo.

   f. A: *Kunu yanmee ya ichi ga { noo / noora / nooi } ra.*

      B: *Shiwaa { san / shi / santi } n shimu sa. Shigu nooi sa.*

4. Match the following pairs of Okinawan phrases with their English meanings.

   a. (___) *Yumee wakai sa.*   A. If you read…

   (___) *Yudi n wakaran sa.*   B. Even if you read…

   b. (___) *Taa n naran.*   A. Anyone can…

   (___) *Taa yati n nain.*   B. No one can…

   c. (___) *ʔwiiji-yuusun.*   A. He can swim.

   (___) *ʔwiiga-riin.*   B. Swimming allowed.

5. Change the following active sentences to passive sentences. Fill in the (___) with the appropriate particles. If no particle is necessary, place an X in the (___).

   a. *Uchinaa wuti bingata chukuin.* (inset)

   → *Bingata ya Uchinaa wuti*

   [_____].

   b. *Shiija ga uttu nkai naraasun.*

   → *Uttu (_____) shiija (_____)*

   [_____].

   c. *Nusudu ga ari ga jin tuitan.*

   → *Ari ga jin (_____) nusudu (_____)*

   [_____].

   → *Aree nusudu (_____) jin (_____)*

   [_____]. (Adversity Passive)

   d. *Uttu ga waa juusu numutan.* (PAST-2)

   → *Waa juusu (_____) uttu (_____)*

   [_____]. (Use PAST-1)

   → *Wannee uttu (_____) juusu (_____)*

   [_____]. (Adversity Passive, use PAST-1)

194 PART I Conversation

6. Using the item in [__] as a focus, rewrite the following as focus sentences.

   Example: [Ari] ga Orion numun.　　　　[Nuu] chukui ga?
   → [Ari] ga **ga** Orion numura].　　→ [Nuu] **ga** chukuira.

   a. [Taa] ga ichiban jooji ya ga? → _____

   _____

   b. Higa sannoo [akaa muumuu] kooin. → _____

   _____

7. Fill in the blanks with the appropriate conditional forms.

   Example: A: Achaa ya Machigwaa nkai ika ndi umutoon.
   　　　　　B: **Ichu-raa**, kubushimi kooti-tchi kwiri yoo.

   a. A: Amirika nkai ichibusa ssaa.

      B: ʔYaa ga (_____), wannin sooti iki yoo.

   b. A: Kunu gurukunoo ippee yassa shiga, kooi ga yaa.

      B: (_____), wan nin kooi sa.

   c. A: Utaa joojee aran shiga utai sa.

      B: Yam-i? (_____), wannee utain doo.

   d. A: Waa konpyuutaa, taagana kooran gayaa.

      B: (_____), waa ga kooi sa. (if you would *sell* ~)

8. Complete the table of exalting and humble forms:

Meaning	DIC.FORM	Exalting form	Humble form
'to go/come'	ichun/chuun		
'to be (existence)'	wun		wu-ibiin
'to bring (someone)'	sooti ichun / sooti chuun	sooti mensheen	
'to be (copula)'	yan		(ya-ibiin)
			unnukiin

Meaning	DIC.FORM	Exalting form	Humble form
		usagain/ usaga-misheen	kwatchii sabiin / (sidiyun)
'to give to me'		kwi-misheen	—
'to do'	sun	shi-misheen	sabiin

9. Fill in the blanks with the appropriate honorific forms.

   Example: *Anu tchoo Asatu shinshii* **yan**. → **yamisheen**;
   Wannee UH nu shiitu **yan** → **yaibiin**

   a. *Asatu shinshii ya chuu shiken nu hanashii* **sun**. → _____

   b. *Asatu shinshii ya ippee churaaku jii* **kachun**. → _____

   c. *Asatu shinshii ga shiitu nkai kwaashi* **kwiin**. → _____

   d. *Asatu shinshii ga shiitu nkai Uchinaaguchi naraachi* **kwiin**. →

   _____

10. Fill in the (__) with the appropriate (contracted) particles and write the appropriate wh-words in the [__].

    a. **"Gooyaa baagaa" vs. "Nuuyaru baagaa"** [inset; left vs. right]

       Gooyaa baagaa (_____) *Nuuyaru baagaa* (_____)

       [_____] *maasa ga?*

       Gooyaa baagaa (_____) *Nuuyaru baagaa nu* (_____) *maasaru.*

    b. **Rooma (Rome) vs. Pari (Paris)**

       Rooma (_____) *Pari* (_____) [_____] *nkai naahin ichibusa ga?*

       'Which one do you want to go more, Rome or Paris?'

       Rooma (_____) *Pari* (_____) (_____) *ichibusaru.*

    c. **Playing sports vs. watching sports**

       Undoo ya su shi (_____) *nnju shi* (_____) [_____] *mashi yaru?*

    d. **Among all your friends**

       Dushigwaa nu naaka (_____) [_____] *ga ichiban dekiyaa ya ga?*

✎ The *nuuyaru baagaa* refers to the famous Jef hamburger in Okinawa, whose name was created as a play on words where *nuu yaru baa* means 'what on earth is it?'. An anecdote has it that when the creator named a burger with *gooyaa* "*gooyaa baagaa*" 'gooyaa hamburger', another person asked, pointing to the other burger, '*(kuree) nuu yaru baa ga?*'. From that exchange came the name *nuuyaru baagaa*, thus resulting in the hamburger pair in the picture.

LESSON 9

Tug of War Festival

Niko is joining Yuna and her friend for the Tug of War Festival. It is a popular summer activity in Okinawa in which the East and the West teams compete by pulling a rope as a test of strength. Before the competition, there are dances and other activities to invigorate the teams' fighting spirits. See [Cul1] for more information.

DIALOGUE A

Shogo is Yuna's childhood friend and Niko's current classmate. Shogo came to see Niko and Yuna at Yuna's house. Then, they all went to the Tug of War Festival, where they ran into Shogo's friend, Kenta.

(At home)

Shogo: *Chuu ya Yunabaru **wuti** china nu **a** kutu, ika yaa.* They have tug of war in Yonabaru today. Let's go.

197

PART I Conversation

Niko & Yuna: Ii, ii. Ichibusan. — Yeah, yeah. I'd love to go.

(At the festival location)

Kenta: Ai, Shogo! miiduusa (nu). Ganjuu sootii? ʔyaa ya kujoo **nuunchi** kuun ta ga? — Oh, Shogo, long time no see! How have you been? Why didn't you come last year?

Shogo: Kujoo ichunasanu, ku(u)raran du ataru. — Last year I was busy, so I couldn't come.

Kenta: ʔyaa ga kuun ta kutu du makitan doo. Kujoo wattaa satta kutu, kutushee jifi katan nee naran. — Because you didn't come, we lost. We lost last year, so we must win this year.

Shogo: ʔyaa ya junni china shichi yan yaa. Chuu ya kachuru **tami ni**, dushi gwaa n sooti chooru **munnu** katchu {sa/n tee}. — You really like the tug of war. To win this year, I also brought friends, so we will win.

(Niko and Kenta greet each other and Kenta says to Niko and Yuna:)

Kenta: Ittaa n wattaa kashii sshi kwiri yoo. — Please help us (to win)!

CORE VOCABULARY

[place] *wuti…an*	'(event) happens / takes place in/at [place]'[1]
Yunabaru	place name, Yonabaru
miiduusa(nu)	← *miiduusan* 'long time no see'
ganjuu s-oo-ti-i	← 'be in good health' + *oo* (ASP) + *ti* (PAST) + *i* (QP)
kujoo	← *kuju* 'last year' + *ya* (TOP)
nuunchi	'why?' [A1]
ichunasanu	← *ichunasa* 'busy' + *nu* 'since'
ku(u)ra-ran	← *ku(u)ra* 'come.POT' + *ran* (NEG)
~ du ataru (ADNOM.FORM)	Focus Construction [L4(A4)]
makitan (PAST-1)	← *makiin* 'lose'
kutushee	← *kutushi* 'this year' + *ya* (TOP)
katan nee naran	← *katan* 'win (NEG)' + *nee naran* 'must' [L6(C3)]
china	'rope, tug of war'
shichi	'like, be fond of'
sooti ch-ooru (ADNOM.FORM)	← *sooti ch* 'bring (a person)' + *ooru* (ASP)
munnu	'because' [A3]
kashii sshi (G.FORM)	← *kashii sun* 'help'

[1] This is a nonexistential use of *an*. Thus it does not mean that a big rope exists, but it means that an event (of the tug of war) happens at a location.]

GRAMMAR A

1. Wh-word: *nuunchi?* 'why?'

The word *nuunchi* 'why?' forms a wh-question. Thus *nuunchi* sentences end with the particle *ga*. If it is a self-addressed question, *gayaa* will be used [L3(B5)]. Here are some examples.

- *ʔyaa ya kujoo **nuunchi** kuunta **ga**?*   'Why didn't you come last year?'
- *ʔyaa ya **nuunchi** wan sooti ikan ta **ga**?*   'Why didn't you take me (there)?'
- *Kujoo **nuunchi** wattaa ya maki ta **gayaa**.*   'I wonder why we lost last year.'
- *Ari ga chukui shee **nuunchi** anshi maasa **gayaa**.*   'I wonder why what he makes is so tasty.'
- A: *Kunu warabee **nuunchi** nachoo **ga**?*   'Why is this child crying?'
  B: *Uya ga wuran nata kutu du nachooibiiru.*   'It is because his parents are gone that he is crying.'

2. Purpose expression: [V₁ (ADNOM.FORM) + *tami ni* V₂] 'in order to do V₁, do V₂'

This is a construction in which [V₁ + *tami ni*] expresses a purpose for V₂. The V₁ is always in the Adnominal Form. Further, the tense of V₁ is always present tense regardless of the tense of V₂ [Part II Topic 6].

Here are some examples:

- *Chuu ya attaa makasuru **tami ni**, dushi gwaa sooti chan.*   'In order to beat them, I brought my friend (to help us).'
- *Uchinaaguchi narairu **tami ni**, Uchinaa nkai chan doo.*   'In order to study Okinawan, I came to Okinawa.'
- *Yaan Amirika nkai ichuru **tami ni**, wannee eego naratoon.*   'In order to go to America next year, I am studying English.'

3. Contrast/Reason: [V₁ (ADNOM.FORM) + *munnu* V₂] (a) 'V₁ but V₂' (b) 'V₁ so V₂'

Munnu can express either a contrastive meaning ('but', 'however') or a reason ('so', 'because').

a. *Munnu*: 'but' or 'however'

- *Chuu ya yii ʔwaachichi yaru **munnu**, nuunchi huka nkai ikan ga?*   'Today is a nice day (so I expect you would go outside), but why don't you go outside?'

- *Chuu ya n(n)na chuuru **munnu**, nuunchi ʔyaa ya kuun ga?* — 'Everyone is coming today (so I expect you would also come), but why aren't you coming?'

b. *Munnu*: 'so' or 'because'

- *Chuu ya Amirika kara chooru dushi gwaa n sooti chooru **munnu**, kachu sa.* — 'I brought my friend from America today, so we will win.'
- *Ari n naran **munnu**, wangaa jooi naran sa.* — 'He can't do it, so I can't definitely do it.'
- *Chuu ya achisaru **munnu**, huka nkai ʔnjiran gutu, yaa nkai wutoochu sa.* — 'It is hot today, so I will stay home without going outside.'

Which one of the meanings *munnu* expresses depends on what follows [Part II Topic 6]. See below.

- *Chuu ya ami nu fuin (n)di ʔyuru **munnu**, {kusaa karan shee mashi ya sa. / kusa kain naa?}* — 'They say it'll rain today, {so it is best to not cut the grass / but you (still) cut the grass?}'

ADDITIONAL VOCABULARY

atarasan 'precious'
jooi 'out of the question'
makasun 'beat'
yaan 'next year'

EXERCISES A

1. Complete the following 'why' questions by filling in the blanks.

    a. *ʔyaa ya nuunchi Uchinaaguchi (_____) ga?*
    'are you studying'

    b. *Uchinaa ya (_____) anshi (_____) gayaa.* 'is hot'

    c. *Chuu ya (_____).* 'I wonder why I can't sleep'

    d. *(_____) ga?* 'Why don't you listen to what I say?'

    e. *Uchinaa-guchi shee (_____) kitaa (_____) ga?* (cf. [Cul2])
    'Why do (they) say (north) as "nishi (= 'west' in Japanese)"?'

2. Combine the two given sentences using *munnu* and identify if it means 'so' or 'but' by check-marking your choice.

   Example: *Chin dateen chichoon. Achisa sa.*
   Chin dateen chichooru munnu achisasa. (√'<u>so</u>' / 'but')

   a. *Muuchii biisa yan. Hiisa sa.*

   [_____] (__ 'so' / __ 'but')

   b. *Maasan. Nuunchi kaman ga?*

   [_____] (__ 'so' / __ 'but')

   c. *Chuu ya anmasan ndi iin. Gakkoo yashiman naa?*

   [_____] (__ 'so' / __ 'but')

   d. *Nachijin nu sakuraa churasan. N(n)na saani ika yaa.*

   [_____] (__ 'so' / __ 'but')

DIALOGUE B

Shogo and Kenta are talking as the procession approaches.

(The processions approach)

Shogo: *Ee, Nnchi ndee. Ama nkai shitaku nu miiyu sa. Paarankuu n chikarii sa.*

Oh, look! You can see *shitaku*. You can hear *paarankuu*.

Kenta: *Shitaku nu chuun doo. Surii nu chibiraasa yoo! Agaree Gosamaru, Irii ya Amawari yan yaa.*

The *shitaku* are coming. How gorgeous is the procession! The East team is *Gosamaru*, West is *Amawari*, right?

Shogo: *Nkashee yaa, watttaa n an gutu sshi china* **katamirasattan** *doo yaa.*

We were made to carry a rope like that before, right?

Kenta: *Yatan yaa. Wattaa yatchii n kutushi karaa yoo, chakushi nkai paarankuu* **shimitoo** *sa.*

Right. My elder brother has his oldest son to do *paarankuu* from this year.

CORE VOCABULARY

ee	interjection, attention-getter
nnchi ndee	← *nnchi* 'see (G.FORM)' + *ndee* 'try to (IMP)'
shitaku	'people on the rope' [Cul1]
miiyu (APO.FORM)	← *miiyun* 'can be seen'[1]
paarankuu	'percussion' (inset in [B] above)
chikarii (APO.FORM)	← *chikariin* 'can be heard'
surii	'procession'
chibiraasa	← *chibiraasan* 'splendidness'
yoo[2]	SFP (exclamation) (attention getter)[2]
Gosamaru	proper noun (historical figure)
Irii	'West'
Amawari	proper name (historical figure)
Agaree	← *Agari* 'East' + *ya* (TOP)
nkashee	← *nkashi* 'long time ago' + *ya* (TOP)
yaa[2]	← 'you know' (particle)[2]
katami-rasat-tan	← *katami* 'carry' + *rasarit* (CAUS.PASS) + *an* (PAST1) [B2]
yoo[3]	'you see' (particle)[2]
chakushi	'the eldest son'
shimi-too (APO. FORM)	← *shimi* 'do (CAUS)' + *too* (ASP)

[1] The verb *miiyun* is the potential verb 'can see'. Its alternative form is *miin*.

[2] *Yoo* appears twice in this dialogue. Both are new types of *yoo* and different from *yoo*[1] which is used with the imperative form as described in [L8(A3)]. The first *yoo*[2] that appears in Kenta's first sentence is a sentence-final particle attached to the Apocopated Form of an adjective and expresses the speaker's surprise and exclamation. On the other hand, the *yoo*[3] that appears in Kenta's last sentence in the dialogue is used in the middle of a sentence to call for an attention of the hearer, functionally comparable to English *you know*. *Yaa*[2] in Shogo's second statement is similar to *yoo*[3] (cf. Part II, Topic 7).

GRAMMAR B

1. Causatives

Causatives mean 'someone makes/lets someone else do something', e.g., 'I made my younger brother cry' and 'Dad let me use his car.' In these sentences, 'I' and 'Dad' are **causers** and 'my younger brother' and 'me' are **causees**.

a. The Causative Verb Form: [INT.FORM + *sun*]

To make a causative sentence, you need to know the causative verb form, which you can make by adding *-sun* to the Intentional Form (*-shimiin* is also possible). Passive and causative forms have the following close relationship.

PASSIVE		CAUSATIVE	
• *irira-***riin**	'be put in' → *irira-***sun**	'make someone put in'
• *kama-***riin**	'be eaten' → *kama-***sun**	'make someone eat'

More examples in the order of DIC.FORM → INT.FORM → PASSIVE → CAUSATIVE. The forms with * indicate items for extra attention.

	DIC.FORM	INT. FORM	PASSIVE (INT.FROM + RIIN)	CAUSATIVE (INT.FROM + SUN)	Meaning of Causative
V	*maga-in*	*magara*	*magara-***riin**	*magara-***sun**	'to make something turn'
V	*sugu-in*	*sugura*	*sugura-***riin**	*sugura-***sun**	'to make someone hit someone'
C-1	*ʔwiij-un*	*ʔwiiga*	*ʔwiiga-***riin**	*ʔwiiga-***sun**	'to make someone swim'
C-2	*ninj-un*	*ninda*	*ninda-***riin**	*ninda-***sun**	'to make someone sleep'
C-3	*kunj-un*	*kunda*	*kunda-***riin**	*kunda-***sun**	'to make someone tie up…'
C-4	*kach-un*	*kaka*	*kaka-***riin**	*kaka-***sun**	'to make someone write…'
C-5	*tach-un*	*tata*	*tata-***riin**	*tata-***sun**	'to make someone stand…'

	DIC.FORM	INT. FORM	PASSIVE (INT.FROM + RIIN)	CAUSATIVE (INT.FROM + SUN)	Meaning of Causative
C-6	turas-un	turasa	turasa-**riin**	tura-**shimiin***[1]	'to make someone give…'
C-7	yub-un	yuba	yuba-**riin**	yuba-**sun**	'to make someone invite…'
C-8	yum-un	yuma	yuma-**riin**	yuma-**sun**	'to make someone read…'
IRG	ichun	**ika**	ika-**riin**	ika-**sun**	'to make someone go'
IRG	chuun	**ku(u)ra**	k(u)ura-**riin***[2]	k(u)ura-**sun***[2]	'to make someone come'
IRG	ʔyun / iin	**ira**	ira-**riin**	ira-**sun**	'to make someone say…'
IRG	sun	**sa**	sa-**riin**	**shimiin***[3]	'to make someone do'

[1] *turashimiin* is irregular.
[2] Both *kurariin / kurasun* and *kuurariin / kuurasun* are possible.
[3] *shimiin* is irregular, ˣ*sa-sun* /ˣ*sa-shimiin* are not possible.

b. The Causative Sentence Structure: [N₁-*ga/ya* N₂-*nkai* CAUSATIVE VERB] 'N₁ makes N₂ do something'

In a causative sentence the causer is the subject and marked by *ga/ya* (the subject/topic particles) and the causee is marked by *nkai*. The sentence ends with the causative verb form.

Here are examples:

- *Wannee chakushi nkai paarankuu* **shimitoo** *sa.* 'I'm making my firstborn son play percussion.'
- *Warabi nkai chimushinji* **numasun**. 'I will make a child eat the liver soup.'
- *Warabi nkai andaagii* **agirasun**. 'I'll make a child deep fry Okinawan doughnuts.'
- *Chuu ya shiitu n chaa nkai Eego nu eesachi* **naraasun** (← [r-drop] **nara-ra-sun**). 'I will teach students English greetings today.'

2. Causative-Passives

Causative-passives mean 'someone is made/let to do something by someone else.' (e.g., 'I was made by my mom to clean the floor.')

a. The Causative-Passive Verb Form: [INT.FORM + *sariin*]

To make a causative-passive sentence, you need to add the causative-passive suffix -*sariin* to the Intention Form.

- *tura* + **sariin** → *tura-sariin* 'be made to take'
- *kama* + **sariin** → *kama-sariin* 'be made to eat'

b. The Causative-Passive Sentence Structure: [N₁-*ga/ya* N₂-*nkai* CAUSATIVE-PASSIVE VERB] 'N₁ is made to do something by N₂'

As shown below, while the causative puts the causer (X) in the subject position, the causative-passive puts the causee (Y) in the subject position with *ga/ya* (the subject/topic particles), and marks the causer (X) by *nkai* followed by the causative-passive verb.

- Causative: X-*ga/ya* Y-*nkai* V<small>CAUS</small>   'X made Y to do V'
- Causative-Passive: Y-*ga/ya* X-*nkai* V<small>CAUS-PASS</small> 'Y is made to do V by X'

In dialogue [B], you see one causative-passive sentence with PAST-1 (the speaker's experience): *katami-rasat-tan*. See various verb forms built on the root *katami* 'carry something on the shoulder'.

- *katami-in*   'carry something on the shoulder' (DIC.FORM)
- *katami-ran*   'not carry something on the shoulder' (NEG.ROOT + NEG.SUFFIX)
- *katamira-riin*   'be carried on the shoulder' (INT.FORM + PASS.SUFFIX)
- *katamira-sun*   'make someone carry something on the shoulder' (INT.FORM + CAUS.SUFFIX)
- *katamira-sariin* 'be made to carry something on your shoulder' (INT.FORM + CAUS-PASS SUFFIX)

Note the PAST-1 of the causative-passive, *katamirasariin,* is *katamirasari-tan,* which then goes through two sound changes as below.

- *katamirasari-tan* 'be made to carry something on the shoulder' (causative. passive, PAST-1)
  → *katamira-sar-tan* (*i* deletion: **r[i]-tan** → r[ ]-tan)
  → *katamira-sat-tan* (*r* assimilating to *t*: [r]-tan → [t]-tan)

If the speaker's observation is about a third person, then the PAST-2 suffix (evidential past [L3(B1)]) -*sari-i-tan* is used. This form does not involve the *i* deletion nor the *r* to *t* assimilation described above.

- ***Wattaa** n china **katamira-sat-tan** doo yaa.* (PAST-1)   '**We** were also made to carry the rope, you know?'
- ***Attaa** n china **katamira-sari-i-tan** doo yaa.* (PAST-2)   '**They** were made to carry the rope, (I witnessed it,) you know?'

More examples follow:

- *Wattaa ya yuu **naraasattoon** yaa*   'We were made to learn well (= they taught us well).'
- *Warabi nu tuchi nee, yuu yaa nu tiganee **shimirasattan**.*   'When we were little, we were often made to do household chores.'

- *Nkashee Uchinaaguchi chikai nee,* **tatasattan** *doo yaa.*

  'In the old days, when we used Okinawan, we were made to stand (outside the class for a punishment).'

- *Anshikara, tiichi yatin kanji machigeei nee, muru* **hyakkai kakasattan** *doo yaa.*

  'And then, even if we missed just one kanji, we were made to write each kanji a hundred times.'

ADDITIONAL VOCABULARY

machigeein 'make mistakes'   **tuchi** 'time'

EXERCISES B

1. Fill in the blanks to complete the table for the following verbs.

DIC. FORM	Meaning	CAUSATIVE	CAUSATIVE-PASSIVE
atch-un			
		kaka-sun	kaka-sariin
fich-un			
ichun			
i-in ('say')			

2. Change the following causative sentences into causative-passive sentences and translate them into English.

   a. *Shiija ya uttu nkai kusui numasun.* _____

   _____

   English: _____

   b. *Uya ya chakushi nkai wakamiji kumii ga ikasun.* _____

   _____

   English: _____

LESSON 9   Tug of War Festival

c. *Ayaa ga warabi-n-chaa nkai muuchii chichimasun.* _____

   English: _____

d. *Shinshii ga meenachi shiitu nkai "Tinsagu nu Hana" utaasun.* _____

   English: _____

e. *Wannee warabi-n-chaa nkai Ufugushiku nu tanmee unchikee shii ga ikachan* (PAST-1 of *ikasun*). _____

   English: _____

DIALOGUE C

Niko, Yuna, Kenta, and Shogo are joining the East team for the tug of war competition.

(The race starts)

Kenta: (To Niko and Shogo) *Hajimain doo.*   It will start now.
             Chimu dakudakuu sun yaa.   I feel excited.
          (To his own team) *Nama doo, fikee!*   Now, pull!

(Kenta's team loses)

Kenta:	*Agaree mata n* **makiti neen** *sa. Chirudai su ssaa.*	The East team lost again. I am very disappointed.
Yuna:	**Santi n** *shimu sa. Nama* **makiti n** *naa chukeenoo a sa. Uri, mata hajimain doo!*	Don't be disappointed. Though we have lost now, there is one more match. Now, we begin.

(After the second match)

Yuna:	*Uri, katchee* **ee sani**! *Chimu fuji-i?*	Hey, we won. Are you satisfied?

CORE VOCABULARY

hajimain	'start' (INTR), *hajimiin* (TR)
dakudakuu / saasaa	'heart-pounding'
fikee (IMP)	← *fichun* 'to pull'
makiti neen	'end up losing' [C1]
chirudai su (APO.FORM)	← *chirudai sun* 'to get disappointed'
santi n shimun	'okay not to be disappointed' [C2]
makiti n	'even if (we) have lost' [C2]
chu-keenoo	← *chu-keen* 'once' + *ya* (TOP)
katch-ee (APO.FORM)	← *katch* 'win' + *een* (RES)
ee sani	SFP [C3]
fuji-i	← *fuji* 'satisfied, G.FORM of *fujun*' + *i* (QP)

GRAMMAR C

1. Completive Aspect: [G.FORM + *neen*] 'end up ~'

This construction expresses a completion of action, which the speaker often regards to be a regrettable or disappointing result. Here are some examples:

- *Agaree mata n* **makiti neen** *sa.*
  'The East team has lost again (to my regret)!'

- A: *?yaa mun du yati-i? Kuneeti kwiri yoo.* **Kadi neen** *sa.*
  'Was this yours? Forgive me. I have eaten it all (to my regret).'

  B: *Atarasa sshi nukucheetaru munnu.* (*atara sun* = 'treat something as precious' [L10(B4)]
  'I have left it as something precious, but…'

2. Concessive Conditional (2): [G.FORM (V/ADJ) + n] 'even if...'

In [L7(B2)], we introduced the concessive conditional patterns [wh-word + *yati n*] 'no matter who/what/where' etc. and [Noun + *yati n*] 'even if (it is (for) Noun).'

- *Taa yati n, nain.* '**No matter who it is**, he/she can do it.' / '**Anyone** can do it.'
- *Warabi yati n nain.* '**Even if** it is a child, he/she can do it.' / '**Any** child can do it.'

This lesson introduces new kinds of concessive conditionals with the verbal and adjectival Gerund Form, both in affirmative and negative forms. These new concessive patterns carry the same concessive meaning of 'even if'.

Verbs

Use the Gerund Form with *n* (*kadi n* 'even if I eat...') or the Negative Gerund Form (the NEG.FORM + *ti*) with *n* (e.g., *kaman-ti n* 'even if I do**n't** eat...').

- *Nama **makiti n** naa chukeenoo a sa.* 'Even if we lose now, we have one more chance.'
- *Achaa ya, ami **futi n** ichumi?* 'Even if it rains tomorrow, are you going?'
- *Achaa ya, yii ʔwaachichi **naranti n** ichumi?* 'Even if the weather doesn't improve, are you going?'

Adjectives

Add *ti* to the Apocopated Form of the adjective (***achisa-ti n*** 'even if it is hot...') or to the Negative Form (***achikooneen-ti n*** 'even if it is not hot...').

- ***Takasati n**, kooi sa.* 'Even if it is expensive, I will buy it.'
- ***Yashikooneenti n**, kooi sa.* 'Even if it is not cheap, I will buy it.'

3. Sentence Final Particle: *ee sani*

You can add this SFP to the Apocopated Form when you intend to counter someone's comment or assumption you do not agree with. See the following English exchange first:

- A: She is not coming.
  B: She *is* coming!
  (When she shows up)
  B: **See**, she *is* here, **I told you so**.

This exchange in Okinawan is like this:

- A: *Pensy ya kuun sa.* 'Pensy is not coming.'
  B: *Chuun yoo…* 'She is coming, I'm telling you…'
  (Pensy shows up).
  B: *Uri, chee ee sani.* '**See**? She has come. **I told you so.**'

With a rising (question) intonation, the speaker can simply express his/her opinion in an effort to solicit the listener's agreement.

- *Chuu ee sani?* '(I believe) she is coming. Don't you agree?'

Here is another exchange from the dialogue:

- A: *Agaree mata n **makiti neen** sa. Chirudaisu ssaa.*
  B: *Uri, katchee **ee sani**? Chimu fujii?*

ADDITIONAL VOCABULARY

fee 'south'	*muru* 'all'
kuneein 'put up with', 'forgive'	*nishi* 'north'
kweeyun 'become fat'	

EXERCISES C

1. Respond to X's utterance using [G.FORM + *neen*].

   a. X: *Uma nkai waa kwaashi nu ata ee sani?*

      Y: *Ai, wan ga (_____)*. ('ended up eating')

   b. X: *Maasu ya naa neen du arui?*

      Y: *Ai, wan ga muru (_____)*. ('ended up using it all')

   c. X: *Chinuu doru 'dollar' kooin (ndi) iita siga, kootii?*

      Y: *Yii yii, Chuu ya (_____) sa*. ('ended up rising')

   d. X: *Chuu ya yii ʔwaachichi yata kutu, sentaku sa shiga…*

      Y: *(_____) yaa*. ('ended up raining')

2. Study the examples, then complete B's responses by filling in the blanks (__) with the appropriate concessive conditionals and the [__] with the English translations.

Example:

> A: *Achaa ya achiku nai shiga, ichumi?*
> B: *Ii. (**Achiku natin**), ichun doo.* ['Yes. Even if it becomes hot, I will go.']
> A: *Kunu iyoo takasa ssaa. Chaa su ga? Kooimi?*
> B: *Ii. (**Takasa tin**), kooin doo.* ['Yes. Even if it is expensive, I will buy it.']
> A: *Naa chukeen yumee, wakai sa.*
> B: *Yii yii. (**Naachukeen yudin**), wakaran sa.* ['**No. Even if I read one more time, I won't understand.**']

a. A: *Chuu ya kaji fuchu shiga, umi nkai ichun naa?*

  B: *Ii.* (_____), *umi nkai ichun.*

  [ ]

b. A: *Maasaru munnu, naa ufee kaman naa?*

  B: *Yii yii.* (_____), *kamee kweeyu kutu, kamaran sa.*

  [ ]

c. A: *Naa chukeen chikee, wakai sa.*

  B: *Yii yii. Naa chukeen* (_____), *wakaran sa.*

  [ ]

d. A: *Karasaree, kaman gayaa.*

  B: (_____), *wattaa warabee kamun. Aree karasa shi shichi ya kutu.*

  [ ]

3. In the exchanges below, complete A's question with the appropriate form of the verb given. Then, complete B's response based on the English translation provided.

   a. A: *Achaa ya ʔyaa n karaoke nkai* (_____) *ee sani?* (use *ichun*)

     B: *Ika ndi umutoota shiga,* (_____) *sa.* 'I thought I was going, but (**I ended up**) **not being able to go**.'

   b. A: *Ama nu denwa bangoo* 'phone number' *ya nuu ya ta ga?* (_____) *ee sani?*

     B: *Ai, nama madi ubitoota shiga,* (_____). 'Oh, I remembered until now, but **forgot it completely**.'

APPLICATIONS

1. Were there things your parents forced you to do when you were small? Discuss it with your peer(s).

   A: *Warabi nu tuchi, shimirasattaru kutu nu ami?*

   B: *Ii, an doo. Wannee…*

   e.g., *piano naraasattan* 'made to learn how to play the piano'
   udui naraasattan 'made to learn how to dance'

2. Role Play: Student A is a parent, and Student B is a child. B says (s)he does not want to do ~ (e.g.. eating vegetables). A forces B to do ~.

   Example:

   Mom: *?yaa ya nuunchi gooyaa kaman ga?*

   Child: *Ufee njasaibii ssaa.*

   Mom: *Njasa kutu du kusui nairu. Kunchi n chichun doo.*

   Child: *Anshi jootuu yaibii raa, waa munu n unju usagami soorani?*

CULTURAL NOTES

1. Tug of War Festival

The Tug of War Festival is a summer event with a long history dating back to the sixteenth century. In Yonabaru, the East and the West teams compete in matches. Avid participants are often referred to as *china mushi* 'tug of war warriors' (see inset). Before the matches, there is dancing and music called *gaa ee* to raise the *china mushi*'s fighting spirit. The people on top of the giant rope called *shitaku* proceed to the main competition stage. The giant rope that the young men carry is about 90 meters long and wide enough for people to stand on. After the matches, sometimes people take home small branches from the main rope as a good luck charm. The *shitaku* dress up as historical figures such as Gosamaru and Amawari, or as famous athletes (e.g., karate athletes). The Naha tug of war made it into the Guinness World Records as the

biggest rope in the world, and the Yonabaru tug of war has received a prestigious award from the Japanese government.

- Research the history of the Tug of War festival in Okinawa.
- Research the origin of tug of war. (Where did it start? Why?)
- Research historical figures like Gosamaru, Amawari, Momoto Fumiagari, etc.

2. East-West-South-North

The four directions in Okinawan are as follows.

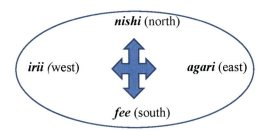

Here are some place names in Okinawa with directional names (cf. Kinjō [1950] 1974):

- Fee-baru / Hae-baru   (lit. 'south wind field')
- Iri-umuti / Iri-omote   (lit. 'west face')
- Agari-hama   (lit. 'east beach')
- Nishi-hara / Nishi-baru   (lit. 'field in the north of Shuri')

3. Summer Events: *O-bon* and *Eisaa*

People in Okinawa celebrate *O-bon* in summer according to the lunar calendar. It lasts three days. The first day is called *unkee* ('welcoming back the ancestors') and the last day is called *uukui* ('sending them back'). Families gather and pray with food in front of the family altar at home (L8).

Around the same time, *Eisaa* festivals will take place in different locations throughout the island. People march playing percussion instruments. Traditionally, it was meant to send off the ancestors in high spirits, but now it has become a great entertainment activity with energetic dance and lively percussion. Many local groups gather and compete with each other at the main *Eisaa* competition sponsored by the prefecture (cf. Hijirida and Oshiro 2011: Lesson 6).

- Are there any notable summer events in your hometown?

LESSON 10

Farewell:
"Once We Meet, Brothers and Sisters Forever"

Niko is joining the 97th birthday celebration for the most senior member of the host family, the great-grandmother. This is a happy occasion indeed, but Niko's departure for America is also fast approaching.

DIALOGUE A

Niko: *Ufuʔnmee sai, kajimayaa nu u-yuuwee unnuki yabira. Ichi ichi* (or *hyaaku hatachi*) *madi n chaa ganjuu sshi utabimisheebiri.*

Great-Grandmother, I'd like to congratulate you on the occasion of *kajimayaa*. May you have a long and healthy life!

Great-grandmother:	*Kafuushi doo. Chuu ya aka-jin* **chichi**, *aka hachimachi n* **shimiti**, *ufee hajikasaa a shiga…*	Thanks. I am a bit embarrassed wearing a red kimono and putting on a red hairband, but…
Niko:	*Wuu wuu, ippee uchatooibiin doo. Wattaa nkai n ayakaarachi utabimisheebiri.*	No, no. You look very good (with the outfit). Please allow us to receive your (longevity).
Great-grandmother:	*Naa ufee yoonnaa tushi tura ndi umutoota shiga, iina kujuu shichi nati neen sa. Fee-ʔnma nu hairu {***gutu** *du aru /* **gutoo** *sa}.*	I was going to age more slowly, but I am already 97 years old. It's as if a fast horse is running.
Niko:	*Junni chichi fi nu tachu shee feesaibiin yaa. Wannin kuma nkai* **chi kara**, **naa** *ichinin naibiin.*	Time flies. It has been one year since I came here.

CORE VOCABULARY

ufuʔnmee	'great-grandmother'
kajimayaa	'97th birthday celebration (by lunar calendar)'
u-yuuwee	'congratulatory remarks'
unnukiyabira (INT.FORM.POL)	← *unnukiin* 'to say' (HUM)
ichi ichi madi n	'many years to come'
chaa	'always'
ganjuu sshi (G.FORM)	← *ganjuu sun* 'to be in good health'
utabimisheebiri (IMP)	← *utabimisheen* 'to give' [L8(B2)]
kafuushi	'thanks' (said to younger)
aka-jin	← *aka* 'red' + *chin* 'robe'
chichi (G.FORM)	← *chiin* 'wear' [A1]
hachimachi	'headband'
hajikasaa a shiga	← *hajikasa* (embarrassment) + *ya* (TOP) + *a* 'exist' + *shiga* 'but'
shimiti (G.FORM)	← *shimiin* 'wear (on head, around the neck)'
ucha-too-ibiin	← *ucha* 'suit, becoming' + *too* (ASP) + *ibiin* (POL)
ayakaa ra-chi (G.FORM)	← *ayakaraa* 'share' (INT.FORM) + *ra* (PASS) *chi* (CAUS) 'let me receive'
yoonnaa	'slowly'
tura (INT.FORM)	← *tuin* 'to get'

nati neen	'to end up becoming' [L9(C1)]
fee-ʔnma	'fast'-'horse' ← feesan 'fast'
hairu (ADNOM.FORM) + gutu	← hain 'to run' + gutu 'like' [A3]
chichihi	'days'
chi kara	← chi 'come' + kara [A2]
naa	'already' [B1]

GRAMMAR A

1. Verbs of Clothing

English uses 'wear' for all clothing items. Okinawan, on the other hand, has multiple clothing verbs. Which verb to use depends on what type of clothes you wear:

- On the head (e.g., *booshi* 'hat'): **kanjun** (G.FORM: **kanti**)
- From waist above, or top and bottom as a unit (e.g., *chin* 'kimono'): **chiin** (G.FORM: **chichi**)
- From waist below (e.g., *hakama* 'Japanese-style formal pants', *zubon* 'Western-style pants', *sukaato* 'skirt'): **hachun** (G.FORM: **hachi**)
- Footwear (e.g., *kutsu* 'shoes', *geta* 'clogs', *saba* 'slippers'): **kumun** (G.FORM: **kudi**)
- Small items: *ganchoo* **kakiin/hachun** 'to wear glasses' (G.FORM: **kakiti/hachi**); *hachimachi* **shimiin** 'to wear a headband', (G.FORM: **shimiti**)

Clothing verbs are often used with the aspectual form *(t)oon*. It is usually interpreted with the resultative meaning: you put on clothing prior to the present moment and as a result, you now have that clothing on you. It sometimes can also express the progressive meaning, '(someone) is putting (something) on'. The table below shows the *(t)oon* form for all the clothing verbs.

	DIC.FORM	G.FORM	Aspectual	Meaning
V	shimi-in	shimi-ti	shimi-**toon**	'to wear (a headband)'
V	kaki-in	kaki-ti	kaki-**toon**	'to wear (glasses)'
V	chi-in[1]	chi-chi*	chi-choon*	'to wear (a kimono)'
C-2	kanj-un	kan**ti**	kant-**oon**	'to wear (a hat)'
C-4	hach-un	ha**chi**	hach-**oon**	'to wear (pants, glasses)'
C-8	kum-un	ku**di**	kud-**oon**	'to wear (shoes)'

[1] *chi-in* is a V-verb, but its conjugation is irregular.

Here are some examples:

- *Chuu ya aka-jin **chichi**, aka hachimachi n **shimiti**, ufee hajikasaa ashi ga…* — 'I'm a bit embarrassed by wearing a red kimono, and headband…'
- *Feeku kutsu **kumee**. Naa ichun doo.* — 'Put on your shoes quickly. I'm going already.'
- *Chuu ya achisa kutu, booshi **kanti**, iki yoo.* — 'Since it's hot today, you should put on a hat when you go.'

2. Temporal clause: [G.FORM + *kara*] 'since/after doing ~'

This construction indicates the following two related temporal meanings.

a. 'Since ~'

- *Kuma nkai **chi kara**, naa ichinen naibiin.* — 'It's already been a year **since** I came here.'
- *Ari ga **keeti kara**, hantushi nain.* — 'It's been half a year **since** he returned.'

b. 'After ~'

- *Chuu ya, yuuban **chukuti kara**, ashibii ga ichu sa.* — '**After** preparing dinner, I go to play.'
- *Taarii ga **usagati kara**, wattaa ya kamun.* — '**After** my father has eaten, we eat.'

Here are some more examples:

- *Muuchii **chichidi kara** ʔnbusun.* — 'After wrapping the *muuchii*, then you steam them.'
- ***Tii aachi kara**, usandee sun.* — 'After praying, then you receive the offering.'
- *Jiibu nu tanmee **unchikee sshi kara**, u-haka nkai ichabiin.* — 'After picking up the elderly Gibo, then we go to the grave.'

✎ The conjunction, *anshikara* [L1(DialA)] comes from the 'gerund + *kara*' pattern as well: *an* 'that' + *sshi* 'do: G.STEM' + *kara*.

3. The *gutu* expressions

a. [N (*nu*) *gutu*] 'like N'

This construction is used as an adverbial phrase. See the examples below:

• *Uchinaanchu nu **gutu** Uchinaaguchi chikain.*	'He uses Okinawan like an Okinawan person.'
• *Osaka Naomi nu **gutu** jooji yaree yaa…*	'If I were good at (tennis) like Osaka Naomi…'
• *Kiyuuna Ryoo nu **gutu** chuusaree yaa…*	'If I were strong like Kiyuna Ryo.'

☞ The particle *nu* does not appear after *an*, *kun*, *un* (e.g., *un gutu* 'like this/that', ˣ *an nu gutu*).

• *Un **gutu** churasa-ree, ichibusan.*	'If it is beautiful like that (as you say), I would like to go.'

b. [N *nu* + *gutoon*] 'it is like ~ / it appears ~'

When this construction appears as the predicate of a sentence, it means that 'X is similar to N' or 'X is comparable to N'. When it appears as a modifier to describe another noun, it changes to *gutooru* as in the second instance in the first example, *~ gutooru tchoo*.

• *Anu tchoo chimu jurasanu, kami nu **gutoon**. Anu tchu nu **gutooru** tchoo nakanaka wuran yaa.*	'That person has a kind heart, and is like a god. There aren't people like that person.'
• *Chuu ya achisa nu, nachi nu **gutoon**.*	'It's hot today; it is like the summer.'

c. [N *nu* + *gutu du aru*] 'it is really like ~ / it really appears as if ~'

This is an emphatic version of (b) with the focus construction [L4(A4)]. Here, what is focused on is what precedes *gutu*.

• *Anshi hisa nu feesanu, fee-ʔnma nu **gutu** du **aru**.* (← *fee-ʔnma nu **gutoon***)	'(The sprinter was) so fast, she was really like a fast horse!'
• *Muuchii biisa ndi ichi n, chuu ya achisa-nu, nachi nu **gutu** du **ataru**.*	'Although it was called the coldest season, it was hot today, so it was really like summer.'
• *Aree sanmin nu feesanu, konpyuutaa nu **gutu** du **aru**.*	'He calculates so fast that he really appears as if he is a computer.'

ADDITIONAL VOCABULARY

arain 'to wash'
booshi 'hat, cap (Jp. loan)'
ganchoo 'eyeglasses'
geta 'clogs (Jp. loan)'
hakama 'Japanese formal garments worn from waist down (Jp. loan)'
hachun 'to wear (pants, glasses)'
hantushi 'half year'
kakiin 'to wear (glasses)'
kanjun 'to wear (a hat)'
kumun 'to wear (shoes)'

kutsu 'shoes (Jp. loan)'
saba 'slippers'
sanmin 'calculation'
sukaato 'skirt (Jp. loan)'
sutumiti mun 'breakfast'
suuji 'celebratory gathering'
ukiin 'to get up (INTR)'
ukusun 'to wake up (TR)'
yuin 'stop by'
zubon 'pants (Jp. loan)'

EXERCISES A

1. Fill in the blanks with the appropriate verb of clothing. Pay attention to the verb form.

    a. *Kundu nu suuji nee bingata* (_____). [cf. see inset in Lesson 1, Dialogue A]

    b. *Asato sanoo ganchoo* (_____) *doo.*

    c. *Chuu ya umi nkai ichu kutu, saba* (_____) *shee mashi yan yaa.*

    d. *Kunu chinoo arata kutu gumaku nati, naa* (_____) *sa.*

    (← a challenging question)

2. Fill in the blanks with the [G.FORM + *kara*] using the verb and pictures given. Refer to the additional vocabulary on the previous page.

    a. ① → ② *Asa* (_____) *chira arain.*

    b. ② → ③ *Chira* (_____) *sutumiti mun kamun.*

    c. ③ → ④ *Sutumiti mun* (_____) *gakkoo nkai ichun.*

    d. ⑤ → ⑥ *Gakkoo nu atu, tushukwan kai* (_____), *yaa nkai keein.*

e. ⑥ → ⑦ *Yaa nkai* (_____) *shukudai sun.*

f. ⑧ → ⑨ *Yuroo,* (_____) <u>*ninjun*</u>.

3. Using ~*gutoon* or ~*gutu du aru*, compose short sentences to describe a person (e.g., Edie, Lina). For (c), (d) and (e), you can make up similar sentences.

   a. *Edie ya yumu shi nu feesanu,* _____.

   ('like a computer')

   b. *Lina ya ippee churasanu,* _____.

   ('like Nakama Yukie')

   c. *Leo ya ʔwiijushi nu feesa nu* _____.

   ('like a fish (= *iyu*)')

   d. _____.

   e. _____.

DIALOGUE B

Yuna:	*Kuree, tachichee (tachichi + ya), Amirika nkai keeyabiin doo.*	He is going back to America next month.
Great-grandmother:	**Naa** *unu shichi natoomi?* **Maada** *mi chichi guree sachi du yaru ndi umutoota shiga…*	It's already that time? I thought it'd be about three more months from now.
Niko:	*Unju naa taa* **tu** *ichati, unjunaataa yaaninju nkai* **kanasa satti***, wannee ʔippee kafuu na mun yaibiin.*	I met you all and all of your family took care of me, so I feel I am a very lucky guy.
Great-grandmother:	*ʔyaa ga wuran nai-***nee** *shikara-ashiku nai sa. Naa ifee urarani?*	If you are gone, we all will miss you. Can you stay a little longer?
Niko:	*Wannin wuibusaa aibii shiga, uya nu chaa n* **machikantii sooru** *haji yaibii kutu, keeran nee naibiran.*	I want to stay (longer), too, but my parents are waiting, so I must go home.

CORE VOCABULARY

tachichi	'next month'
shichi	'time, season'
maada/naada	'still' [B1]
mi-chichi	'three months'
guree	'about'
sachi	'later, ahead'
ichati (G.FORM)	← *ichain* 'to meet'
kanasa	← *kanasan* 'lovely, dear' [B4]
satti (G.FORM)	← *sa* 'do' + *riti* (PASS [G.FORM])

nee	'if / when' [B2]
kafuu na mun	'lucky guy'
wura-ran-i	← *wura* 'stay' + *ran* (NEG) + *i* (QP)
wuibusaa -aibii (APO.FORM)	← *wui* 'stay' + *busa* 'want' + *ya* (TOP) -*aibiin* (POL)
machi-kantii sooru	'difficult to wait' [B3]
keeran nee naibiran	'must return' (L6)

GRAMMAR B

1. *Naa* 'already' and *maada/naada* 'still'

These adverbs appear both with negative and positive predicates and express distinct meanings.

- *naa* + positive = 'already'
  Naa nachi natoon. 'It has become summer **already**.'

- *naa* + negative = 'not anymore'
  Wannee naa wakakoo neen. 'I'm **not** young **anymore**.'

- *maada/naada* + positive = 'still'
  Aree {maada / naada} video game soo sa yaa. 'He's **still** playing video games.'

- *maada/naada* + negative = 'not yet'
  Aree {maada / nadaa} kuun sa yaa. 'He's **not** here **yet**.'

Here are some more examples:

Uma nkai chi kara, **naa** *ichinen naibiin.*	'It's been a year **already** since I came here.'
Naa *unu shichi natoomi?*	'It's **already** that season?'
Urijin natooru munnu, **naa** *hiikooneen sa.*	'It's become *urijin* (= spring/early summer [L7(Cul1)]), so it would not be cold **anymore**.'
Wakanachi natooru munnu, **maada** *achikooneen yaa.*	'Although it is *wakanachi* (= early summer), it is **not** hot **yet**.'
Maada *ta chichi*[1] *guree sachi du yaru ndi umutoota shiga.*	'I thought it is **still** about two months later, but ...'

[1] *tachichi* = next month; *ta chichi* = two months.

2. Habitual Conditional: [ADV.FORM + *(i)nee*] 'when/whenever'

a. With verbs

To make the habitual conditional clause, add *nee* to the Adverbial Form. In the case of C-verbs, add an extra *i* after the Adverbial Form. Special irregular verbs (*an, yan, wun*) have no extra *i*.

- *tu-in*   → ***tu-i*** (ADV.FORM)   + *nee*   → tuinee   (V-verb)
- *kach-un* → ***kach-i*** (ADV.FORM) + *i* + *nee*   → kachiinee   (C-verb)
- *ich-un* → ***ich-i*** (ADV.FORM) + *i* + *nee*   → ichiinee   (IRG -verb)

	DIC.FORM	ADV.FORM	Habitual Conditional	Meaning
V	tu-in	tu-i	tui-**nee**	'when(ever)…take…'
V	maga-in	maga-i	magai-**nee**	'when(ever)…turn…'
1	kuuj-un	kuuj-i	kuuji-i-**nee**	'when(ever)…row (a boat)'
2	ninj-un	ninj-i	ninji-i-**nee**	'when(ever)…sleep'
3	kunj-un	kunj-i	kunji-i-**nee**	'when(ever)…tie up…'
4	kach-un	kach-i	kachi-i-**nee**	'when(ever)…write…'
5	much-un	much-i	muchi-i-**nee**	'when(ever)…hold…'
6	turas-un	turash-i	turashi-i-**nee**	'when(ever)…give…'
7	yub-un	yub-i	yubi-i-**nee**	'when(ever)…invite…'
8	yum-un	yum-i	yumi-i-**nee**	'when(ever)…read…'
IRG	ichun	ich-i	ichi-i-**nee**	'when(ever)…go'
IRG	chuun	chi-i	chi-i-**nee**	'when(ever)…come'
IRG	sun	shi-i	sh-i-i**nee**	'when(ever)…do…'
IRG	an	a-i	**ai-nee**	'when(ever)…exist'
IRG	yan	ya-i	**yai-nee**	'when(ever)…is/are/am…'
IRG	wun	wu-i	**wui-nee**	'when(ever)…exist'

Examples:

- *Chiburu yami-**i-nee**, kusui numun.* 'Whenever I have a headache, I take medicine.'
- *Ami yai-**nee** (ˣ yai-i-nee), muchikasan.* 'When it rains, it's difficult.'

b. With adjectives

The Adverbial Form for adjectives is Apocopated Forms followed by *i*. Note the extra *i* that was needed for the C-verbs is not necessary for adjectives.

- *maasan* → *maasai* → *maasai nee*
- *shikaraasan* → *shikaraasai* → *shikaraasai nee*

- *Anmasai **nee**, ninju shee mashi doo.* 'When(ever) you feel sick, you'd better sleep.'
- *Maasu nu ikirasai **nee**, naa ufee (←ufi+ya) iriin.* 'When(ever) salt is not enough, I put more in.'

3. "Difficulty" expression: [ADV.FORM + *kantii sun*] 'difficult to ~'

This pattern expresses difficulty of carrying out the activity described by the verb. See a similar expression with *gurisan* in [L5(A2)]. Compared to *gurisan*, which objectively states a difficulty involved in a situation, *kantii sun* adds a nuance of 'no matter hard I/someone try/tries'. Here are some examples:

- *Asa nu go-jee **uki(i)kantii sun**. Yakutu, chaa dushi nkai ukusattoon.* 'I have a hard time getting up at 5:00 a.m. So I'm always getting my friend to wake me up.'
- *Takasaru tukuma nkai ukee, warabi gaa **tuikantii sun**.* 'If you put it on a higher place, kids have a hard time getting it.'
- *Uya nu chaa ga **machikantii sooru** haji yaibiin.* 'It might be the case that my parents can hardly wait to see me.'
- *Unu shikuchee chui shee **shiikantii su** kutu, ʔyaa tiganee shi kwiriyoo.* 'It's difficult to carry out this task alone, so would you help him out?'
- *Kunu gooyaa juusu ndi shee njasanu, warabi-n-chaa ya **numi kantii su** kutu, ufee saataa irii shee mashi yaa.* 'This *goya* juice is bitter and difficult for children to drink, so it would be good to add sugar.'

4. Derived verbs: [(adj. of emotion/sensation) APO.FORM] + *sun*

Some adjectives of emotion/sensation/values can be turned into related verbs by adding the verb *sun* to their Apocopated Form (Part II, Topic 4):

- *kanasa* 'dear, affectionate' + *sun* → *kanasa sun*   'love', 'take a good care of'
- *atarasa* 'precious, valuable' + *sun* → *atarasa sun*   'use sparingly', 'use with care'
- *shikaraasa* 'lonely' + *sun* → *shikaraasa sun* 'miss someone'
- *hirumasa* 'strange' + *sun* → *hirumasa sun* 'think ~ as strange'
- *achisa* 'hot' + *sun* → *achisa sun* 'act as if one is hot'
- *yaasa* 'hunger' + *sun* → *yaasa sun.* 'starve'

- *Unju naa taa yaaninju nkai **kanasa satti**, wannee ʔippee kafuu na mun yaibiin.*   'All of your family took care of me, so I feel I am a very lucky guy.'
- *Anu warabee **yaasa soo** sa. Nuugana kamashee.*   'That child is starving. Give something to him (lit. make him eat something).'

ADDITIONAL VOCABULARY

kuujun 'to row (a boat)'

maniaain 'to be on time'

EXERCISES B

1. Complete the following sentences. For the first blank in all the sentences, write the appropriate *nee* conditional form based on the English cues. Complete the second blanks in (d) and (e) with your own phrases.

    a. *Muuchii nu shichi (_____) nee, hiiku nain.* (hint: 'become')

    b. *Paarankuu nu (_____) nee, naa shigu chinahichi yan.* ('be heard')

    c. *Diigu nu hana nu dateen (_____) nee, ufu kaji nu ufooku nain.* (*sachun* 'bloom') [L7(Cul1)])

    d. (_____) *nee,* (_____). ('hot' for the first blank)

    e. (_____) *nee,* (_____). ('wind blows hard' for the first blank)

LESSON 10 Farewell: "Once We Meet, Brothers and Sisters Forever"   227

2. Complete the sentences using ~ kantii soon.

   Example: *Nbusanu, tanmee ya muchikantii soomisheen.* ('hard time carrying')

   a. *Shishi nu magisanu, anu warabee (_____) sa.* ('eating')

   b. *Jii nu gumasanu, (_____).* ('reading')

   c. *?waa 'pig' ya iishi nu muchikasanu, (_____).* ('saying')

   d. *Muuchii 100 (hyaaku) chukuran nee naran shiga, chui shee*

      (_____). ('make')

   e. *Umaa michi nu wassanu, saba shee (_____).* ('walk')

3. Choose the appropriate word.

   a. *(naa / maada) shiwaashi natoon. Uri kara meenachi hiiku nain yaa.*

   b. *(naa / maada) aree kuuni? Nama ikanee maniaaran doo.*

   c. *Aree (naa / maada) binchoo soon naa? Dikiyaa ya chigain yaa.*

   d. A: *?yaa ya nuunchi waa ga 'san ki yoo!' ndi shi su ga?*

      B: *Taarii tai, (naa / maada) sabiran sa. Kuneetikwimisoori.* 'Forgive me'

   e. A: *"Wannee Mayaa du Yaru" ya (naa / maada) ?njitoomi?*

      'Has the book called *Wannee Mayaa du Yaru* gone out

      (= published) yet?'

      B: *(Naa/Maada) yaibiin.* ('not yet')

4. Choose two adjectives from [B4] and make two short sentences.

   _____

   _____

   _____

   _____

DIALOGUE C

Niko:	Yashiga, ama nkai ʔ**nji atu** n mata **muduti (t)chi n shimabii** gayaa.	But, after I go back, is it OK to come back again?
Great-grandmother:	Ataimee du yaru. 'Ichariba choodee' ndi iru kugani kutuba nu gutu, **ichairu mee** ya, shiran tchu du yata shiga, namaa yaaninju du yan doo. Shiran tchu **natee naran** doo.	Of course. Like the saying, 'Once we meet, we are all brothers and sisters', we are strangers before we meet, but we are now family members. Don't be strangers (again).

(Looking at Niko, whose eyes welled up with tears, Yuna says to him)

Yuna:	Mii nada guruguruu sshi, nachi**gisaa** soon yaa. Wannee amirika nkai ʔnjaru **kutoo neen** kutu, yaan ya ichibusa ssaa. Amirika nkai ichiinee visaa **turantin shimu** ee sani.	Your eyes welled up with tears, and you look like you are going to cry. I have never been to America, so I want to go there next year. When I go to America, I don't need to get a visa, right?
Niko:	Ii, shimun doo. Yakutu, jifi kuu yoo.	Yeah. That's right. So, please come by all means.

(Niko looking at everyone)

Niko:	Unjunaa taa n majun mensoori yoo.	Everyone, please come to visit.
Yuna:	Anshee ʔyaa ga wuru ʔ**weeda** ni eego nararan nee naran yaa.	Then while you are here, we have to study English.

CORE VOCABULARY

yashiga	'but' (continued from [B])
ʔnji atu	'after going' [C1b]
muduti (G.FORM)	← *muduin* 'return'
(t)chi n shima-bii (APO.FORM-POL)	← *tchi* 'come' + *n* 'also' + *shimun* 'OK' [C2a]
ataimee	'no question, of course'
ichariba choodee	[Cul3]

kugani kutuba	'words of wisdom'
ichairu mee	'before meet' [C1a]
shiran tchu	'stranger'
~ *natee naran*	'shouldn't become ~' [C2d]
nada	'tears'
mii nada guruguruu	'tears welling up in the eyes'
nachi-gisaa s-oon	← *nachi* 'cry' + *gisaa* 'looks like' + *s* 'do' + *oon* (ASP) [C4]
~ *ʔnjaru kutoo neen*	'have never been to ~' [C3]
yaan	'next year'
ʔweeda	'during the time' [C1c]

GRAMMAR C

1. **Temporal Relations**

    a. [ADNOM.FORM (present) + *mee*] 'before ~'

This construction means '(A happens) **before** B.' The subjects of two clauses before and after *mee* could be different. The verb form before *mee* must be in the Adnominal Form.

- *yumuru mee . . .*   'before reading'
- *ninjuru mee . . .*   'before going to bed'
- *keeiru mee . . .*   'before going home'
- *sagiiru mee . . .*   'before hanging something'
- *shikuchi suru mee . . .*   'before working'

The Adnominal Form before *mee* is always in the present tense even if the main verb is in the past tense. You specify the tense of the sentence at its end.

- *Hun yumuru mee munu **kamun**.*   'I eat before reading a book.'
- *Hun yumuru mee munu **kadan**.*   'I ate before reading a book'
- ***Ichairu mee** ya, shiran tchu du yataru.*   'Before we met, we were strangers.'
- *Uchinaa nkai **chuuru mee**, wannee Tookyoo nkai wutan.*   'Before I came to Okinawa, I was in Tokyo.'
- *U-shiimii **suru mee**, u-haka nu kusa karan nee naran.*   'Before we do *u-shiimii* gathering, we have to cut the grass around the grave.'
- *Okinawa ken nkai **nairu mee** ya, Ryūkyū koku yatan.*   'Before it became Okinawa Prefecture, it was the Ryukyu Kingdom.'

b. [G.FORM + *atu*] 'after ~'

The conjunction *atu* appears between two clauses, A *atu* B. The whole sentence means 'After A happens, B happens'. In other words, **A *atu* B** ('B after A') and **B *mee* A** ('A before B') express the same time relation between A and B. The verb form before *atu* must be the Gerund Form.

- yu**di** atu ...   'after reading'
- nin**ti** atu ...   'after going to bed'
- shikuchi **sshi** atu ...   'after working'
- ka**ti** atu ...   'after cutting (grass)'
- sagi**ti** atu ...   'after hanging (something)'

Like the *mee* clauses, you specify the tense of the sentence at the end.

- Hun yudi atu munu **kamun**.   'I will eat after reading a book.'
- Hun yudi atu munu **kadan**.   'I ate after reading a book'

A few more examples follow.

- Ama nkai **ʔnji atu**, mata muduti chuun.   'After I'm gone there, I will come back.'
- Afakee **tuti atu**, hama wuti ashibun.   'After we dig clams, we play on the beach.'
- Muuchii **chukuti atu**, tinjoo kara sagiin. 'After we make *muuchii*, we hang them from the ceiling.'
- Shukudai **sshi atu** du ashiburu, **suru mee** ni ashibu shee aran.   'You should play after doing homework, not before you do (your homework).'

c. [ADNOM.FORM (PRESENT) + *ʔweeda/ ʔweema*] 'while ~', 'during the time ~'

This construction means 'while an activity or a situation [A] goes on, another activity or situation [B] goes on.' The verb before *ʔweeda/ ʔweema* must be in the Adnominal Form, and it is often in the progressive form, i.e., -(t)ooru appears often. In addition, the tense of the Adnominal Form is non-past even when the main verb is in the past tense (e.g., *yudooru* 'reading' in the third example below). The subjects of A and B can be different. Recall this is not the case with -*gachii* (simultaneous actions by the same person [L8(C1)]). Furthermore, the subject is not marked by *ya*, but by *ga*.

- Ari ga munu **chukutooru ʔweeda**, wannee yaa nu sooji soochun.   'While she's making meals, I will clean up the house (in preparation).'
- Wan ga binchoo **sooru ʔweema** ya, uma wuti sawagan ki yoo.   'While I'm studying, do not make noise here.'

- *Ari ga hun **yudooru ʔweeda**, wannee nintootan.* — 'While he was reading, I was sleeping.'
- *Uchinaa nkai **wuru ʔweeda**, meenachi Uchinaaguchi chikara ndi umutoon.* — 'While I'm in Okinawa, I think I'll use Okinawan.'

2. Speech Act Expressions

In our daily lives, we use language to perform various actions involving others: we seek and get permissions and exemptions, and issue prohibitions and obligations. These expressions are speech act expressions.

a. Permission granting: [G.FORM (V/adj.) + n + shimun] 'You may ~ / You can ~'

We learned the concessive construction [G.FORM + n] 'even if…' in [L9(C2)]. When combined with **shimun** 'okay, even if…' it creates the meaning of positive **permission** (i.e., 'may') (e.g., 'You **may** eat my lunch', 'You **may** go home now').

- *yudi n **shimun**…* — 'you **may** read'
- *ninti n **shimun**…* — 'you **may** go to bed'
- *kati n **shimun**…* — 'you **may** cut (grass)'
- *sagiti n **shimun**…* — 'you **may** hang (something)'
- *shigutu sshi n **shimun**…* — 'you **may** work'

b. Permission seeking: [G.FORM (V/adj.) + n + shimum-i?] 'May I / Can I…?'

With this construction, you can request permission from someone to do something (e.g., '**May** I go home now?' '**May** I stay here?').

- *Yudi n **shimumi**?* — '**May** I read…?' (plain)
- *Ninti n **shimumi**?* — '**May** I go to bed?' (plain)
- A: *Kuree **kadin shimabiimi**?* — '**May** I eat this?' (polite)
  B: *Ii, **shimun** doo.* — 'Yes, you **can**.' (plain)

c. Exemption: [G.FORM (neg) + n + shimun] 'You don't have to…'

If you want to relieve someone from doing something ('You don't have to cut the grass', 'You don't have to work today'), you can use the Negative Gerund Form before *n shimun*. Negative Gerund Form is [NEG.FORM + ti].

- *tuin* → *turan* + *ti* → *turanti*   *n shimun* 'you **don't have to** take it'
- *yumun* → *yuman* + *ti* → *yumanti*   *n shimun* 'you **don't have to** read it'
- *ʔnjasun* → *ʔnjasan* + *ti* → *ʔnjasanti*   *n shimun* 'you **don't have to** turn it in'
- *machun* → *matan* + *ti* → *matanti*   *n shimun* 'you **don't have to** wait (for me)'
- *sun* → *san* + *ti* → *santi*   *n shimun* 'you **don't have to** do it (now)'

- A: *Shukudai ya chuu ʔnjasanti n shimabiimi?*   'Is it OK not to turn in homework today?'
- B: *Yii yii chuu ʔnjasan nee naran sa. Achaa ya naran doo.*   'No. You must turn it in today. Tomorrow is no good.'

d. Prohibition: [G.FORM + *ya* (= G.ROOT + *ee*) + *naran*] 'You may not ~'

Use this construction to prohibit someone from doing something ('you may not enter this room'). The verb form is in the Gerund Form and it is followed by the topic particle *ya*. Since all Gerund Forms end in *-i*, the [*-i + ya*] combination changes to [*-ee*].

- *tuin* → *tuti* + *ya* → *tutee naran*   'you **may not** take it'
- *yumun* → *yudi* + *ya* → *yudee naran*   'you **may not** read it'
- *kachun* → *kachi* + *ya* → *kachee naran*   'you **may not** write it'
- *machun* → *matchi* + *ya* → *matchee naran*   'you **may not** wait (here)'
- *ninjun* → *ninti* + *ya* → *nintee naran*   'you **may not** sleep (here)'
- *nnjun* → *nnchi* + *ya* → *nnchee naran*   'you **may not** look at (her)'
- *sun* → *sshi* + *ya* → **shee naran*   'you **may not** do it (here)'

- A: *Ooruu pen shi **kachin shimabiimi**?*   '**May** I write with a blue pen?'
- B: *Ooruu shi **kachee naran** sa. Kuruu sshi kakee.*   'You **may not** write with a blue (pen). Write with a black (pen).'

Don't confuse this with the '**obligation**' sentence we learned earlier [L6(B1)]. If what precedes *naran* is [INT.FORM + *nee*], the meaning is 'must' (e.g., 'you must enter this room').

e. Obligation: [N.FORM + *nee/daree naran*] 'must' [L6(B1)]

Compare the pair below.

- Obligation: *kunu kusui **numan daree/nee naran**.*   'You **must** take this medicine.'
- Prohibition: *kunu kusui **nudee naran**.*   'You **may not** take this medicine.'

- *tuin* → *turan* + *nee naran* → *turan **nee naran**.*   'you must take it'
- *yumun* → *yuman* + *nee naran* → *yuman **nee naran**.*   'you must read it'
- *kachun* → *kakan* + *nee naran* → *kakan **nee naran**.*   'you must write it'
- *nnjun* → *nndan* + *nee naran* → *nndan **nee naran**.*   'you must look at (her)'
- *sun* → *san* + *nee naran* → *san **nee naran**.*   'you must do it (now)'
- *machun* → *matan* + *nee naran* → *matan **nee naran**.*   'you must wait (here)'
- *ninjun* → *nindan* + *nee naran* → *nindan **nee naran**.*   'you must sleep (now)'

☞ The above could be *tura nee naran, yuma nee naran,* etc. after the collapse of *nn* to *n*.

Observe a variety of speech act expressions in the examples below.

- A: *Kunu konpyuutaa* **chikati n shimabiimi**?   'May I use this computer?' (permission seeking)

  B: *Kunu konpyuutaa ya* **chikatee naran** *shiga, aree* **chikati n shimu sa**.   'As for his computer, you may not, but that, you may.' (prohibition/permission)

- A: *Kuruma* **kati n shimabiimi**?   'May I borrow your car?' (permission seeking)

  B: *Ii,* **shimun** *doo*.   'Yes, you may.' (permission)

  Anshiga, kuruma muchu raa, nama saki **nudee naran** *doo*.   'But if you drive, you must not drink.' (prohibition)

- A: *Kuree chuu madi ni* **san nee naibirani**?   'Do I have to do this by today?' (obligation question)

  B: *Yii yii, chuu* **santi n shimun** *doo*.   'No, you don't have to do it today.' (exemption)

3. Experiential expressions:
(a) [ADNOM.FORM (PAST-1) + *kutu nu an*] 'I have done ~';
(b) [ADNOM.FORM (PAST-1) + *kutoo* (← *kutu ya*) *neen*] 'I haven't done ~'

These constructions express one's experience: 'have done ~before' / 'haven't done ~ yet.' The form before *kutu* is the Adnominal Form in its simple past (PAST-1) regardless of the subject. Remember the simple past is made with the Gerund Root + *an*.

- *tuin* → *tut-an* → **tutaru kutu** *nu an*   'I have taken (*chimboora*) before'
- *kamu* → *kad-an* → **kadaru kutu** *nu an*   'I have eaten (it) before.'
- *ichun* → *ʔnj-an* → **ʔnjaru kutu** *nu an*   'I have been (to a place) before.'
- *sun* → *s-an* → **saru kutu** *nu an*   'I have done (it) before.'
- *Wannee china* **ficharu kutu nu an** *doo*.   'I've pulled the rope (in the tug of war match).'
- *Wannee haarii* **nncharu kutu nu an** *doo*.   'I have seen a *haarii* (boat race) before.'
- *Wannee funi* **kuujaru kutu nu an** *doo*.   'I have rowed a boat before.'

The negative counterpart of *kutu nu an* is *kutu ya neen* → *kutoo neen* 'I haven't done it yet.'

Here are examples from the dialogue as well as additional examples:

- *Wannee amirika nkai njaru **kutoo neen**.* 'I've never been to America'
- *Aree haarii **nncharu kutoo neen** (n)di iitan.* 'He said he's never seen a *haarii* (boat race).'
- *ʔyaa n kachaashii **saru kutoo neen** naa?* 'You haven't danced a *kachaashii* yet?'

4. Visual Evidential:
(a) [ADV.FORM (V) + *gisan*] 'looks as if ~' / 'about to ~';
(b) [APO.FORM (Adj) + *gisan*] 'looks as if ~

You can use this construction when you feel that something is going to happen based on visual observations. For instance, in the first example below from the dialogue, the speaker is witnessing tears welling up in Niko's eyes. In this sentence, the Adverbial Form of the verb *nachun* 'to cry' is used before *gisan*. In the second example, the Apocopated Form of the adjective *achisan* 'hot' is used.

- *Mii nada guruguru sshi, nachi**gisaa** soon yaa.* 'Your eyes welled up with tears, and you look like you are going to cry.'

✒ When *gisa* is followed by *soon*, the last vowel is lengthened as in *gisaa soon*.]

- *Aree dateen chichi, achisa**gisa** ssaa.* 'He's wearing a lot and looks so hot!'

The [ADV.FORM (V) + ***gisan***] is semantically similar to [DIC.FORM + *nee sun*] [L6(B4)] as both express speakers' conjectures. However, while *gisan* relies on the speaker's observation (visual evidential), *nee sun* relies more on his/her gut feelings.

- *Tin nu makkuuruu sshi, ami nu **fuigisan**.* 'The sky is dark, and it appears it'll rain (soon).'
- *Wakaran shiga, ami nu **fuin nee sun**.* 'I don't know why, but it seems it is about to rain.'

Here are more examples:

- *Kuree **maasagisan** yaa.* 'It looks like this is delicious.'
- *Aree dikiyaa ya kutu, kunu muchikasaru shikuchi n **naigisa** ssaa.* 'He is smart, and it looks like he can do this difficult job.'
- *"Numan ki yoo" ndi icha shiga, aree nama **numigisa** ssaa.* 'I told him not to drink, but it appears that he is going to drink.'

ADDITIONAL VOCABULARY

awatiin 'to get excited', 'to panic'	**machun** 'to spray, sprinkle (e.g., water)'
haniin 'to be hit by a car'	**sawajun** 'to make a racket'
kangeein 'to think'	**uchun** '(animal) bites'

EXERCISES C

1. Match the expressions on the left with their correct interpretations/situations on the right.

    a. (___) *Kadee naran.*   A. Permission

       (___) *Kadin shimun.*   B. Prohibition

    b. (___) *Kaman nee naran.*   A. Obligation

       (___) *Kaman tin shimun.*   B. Exemption

2. Using *gisan* and the verbs/adjectives in bold as hints, fill in the blanks. Pay attention to the forms.

    a. X: *Aree kunu shikuchi **nai** gayaa.*

       Y: *Yii yii.* (_____) *ssaa.*

    b. X: *Aree isa nkai tumirattoo kutu, amasa shee **kaman** sa.*

       Y: *Ya gayaa. Nnchi ndee.* (_____) *doo.* (inset)

    c. X: *Anu karee ya **karasa** gayaa.*

       Y: *Ii,* (_____) *ssaa.* (inset)

3. Choose the correct word to complete each sentence.

    a. *Uchinaaguchi binchoo* (*shi kara* / *sshi atu*), *naa gu nin naibiin.*

    b. *Shinshii taa yaa nkai* (*ichuru* / *njaru*) *mee ni, chitu kootan.*

    c. *Kuju* (*makiti* / *makiiru*) *atu ya, jifi katan nee naran.*

    d. *Afakee* (*tuti* / *tuiru*) *atu, nna saani kamu shee tanushimi yan.*

    e. *Tinchi yohoo nndan ta kutu, ami nu* (*futi* / *fuiru*) *mee, kusa nkai miji machi neen sa.* 'Since I didn't check the weather forecast, I watered the grass before it rained.'

4. Translate the following into English. Underline the patterns you recognize (e.g., *ichaibusan* 'would like to meet').

    Wannee naada iriomote yanameko ndi shi nncharu kutoo neeyabiran. Unu mayaa ya ippee mijirasaru mayaa nati, muru kara atarasa sattooyabiin. Mushi kunu

236 PART I Conversation

mayaa nu kuruma nkai hanirariiru kutu nai nee, shigu kinkyuu heri ndi shi ga tchi, awatiti byooin (n)kai sooti ichun ndi irattoibiin. Yashiga, tchu nu habu nkai utatti n (← uta-riti n 'bite'-PASS-'even if'), *taa n awatiran (n)di nu hanashi yaibiin. Unu mayaa nkai chukeenoo ichaibusan (n)di umuyabiin.*

✏️ *iriomote yamaneko* 'Iriomote Mountain Cat'; *kinkyuu heri* 'emergency helicopter'; *byooin* 'hospital'

LESSON 10 Farewell: "Once We Meet, Brothers and Sisters Forever" 237

APPLICATIONS

1. Students A and B are talking about other people in the lounge. A asks B a name of a person in the distance by describing him/her by his/her clothing and accessories.

A: *Anu ganchoo kakitooru tchoo taa ya ga?*
B: *Anu akaa chin chichooru tchu naa?*
A: *Yii yii, ooruu chin chichoo shi, yoo.*
B: *Aa, aree XX-san ya sa.*

Using the picture, continue to carry out the conversation. You can describe the person you have in mind by their clothing or by their actions.

2. Ask your classmate about his/her experience as below:

   a. Have you been to places X, Y, and Z?

   b. Have you made foods X, Y, and Z?

   c. Have you seen movies X, Y, and Z?

   Also discuss what needs to be done **before** doing these actions and what one would do **afterwards**.

3. Student A invites Student B to go with him/her to a fun activity. Student B declines the invitation, citing various things he/she has to do. Compose your own exchanges paying attention to the bold structures (obligation, exemption, etc.)

   A: *Kundu nu doyoobi karaoke nkai ikani?*
   B: *Namaa ichunasanu naran saa.*

A: **Nuunchi** yoo.

B: Raishuu shiken nu akutu binchoo **san nee naran**.

A: Anshee, namaa santin raishuu **kara shin shimu ee sani**.

B: Wannee utaa joojee aran kutu...

A: Magiiku **utaranti n shimu** sa...

CULTURAL NOTES

1. *Kugani Kutuba* ('Words of Wisdom')

Choose two *kugani kutuba* from the list below and write your thoughts about the culture and philosophy in Okinawa. Compare these sayings with those found in other cultures.

    http://manoa.hawaii.edu/okinawa/wordpress/wpcontent/uploads/2010/12/Handbook_L3_Proverbs.pdf

    Proverbs Archives—https://www.okinawa.com/blog/category/research/proverbs

_____

_____

_____

_____

_____

_____

_____

_____

_____

_____

2. *Kajimayaa*

Do some research on *kajimayaa* and explain what it means and how it is done. Find out if any other parts of the world have similar celebrations.

3. *Choodee gwaa bushi*
   (Lyrics: Maekawa Chooshoo; Music: Yara Chookyuu)

The title of this lesson comes from *Choodee gwaa bushi* (inset). The lyricist is Maekawa Chooshoo from Yonabaru. Every year in his birthplace, a singing contest featuring this song is held. Both young and old singers show their talent singing this song.

- https://www.youtube.com/watch?v=XZxR2SS9E-o (Song with the lyrics)
- https://yonakan.jimdofree.com
- http://coralway.jugem.jp/?eid=3128

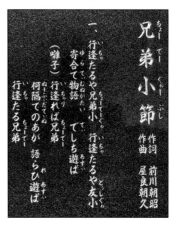

The lyrics in this stone inscription are regarded by many as representative of the essence of Okinawan hospitality and pursuit of global peace.

1. *Ichataru ya   choodee gwaa   ichataru ya dushi gwaa   yurati   munugatai   dii shichi ashiba*
   (Refrain) *Ichariba choodee nuu fidati nu aga kataree ashiba*

2. *Ubijasusa nkashi namani natimiriba nachikashin yurati kataree bushanu*
   (Refrain)

- Using the *Wordbook*, translate the lyrics above into English. Further state your thoughts on the message this song exudes.

_____
_____
_____
_____

- Discuss how the spirit of this song is depicted in Disney Japan's anime *Stitch* (episode 1: *Ichariba Choodee*).

4. Yamanokuchi Baku

Yamanokuchi Baku is a famous Okinawan poet. He blends a few Okinawan phrases into the following Japanese poem.

Tama o Abita Shima** yori* (from ***Shell-Shocked Island)

Romanized Original	Translation by Rie Takagi (2000)
Shima no tsuchi wo funda totanni "*Ganjuui*" *to aisatsu shita tokoro*	The moment I set foot on the island soil and greeted them *Ganjuy*[1]
Hai okage sama de genki desu toka itte Shima no hito wa nihongo de kita noda Kyooshuu wa isasaka tomadoi shite shimatte	Very well, thank you the island people replied in Japanese My nostalgia at a bit of a loss
"*Uchinaaguchi madi n muru ikusa ni sattarubasui*" *to iu to*	I muttered *Uchi nahguchi madhin muru Ikusani sattaru basui*[2]
shima no hito wa kushoo shita no daga Okinawago wa joozu desu ne to kita noda	to which the island people feigned a smile but remarked how well I spoke the Okinawan dialect

[1] How have you been?
[2] Was even your dialect destroyed by war?

- Write down your thoughts about this poem with reference to the theme of this lesson or the Uchinaaguchi eradication movement in the 1950s and '60s and the recent preservation/perpetuation effort (refer to Shinzato 2003b).

_____
_____
_____
_____
_____
_____
_____

REVIEW EXERCISES

Lessons 9 and 10

1. Fill in the verb conjugation chart below.

DIC.FORM	Meaning	NEG	Passive	Causative	CAUS.PASS	ADV.FORM	G.FORM
ka-in	'to cut'			karasun			kati
kuuj-un	'to row'				kuugasariin	kuuji	
chich-un	'to listen'				chikasariin	chichi	
ʔnjas-un	'to take out'				ʔnjasasariin		
ichun	'to go'			ikasun			
sun				shimiin			
wun					wurasariin	wui	

2. The chart below shows how a construction is made by attaching different forms to the Adnominal, Adverbial, or Gerund Form. The example row shows that the verb in Adnominal Form is followed by *tami ni* to create the purposive expression 'in order to V' (e.g., *tuiru* is followed by *tami ni* to create *tuiru tami ni* 'in order to get (it)'). Fill in the blanks in the chart.

Form	Elements to follow	Meaning
Adnominal Form	+ *tami ni*	'in order to V'
	+ *munnu*	

Form	Elements to follow	Meaning
Adnominal Form	+ gutoon	
Adnominal Form (PAST-1)		'have {done/ never done}'
	+ mee	
	+ (i) nee	'if', 'when'
		'difficult to do'
		'looks as if'
	+ neen	
Gerund Form	+ n (e.g., yudi n ~)	
Gerund Form	+ kara (e.g., yudi kara)	
	+ atu (e.g., yudi atu)	'after ...ing'
Gerund Form (AFF)	+ n shimun	
	+ n shimun (e.g., yumanti n shimun)	'don't have to do'
	+ ya naran → ~ -ee naran (e.g., yudi ya naran → yudee naran)	
	+ nee naran (e.g., yuman nee naran)	'you must do'

3. Select the correct forms.

   a. A: *Ee, naa shimu sani?* 'Isn't it enough?'

   Wata nu yamu ndi { iu / iiru / iin } munnu, naahin kamun naa?

   B: *Anshi maasa du { a / aru / an } munnu.*

   b. A: *Kuri { kama / kami / kadi } n shimabiimi?*

   B: *Ii, { kadi / kamee / kaman }.*

   c. A: *Uchinaaguchi binchoo { sshi / sun / su } kara nan nin nai ga?*

   B: *Naa ichi-nin { nai / nairu / nati } neeyabiran.*

   Ichi nin { nai / nairu / nati } n Uchinaaguchee maada jooji natee wuibiran ssaa.

A: *Yashiga, Uchinaa nkai { chuu / chuuru / chi } mee ya,*

   Uchinaaguchi { nara / narati / narataru } kutoo neenta ee sani?

   Uri{ kangeei / kangeeti / kangeeiru } nee, ʔyaa Uchinaaguchee rippa yan doo.

A: *ʔyaa ya daigaku { ʔnjiiru / ʔnjiin / ʔnjiti } atu, nuu suga?*

B: *Shinshii naibusaibiin.*

d. A: *Higasan (n)oo nuu n { nai / nairu / nati } gisan yaa.*

   B: *Ii, Toodai nkai { iin / ii / iiru } tami ni, meenachi dateen binchoo soon doo.*

   A: *Wan ga { [y]a / n } jooi naran ssaa.*

e. A: *Kuree ʔnbusanu { muchi / mutchi / muchuru } kantii su ssaa.*

   B: *Wannin tiganee su sa.*

4. Match the following expressions on the left with their appropriate translations or situations on the right.

   a. (___) *Yassa tin kooran.*   A. If it is cheap, then I will buy it.

      (___) *Yassaree kooin.*   B. Even if it is cheap, I won't buy it.

   b. (___) *Nudee naran.*   A. Permission

      (___) *Nudin shimun.*   B. Prohibition

   c. (___) *ami fuigisan.*   A. It appears that it will rain.

      (___) *ami fuin nee sun.*   B. I don't know why, but I feel that it will rain.

   d. (___) *Maada saki numun.*   A. (He) drinks sake at present …

      (___) *Naa sakee numan.*   B. (He) doesn't drink sake anymore.

   e. (___) *Maada kuun.*   A. late arrival

      (___) *Naa choon.*   B. early arrival

5. Change the following active sentences to causative and causative passive sentences. Fill in the (__) with the appropriate particle. If no particle is necessary, place an X in the (__).

   a. *Warabi ga jii kachun.*

   → *Uya ga warabi (_____) jii (_____) [_____]. (causative)*

   → *Warabee uya (_____) jii (_____) [_____]. (causative-passive)*

b. *Shiitu ga sooji-sun.*

→ *Shinshii ya shiitu (_____) [_____]*. (causative)

→ *Shiitoo shinshii (_____) [_____]*. (causative-passive)

c. *Uttu ga yuuban chukuin.*

→ *Shiija ga uttu (_____) yuuban (_____) [_____]*. (causative)

→ *Uttoo shiija (_____) yuuban (_____) [_____]*.

(causative-passive)

d. *Yunabaru kara Sui madi atchan.* (note this is in the past tense)

→ *Shiija ga wattaa (_____) Yunabaru kara Sui madi [_____]*.

(causative)

→ *Wattaa ya Shiija (_____) Yunabaru kara Sui madi [_____]*.

(causative passive)

6. Fill in the blanks either with *naa* or *maada/naada* and translate the sentences into English.

a. (_____) *nachi natoon. Anshi achisaru.*

English: _____

Shigwachi natoo shiga, (_____) *hiisa ssaa.*

English: _____

b. A: *Aree* (_____) *tabaku fuchoon yaa. Chinuu n fuchoo tan, doo.*

English: _____

B: *Aran doo.* (_____) *tabakoo fukan haji ya shiga. Attaa yatchii ya aran ti-i?*

English: _____

7. Based on the pictures, complete the following short exchanges.

a. A: *Kuma wuti* **munu kadin shimabii** *gayaa.*

B: *Yii yii [_____]*

b. A: *Kuma wuti juusu [_____] gayaa.*

B: *Yii yii* **nudee naran** *doo.*

c. A: *Kuma nji saba* **hachin shimabii** *gayaa.*

   B: *Yii yii* [_____]

d. A: *Chuu ya Uchinaaguchi nu renshuu* [_____] *gayaa.* 'not to practice'

   B: *Yii yii* [_____] *doo.* 'must practice'

8. Study the example and compose your own sentences using ~(i)nee, ~.

   Example: *Michi nkai tchu nu ufusainee atchikantii sun.*
   English: When there are too many people, it is difficult to walk.

   a. [_____]

   English: _____

   b. [_____]

   English: _____

   c. A: [_____]

   English A: _____

   B: [_____]

   English B: _____

PART II

GRAMMAR

TOPIC 1

Typological Introduction

Okinawan shows some notable typological characteristics.

1.1 Demonstratives

A three-way spatial contrast defines Okinawan demonstratives. They indicate proximal, medial, and distal spaces, and are represented by *ku-*, *u-*, and *a-*, respectively. Demonstratives are used pronominally (*ku-ri, u-ri,* and *a-ri*), adnominally (*ku-nu, u-nu,* and *a-nu*), and as locative demonstrative nouns (*ku-ma, ʔn-ma,* and *a-ma*). However, the distinction between the proximal (*ku-*) and medial (*u-*) is not as clear as the one found in the similar Japanese system (Tsuhako 1992:837; Uchima 2011:39–42). See [L1(A1)].

1.2 Personal Pronouns

There are first, second, and third person pronouns in the singular and plural forms: *wan* (1sg.)/*wattaa* (1pl.), *ʔyaa* (2sg.)/*ittaa* (2pl.), *ari* (3sg.)/*attaa* (3pl.). The third person singular pronoun is identical to the distal demonstrative pronoun (*ari*). In addition, the second person has Polite Forms: *unju* (2sg.)/*unju(naa)taa* (2pl.).

The genitive pronouns are identical to the forms presented above except for the first person singular (*waa* in addition to *wan*) and the third person singular (*ari ga*). The genitive pronominal paradigm can be shown as follows: *waa* or *wan* (1sg.GEN)/*wattaa* (1pl.GEN), *ʔyaa* (2sg.GEN)/*ittaa* (2pl.GEN), *ari ga* (3sg.) / *attaa* (3pl.GEN). As shown here, unlike regular nouns, most pronouns do not take the genitive particle *ga* or *nu* when they modify a noun except for the third person singular form. There is another exception, which is that the second person polite singular pronoun takes either *ga* or *nu* (*unju ga / nu*) though its plural form does not take the genitive particle (*unju(naa)taa*).

Unlike some other Ryukyuan languages, there are no inclusive and exclusive distinctions in Central Okinawan (Yabiku 1963, Uchima 2011:33-52, Shimoji 2021), the variety on which this book is based. The plural forms (*wattaa, ittaa, attaa*) are used even when the possessor is singular (*wattaa shima* 'our home village' ← 'my home village', *attaa shinshii* 'their teacher' ← 'his/her teacher') (Yabiku 1963:149–153). This happens especially when the modified nouns are senior members of a family (*ittaa taarii* 'your (pl.) father' ← 'your (sg.) father'.

1.3 Constituent Orders

Okinawan is a head-final language, so the predicate appears at the end of a clause (i.e., a simple sentence) including the nominal, adjectival, and verbal predicates. The predicates are in bold in the examples below.

- *Wannee* **Yoshio yaibiin.** 'I am Yoshio.'   (Nominal Predicate)
- *Uchinaa ya* **achisaibiin.** 'Okinawa is hot.'   (Adjectival Predicate)
- *Ami nu* **fuin.** 'It rains.'   (Verbal Predicate)

For a clause with a transitive verb, the constituent order is S-O-V. Okinawan marks a noun for its semantic relation to the verb in the clause with a case particle. Thus, in the next sentence, the subject (S), i.e., *Kaya*, is marked by *ga*. However, it is a notable fact in Okinawan that the direct object (O), i.e., *iyu* 'fish', is unmarked (shown here by Ø).

- *Kaya-ga   iyu-Ø   kooin.* 'Kaya buys fish.'
     S   O   V

Oblique noun phrases can be inserted within a sentence. In the next sentence, an additional phrase, *machigwaa-wuti* 'at the market' is added. The postpositional particle *wuti* (or *wutooti*) following *machigwaa* 'market' shows that the noun phrase indicates a location where the action of 'buying' takes place. See Topic 2 (Part II) for other case-marking particles.

- *Kaya-ga   machigwaa-wuti   iyu-Ø   kooin.* 'Kaya buys fish at the market.'
     S   at the market   O   V

A sentence with a verb of movement follows a similar structure. In the next sentence, the postpositional particle *nkai* following *machigwaa* 'market' indicates the goal of the movement.

- *Kaya-ga   machigwaa-nkai   ichun.* 'Kaya goes to the market.'
     S   to the market   V

For a ditransitive verb, the S-IO-DO-V or S-DO-IO-V orders are possible (IO=indirect object; DO=direct object). In the next two sentences below, the subject appears in the topic form, i.e., *wannee* and *Kayaa* (see [L1(A1)]), and the recipient is marked by *nkai*. Note the particle *nkai* is adjusted to *ninkai* after *wan* 'I'. The same verb *kwiin* 'give' can be used when the first person is a giver or recipient, unlike Japanese which requires different verbs, *ageru* ('I give it to someone') and *kureru* ('someone gives it to me').

- *Wannee kuri-Ø Kaya-nkai kwiin.* 'I give this to Kaya.'
     S   DO   IO   V

- *Kayaa kuri-Ø wan-ninkai kwiin.* 'Kaya gives this to me.'
     S   DO   IO   V

Being a head-final language, a modifier appears before a head noun as in Japanese. Unlike Japanese, however, both adjectives and verbs must be in the Adnominal Form when they modify a noun. The first sentence below has the Adnominal Form of *maasan* 'delicious', which is *maasaru* (non-past) and *maasataru* (past). The second sentence has the past Adnominal Form of *yan* (the copula), which is *yataru*.

- **maasaru/maasataru**   *yaashee*
  delicious / was delicious   vegetable
  'tasty vegetable / the vegetable that was tasty'

- UCLA   *nu*   *shiitu* **yataru** *tchu* 'a person who was a UCLA student'
  (school name)   GEN   student   was   person

When a clause with an internal subject (e.g., *Hanako* in the two sentences below) modifies a head noun, the subject must be marked by a subject marker (not a topic marker) and the verb must be also in the Adnominal Form (non-past or past).

- *Hanako ga*   *machigwaa-wuti*   *kooiru/kootaru*   **iyu**
  (name) SUB   market-at   buy / bought   fish
  'the fish which Hanako buys/bought at the market'

- *Hanako-ga*   *Kaya-nkai*   *kwiiru/kwiitaru*   **sumuchi**
  (name)-SUB   (name)-to   give/gave   book
  'the book which Hanako will give/gave to Kaya'

1.4 Subject and Topic

The sentence, *Wannee* (← *wan + ya*) *Higa yaibiin* 'I am Higa,' can be analyzed as consisting of a topic and a comment: [*Wan ya*]TOP [*Higa yaibiin*]COMMENT. A topic is something or someone which the addressee can identify ('given information') and is further commented on. If *ya* is replaced by a subject marking particle *ga* as in *Wan ga Higa yaibiin*, the logical content is identical, but *wan* 'I' is presented as 'new information,' e.g., 'Who is Mr. Higa?' '*I* am Higa.' The same contrast appears between any sentence pairs that use *ya* (and its variant form, [L1(A2)]) and *ga/nu* (Topic 2). Comparing *Merii ya Hawai-nkai ichun* and *Merii ga Hawai-nkai ichun*, the former represents an unmarked situation, 'Mary is going to Hawaii,' while the latter is used to answer the question 'Who is going to Hawaii?' Note that a topic does not have to correspond to a subject. In [*Orionoo* (← *Orion + ya*)] TOP [*Merii ga numun*] COMMENT 'Orion beer, Mary drinks,' it is a direct object that is being used as a topic. In this case, a sense of contrast is strongly expressed, i.e., '(It is not Kirin beer, or Asahi beer, but) it is Orion beer that Mary drinks.'

The differential marking system for subject and topic is shared with Japanese, but in Okinawan, it is not uncommon to use the topic and subject-marking particles together. This is not possible for Japanese: i.e., *ga ya* ('subject-topic') → *gaa*; *nu ya* (subject-topic) → *noo* ([L7(B3)], Topic 2).

1.5 Agglutinating Morphology

Okinawan is an agglutinating language with rich morphological structures, especially in its verb forms. As an illustration, forms of 'eat' (*kam-*, *kad-*, etc.) with various suffixes are given below (see more details in Topic 3).

kam-un	[BASIC.ROOT-DECLARATIVE.NONPAST]	'eat'
kam-an	[NEGATIVE.ROOT-NEGATIVE.NONPAST]	'not eat'
kamu-tan etc.	[APOCOPATED.FORM- PAST 2]	'(I saw) him eating'

Various auxiliary verbs are also suffixed.

kad-oon	[GERUND.ROOT-ASPECT.NONPAST]	'be eating'
kad-een	[GERUND.ROOT-RESULTATIVE.NONPAST]	'have eaten (and the result still lingers)'
kama-riin	[INTENTIONAL.FORM-PASSIVE.NONPAST]	'be eaten'
kama-rii-tan	[INTENTIONAL.FORM-PASSIVE-PAST 2]	'(I saw, e.g., a small fish) being eaten (by a big fish)'
kama-sun	[INTENTIONAL.FORM-CAUSATIVE.NONPAST]	'make someone eat'
kama-sa-riin	[INTENTIONAL.FORM-CAUSATIVE-PASSIVE.NONPAST]	'be made to eat'
kama-sa-tt-an ← *kama-sa-ri-tan*	[INTENTIONAL.FORM-CAUSATIVE-PASSIVE-PAST1]	'was made to eat', etc.

1.6 Other Points

Part II further discusses case marking (Topic 2), verb morphology (Topic 3), adjectives (Topic 4), questions (Topic 5), clause combining (Topic 6), sentence final particles (Topic 7), and focus concord constructions (Topic 8). Other interesting typological features are also discussed in Part I. These include a transitivity contrast [L3(A2)], the concepts of 'doing' and 'becoming' [L3(Cul3)], special types of passives known as adversity and warning passives (L8), and honorific systems (L8).

TOPIC 2

Case Marking

Okinawan marks nouns in a sentence with postpositional particles. Some particles indicate grammatical roles such as the 'subject', while others indicate adverbial information such as time, location, means, etc. (Okinawan also uses topic [L1(A2)] and additive topic-marking [L2(A3)] particles.)

2.1 Subject: *ga, nu*

When a subject represents given/old/predictable/identifiable information as is often the case, it is either unexpressed or coded as a topic, but when it is new information, the subject must be expressed and is marked by *ga* or *nu*. *Niko* is the new information in the next sentence as it is supplying the information sought by *who*.

- *Niko ga ichun.*   '**Niko** will go.' ← '(Who will go?)'

The choice between the two particles *ga* and *nu* is largely determined by the type of the subject noun phrase. Generally, personal names (such as *Niko* above), kinship terms (such as *wattaa uttu* 'my younger brother/sister' below) and human common nouns (such as *shiitu-n-chaa* 'students' below) are marked by *ga* (Uchima 1994:211; Ishikawa 1996).

- *Wattaa uttu ga ʔwiijoon.*   'My younger brother/sister is swimming.'
- *Shiitu-n-chaa ga huka wuti ashidoon.*   'Students are playing outside.'

As noted above and shown in the first sentence below, personal names take *ga*, but as the second example shows, *nu* may appear in some cases, especially with an honorable subject with an exalting verb (Kinjō [1944] 1974:97).

- *Asatu ga chuun.*   'Asato will come.'
- *Asatu shinshii ga/nu mensheen.*   'Prof. Asato will come.'

Pronouns are invariably coded with *ga* regardless of whether the referent is human or non-human.

- **Waa** ga ichun. 'I will go (if no one else is going).'
- **Ari** ga chuutan. 'He came.'
- **Ama** ga gakoo yaibiin. 'That location is a school.'
- **Kuri** ga mijun yaibiin. 'This is a sardine.'

Nonhuman nouns are marked by *nu* (Kinjō [1944] 1974), but some human nouns may also be marked by *nu*.

- **Mayaa** nu nintoon. 'A cat is sleeping.'
- **Hana** nu sachoon. 'Flowers are blooming.'
- **Wata** nu yamun. 'My stomach hurts.' (Ishikawa 1996:37)
- **Habu** nu wun. 'There is a snake.' (ibid.)
- **Tuji** nu chuun. 'The wife comes.' (ibid.)

This complex system of subject marking can be summarized as in the diagram below.

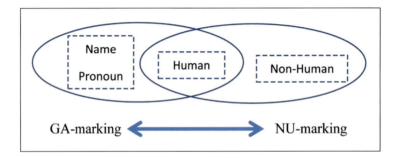

The 'human' category is most variable, and the subject marking is probably influenced by discourse properties such as salience. Discourse saliency sometimes allows non-human nouns such as *tiida* 'the sun' to be marked by *ga*, though in normal conditions usually *nu*-marking would be the norm (Ishikawa 1996:39).

A subject can be emphasized by adding a focus marker *du* or *ga*, which triggers the use of the Adnominal or the Ra Forms in the predicate (see Topic 8).

- Niko ga **du** ichuru. '(Is it Kaya who's going?) It's **Niko** who will go.'
- Niko ga **ga** ichura. 'I wonder if it is **Niko** who is going.'

Finally, *ga* and *nu* can be combined with the topic particle *ya* or additive topic particle *n*. The *ga + ya* and *nu + ya* contract as *gaa* and *noo*, respectively [L7(B3)]. For example, *waa gaa nain* means '(I don't know about others, but) as for me, I can do it,' and *waa ga n nain* 'Even I (who am always clumsy) can do it' (Miyara 2019:86; Tsuhako 1992:83; Kinjō [1944] 1974).

2.2 Possessor: *ga, nu, Ø*

A possessor is normally marked by *ga* or *nu*. The distribution pattern is based on the same principle as for the subject marker described above.

- *shinshii ga naa* vs. *kunu mayaa nu naa*   'teacher's name' vs. 'this cat's name'

However, most personal pronouns are marked by a zero (Ø) marker as shown in the first two examples. Some require *ga* as shown in the last two examples.

- *waa/wan Ø saba*   'my sandal'
- *ʔyaa Ø mun*   'your thing'
- *ari ga / uri ga / kuri ga mun* 'this/that/that (far) person's thing'
- *unju ga naa*   'your name' (*nu* is also possible)
                                   (Ifa 1992:54, Sakihara et al. 2017)

Personal names can also appear as a possessor without any particle (Miyara 2019:85). The last vowel may be elongated as in the second example (*Takashii* ← *Takashi*).

- *Chiruu Ø mun*   'Chiruu's thing'
- *Takashii Ø mun*   'Takashi's thing'

Nouns referring to a quantity of people also require *ga* (Miyara 2019:85).

- *nna ga mun*   'things belonging to everyone'
- *tai ga mun*   'things belong to two persons'

Family terms require *nu* except for terms for mother and father (Miyara 2019:86).

- *tuji nu chin*   'my wife's clothes'
- *shiija nu hun*   'my elder sister/brother's book'
- *duu nu shima*   '(my/our/your/his/her/their) own village'
- *anmaa Ø mun*   'mother's thing'

2.3 Modifier: *nu*

In addition to the typical possessive meaning, *nu* can also form various types of modifier phrases such as:

- *Uchinaa nu hana*   'flowers of Okinawa'
- *Uchinaa nu hun*   'a book on/from Okinawa'
- *Eego nu shinshii*   'an English teacher'

It can also appear in an appositive phrase:

- *waa dushi nu Ken*   'my friend Ken'

It can also appear before a plural-indicating noun such as *chaa*.

- *dushi nu chaa*   'friends'
- *warabi nu chaa* → *warabi-n-chaa*   'children'

2.4 Object: Ø (zero marking)

Okinawan does not mark an object with a particle. Since some other Ryukyuan languages (and Japanese) mark it with a specific particle, Okinawan can be described as a language which marks direct objects with a zero particle (shown as Ø below). In other words, the case marking here is not a consequence of particle deletion.

- *Aree Eego Ø nain.*   'She can speak English.'
- *ʔyaa ga suba Ø kamee.*   'You eat noodles!'
- *Wannnee kunu eega Ø nnji-busaibiin.*   'I want to watch this movie.'

The object for the predicate *fusan* 'want' is often marked by Ø (Uchima 1994:212), but it may be optionally marked by *nu* (Hanazono 2020:93).

- *Nuu Ø fusa ga?*   'What do you want?'
- *Miji Ø / nu fusan.*   'I want some water.'
- *Taruu ya miji Ø / nu fusan ndi iin.*   'Taro said he wants some water.'

2.5 Goal (1): *nkai*

Goals of motion and locations of existence are marked by *nkai* (see Nishioka 2004).

- *Warabi-n-chaa ya gakkoo nkai ichun.*   'Children go to school.'
- *Warabi-n-chaa ya gakkoo nkai wun.*   'Children are at school.'

This particle also marks more abstract goals (e.g., the dative / an indirect object).

- *Kunu sumuchee uttu nkai kwiin.*   '(I) give this book to my younger brother/sister.'
- *Dushi nkai iin.*   '(I) will tell my friend.'

Furthermore, *nkai* also marks the agent in a passive sentence.

- *Wannee uttu nkai anu muuchii kamattan.*   'My brother ate my *muuchii*' (adversity passive)

2.6 Goal (2): *madi*

When the spatial goal is the final destination, *madi* may be used (in place of *nkai*).

- *Wattaa ayaa ya gakkoo madi mensoochan.*   'My mother came (all the way) to school.'

When the goal is a temporal finishing line, *madi* must be used (i.e., *nkai* is not appropriate).

- *Hachiji madi nintootan.*   'I was sleeping until 8.'

2.7 Locative: *wuti / wutooti / nji*

The location where some action takes place is marked by *wuti*, *wutooti*, or *nji* (i.e., 'in/at/on').

- *Achaa gakkoo wuti / wutooti /nji shibainu an.*   'There will be a performance at school tomorrow.'
- *Hawai wutee / wutootee Kona coffee kootan.*   'In Hawaii, (I) bought Kona coffee.'

2.8 Temporal: *ni*

A time when something happens is marked by *ni* ('at/on')

- *Rukuji ni kuu wa.*   'Come at six.'
- *Sangwachi ni Naaku nkai ʔnjan.*   'I went to Miyako in March.'

Temporal adverbs such as *achaa* 'tomorrow', *chinuu* 'yesterday', and *yaan* 'the next year' do not need to be marked by *ni*.

- *Yaanoo wattaa warabee tuu nain.*   'My kid will be ten next year.'

2.9 Origin: *kara* (1)

Both locational and temporal starting points are marked by *kara*.

- *Kuma kara ichun.*   '(I) go from here.'
- *Hiru kara shikuchi sun.*   '(I) work from noon.'

2.10 Passage: *kara* (2)

The passage through/on which one travels is marked by *kara* (e.g., drive on the street, run on the beach).

- *Warabi-n-chaa ya kunu michi kara atchun.*   'Children walk on this street.'
- *Anu michi kara ika.*   'Let's go on that street!'

2.11 Means of Transportation: *kara* (3)

A means of transportation is marked by *kara*.

- *Hikooki kara San Francisco nkai ʔnjan.*   'I went to San Francisco by plane.'

2.12 Instrument: *(s)shi / saani*

A tool with which you perform some activity is marked by *(s)shi* or *saani*.

- *ʔnmeeshi (s)shi / saani sashimi kamun.*   '(I) eat sashimi with chopsticks.'
- *Harusaa ya irana (s)shi / saani wuuji kain.*   'Farmers cut sugarcane with sickles.'

2.13 Companionship: *tu*

Traditional grammar calls this the comitative case. It marks someone with whom one does things.

- *Wannee ʔnmii tu majun muuchii chukuin.*   'I make *muuchii* with my older sister.'
- *Kana-sanoo Jiroo-san tu niibichi sun.*   'Kana will get married to Jiro.'
- *Dushi gwaa tu ichain.*   'I meet with my friend.' (This *tu* can be changed to *nkai*.)

The same particle *tu* can also connect two nouns with the meaning of 'and'.

- *Hawai tu Uchinaa.*   'Hawaii and Okinawa'

Also, this particle can appear in a comparative sentence as follows. Notice the second *tu* is topicalized and appears as *too*.

- *Hawai tu Uchinaa too maa ga achisaibii ga?*   'Which is hotter, Hawaii or Okinawa?'

TOPIC 3

Verbs

This chapter describes how Okinawan verbs are structured to express various meanings and functions.

3.1 Preliminary

The **Dictionary Form** [L1(B2)] is the form found in a dictionary, e.g., *Wordbook*. All dictionary verb forms end in either *-in* (e.g., *tu-in* 'to take') or *-un* (e.g., *kach-un* 'to write'). The *-in* ending verbs are called **vowel verbs**, or V-verbs in short, because the segment before *-in* is a vowel (e.g., *-u-*). The *-un* ending verbs are called **consonant verbs**, or C-verbs in short, because the segment before *-un* is a consonant (e.g., *-ch-*). There are nine sub-groups within the Consonant Verbs as discussed below. In addition, there are a number of irregular verbs which are treated separately. The form without the final *-n* of the Dictionary Form (e.g., *tui-* and *kachu-*) is the **Apocopated Form**. (See more information about these forms in 3.2.2 below.)

3.2 Building Blocks

Building blocks are units that are used in creating various verbal and predicate forms. The three levels of building blocks are **the root**, **the primary form**, and **the construction**.

3.2.1 Roots

There are three types of root.

- Basic Root (B.ROOT):   Dictionary Form minus *-un* / *-in* [L1(B2)]
- Negative Root (N.ROOT): This has to be memorized [L2(C3)]
- Gerund Root (G.ROOT): This has to be memorized [L3(A1)]

The **Basic Root** is the form without *-in* or *-un* (e.g., *tu-* 'to take' and *kach-* 'to write'). The Dictionary Form, Apocopated Form and the Basic Root are presented for comparison.

Verb	DIC.FORM	APO.FORM	B.ROOT
V-verb ('to take')	tu-in	tui-	tu-
C-verb ('to write')	kach-un	kachu-	kach-

The **Negative Root** is used to make the Negative Form and others. For the V-verbs, the Negative Root is identical to the Basic Root.

Verb	DIC.FORM	B.ROOT	N.ROOT
V-verb ('to take')	tu-in	tu-	tu-

For the C-verbs, the Negative Root is identical to the Basic Root for #6–9, but are different for #1–5 and must be memorized.

No.	C-verb	DIC.FORM	B.ROOT	N.ROOT
1	'to swim'	ʔwiij-un	ʔwiij-	ʔwiig-
2	'to sleep'	ninj-un	ninj-	nind-
3	'to tie up'	kunj-un	kunj-	kund-
4	'to write'	kach-un	kach-	kak-
5	'to hold'	much-un	much-	mut-
6	'to give'	turas-un	turas-	turas-
7	'to invite'	yub-un	yub-	yub-
8	'to read'	yum-un	yum-	yum-
9	'to die'	shin-un[1]	shin-	shin-

[1] There is a ninth type of C-verb, *shin-un* '(animals) die,' but it is not included in the rest of this textbook except for this chapter and in Lesson 2. See *Wordbook*, p. xv, p. 161.

The **Gerund Root** is used to make the Gerund Forms and other various forms (see below). For the V-verbs, the Gerund Root is identical to the Basic and Negative Roots.

Verb	DIC.FORM	B.ROOT	N.ROOT	G.ROOT
V-verb ('to take')	tu-in	tu-	tu-	tu-

For C-verbs, Gerund Root endings are all different from the Basic and Negative Roots except for #1 and #4, which have identical endings in their Basic and Gerund Roots, and #9, which has identical Basic and Negative Roots.

	C-verb	DIC.FORM	B.ROOT	N.ROOT	G.ROOT	
1	'to swim'	ʔwiij-un	ʔwiij-	ʔwiig-	ʔwiij-	j-g-j
2	'to sleep'	ninj-un	ninj-	nind-	nint-	j-d-t
3	'to tie up'	kunj-un	kunj-	kund-	kunch-	j-d-ch
4	'to write'	kach-un	kach-	kak-	kach-	ch-k-ch
5	'to hold'	much-un	much-	mut-	mutch-	ch-t-tch
6	'to give'	turas-un	turas-	turas-	turach-	s-s-ch
7	'to invite'	yub-un	yub-	yub-	yud-	b-b-d
8	'to read'	yum-un	yum-	yum-	yud-	m-m-d
9	'to die'	shin-un	shin-	shin-	shij-	n-n-j

3.2.2 Primary Forms

Table 1 below shows nine primary forms (first column), how they are made (the second column), examples (the third and fourth columns), and the lesson in which they were first introduced. The parentheses in the second column indicate a consonant that appears for V-verbs, but not for C-verbs. Some of the primary forms appear in the final position of the main clause (i.e., sentence) (e.g., Finite, Negative, Intentional), while others appear in a non-main clause (e.g., Adverbial, Gerund).

Table 1. Primary Forms

Primary Forms	Morphological Process	V-verb	C-verb	Lesson
Dictionary Form (DIC.ORM)	= headword in dictionary	tu + in	kach + un	L1[B2]
Finite Form (FIN.FORM)	= any *n*-ending form	tu + in	kach + un	L4[A3]
Adnominal Form (ADNOM.FORM)	← change -*n* of Finite Form to -*ru*	tu + iru	kach + uru	L4[A3]
Apocopated Form (APO.FORM)	← drop -*n* from Finite Form	tu + i	kach + u	L1[B2]
Ra Form (RA.FORM)	← APO.FORM + *ra*	tui-ra	kachu + ra	L7[A2]
Negative Form (N.FORM)	← N.ROOT + *(r)an*	tu + ran	kak + an	L2[C3]
Intentional Form (INT.FORM)	← N.ROOT + *(r)a*	tu + ra	kak + a	L5[C2]
Adverbial Form (ADV.FORM)	← B.ROOT + *i*	tu + i	kach + i	L4[A4]
Gerund Form (G.FORM)	← G.ROOT + *(t)i*	tu + ti	kach + i	L3[A1]

(1) The **Dictionary Form** is used as the nonpast tense form.

(2) The **Finite Form** is any -*n* ending form including the nonpast (*kachu-n* '(will) write') and past (*kacha-n* 'wrote') tense forms, and the negative forms (*kaka-n* 'not write').

(3) The **Adnominal Form** is used when a verb modifies a noun as in the relative clause construction (*tuiru tchu* 'a person who takes it'; *tachuru tchu* 'a person who stands'). It is also used in one of the focus constructions with the focus particle *du* [L4(A4)], Topic 8.

(4) The **Apocopated Form** is the Finite Form without the final -*n*, and is used with different ending elements to create, for instance, the PAST-2 (*tui-tan* '(he) took it'; *tachu-tan* '(she) stood') and conjunctive construction (*tui-shiga* '(I) took, but…'; *tachu-shiga* '(I) stood, but…').

(5) The **Ra Form** is used in the second focus construction with the focus particle *ga* ('I wonder if…') [L7(A2)], Topic 8)

(6) The **Negative Form** here means the nonpast negative form, but it can be modified into the past negative by adding -*tan* (*turan-tan* '(I/he/she) did not take it'; *kakan-tan* '(I/he/she) did not write').

(7) The **Intentional Form** is to show the speaker's will to carry out an act ('I will do it') or their intent to invite others ('Let's do it').

(8) The **Adverbial Form** is used in many different constructions (e.g., *tui yassan* 'easy to take'; *tui gurisan* 'hard to take'; *tui yuusun* 'can take it').

(9) The **Gerund Form** is also used in many different constructions (e.g., *tuti-kwiin* 'please give it to (me/him/her)'; *tuti-neen* 'end up taking it').

Table 2 below shows selected primary forms for nine **irregular verbs**, that undergo significant morphological changes.

Table 2. Primary Forms of Irregular Verbs

Primary Forms	'to do'	'to go'	'to come'	'to say' [1]	'to see'	'to be' (COP)	'to be/exist' (animate)	'to be/exist' (INANIM)	'to be, go etc.' (honorifics)
DIC.	sun	ichun	chuun	iin	nnjun	yan	wun	an	-misheen
ADNOM.	suru	ichuru	chuuru	iiru	nnjuru	yaru	wuru	aru	-misheeru
RA	sura	ichura	chuura	iira	nnjura	yara	wura	ara	-misheera
INT.	sa	ika	kuu	ira	nnda	—	wura	—	—
NEG.	san	ikan	kuun	iran	nndan	aran*	wuran	neen	-misooran
ADV.	shii	ichi	chii	ii	nnji	yai	wui	ai	-misheei
GER.	sshi	ʔnji	tchi	ichi	nnchi	yati	wuti	ati	-misoochi

[1] There are alternative forms for 'say', which are *ʔyun* and *iyun*.

3.2.3 Constructions

Roots and primary forms are used as building blocks to create various other forms and constructions. For example, the Basic Root is used to create the Polite Form (e.g., *tu-ibiin* 'will take'), and the Adverbial Form is used to create the Desiderative Construction (e.g., *tui-busan* 'want to take it'). All the constructions introduced in this book appear in two tables in Appendix 2.

3.3 Predicate Forms

This section shows selected predicate forms for both statements and questions in the plain and polite paradigms.

3.3.1 Plain Forms

Table 3 shows different statement forms in the Plain Form while Table 4 shows different types of questions and the hortative form in the Plain Form.

Table 3. Statement Forms

	V-verb	C-verb
Nonpast Affirmative	tuin	muchun
Nonpast Negative	turan	mutan
PAST-1	tutan	mutchan
PAST-2	tuitan	muchutan
Past Negative	turantan	mutantan

Table 4. Question and Hortative Forms

	V-verb	C-verb
Yes/no-question	tuim-i	muchum-i
Wh-question	tui-ga	muchu-ga
PAST-1 yes/no-question	tuti-i	mutchi-i
PAST-2 wh-question	tuita-ga	muchuta-ga
Negative Question	turan-i	mutan-i
Negative wh-question	turan-ga	mutan-ga
Hortative	tura	muta

3.3.2 Polite Forms

The Polite Form is made by adding *-ibiin* to the Basic Root of V-verbs and *-abiin* to that of C-verbs. Both *-ibiin* and *-abiin* behave like V-verbs. Table 5 shows all basic statement forms while Table 6 shows question and hortative forms. Table 7 shows irregular verbs in their Polite Form.

Table 5. Basic Statement Forms

	V-verb	C-verb
Nonpast Affirmative	-ibiin	-abiin
Nonpast Negative	-ibiran	-abiran
PAST-1	-ibitan	-abitan
PAST-2	-ibiitan	-abiitan
Past Negative	-ibirantan	-abirantan

Table 6. Question and Hortative Forms

	V-verb	C-verb
Yes/no-question	-ibiim-i	-abiim-i
Wh-question	-ibiii-ga	-abii-ga
Past yes/no-question	-ibiti-i	-abiti-i
Past wh-question	-ibita-ga	-abita-ga
Negative Question	-ibiran-i	-abiran-i
Negative wh-question	-ibiran-ga	-abiran-ga
Hortative	-ibira	-abira

✍ V-verbs (e.g., *tu-ibiin* 'to take', *wara-ibiin* 'to laugh') have secondary forms (e.g., *tuy-abiin*, *waray-abiin*), and conjugate with the *-abiin* suffix.

Table 7. Irregular Verbs in the Polite Form

'to do'	'to go'	'to come'	'to say'	'to see'	'to be' (COP)	'to be/exist' (ANIM)	'to be/exist' (INANIM)	'to be, go, etc.' (honorifics)
sabiin	*ichabiin*	*chaabiin*	*iyabiin*	*nnjabiin*	*yaibiin*	*wuibiin*	*aibiin*	*-misheebiin*

TOPIC 4

Adjectives

Okinawan adjectives consist of a root and a suffix (Hokama 1971:39). The suffix is *-san* (Type A) or *-shan* (Type B) (cf. Miyara 2019:155–156). The two types of adjectives may not be distinguished in the non-past finite form (OGJ1, p. 82), but are different in the negative and adverbial forms (see the discussion later in this section). In addition, a small number of adjectives (Type C) have an irregular nonpast tense finite form (Miyara 2019:154–156). A few examples are shown below.

(Type A)

- *chura-san*   'beautiful'
- *maa-san*   'tasty'
- *magi-san*   'big'
- *achi-san*   'hot'
- *hii-san*   'cold'

(Type B)

- *uturu-shan/uturu-san*   'fearful'
- *ichuna-shan/ichuna-san*   'busy'
- *kashima-shan/kashima-san*   'annoying'
- *kana-shan/kana-san*   'lovely, affectionate'

(Type C)

Note: What is in ( ) does not exist and is a hypothetical form.

- (*waru-san*) = *wassan*   'bad'
- (*garu-san*) = *gassan*   'light in weight'

Adjectives appear in the Finite, Adnominal, Adverbial, and Apocopated Forms.

4.1. Finite Form

The Finite Form of an adjective ends in *-san/-shan* as noted above. The suffix *-san/-shan* originated from the existential verb *an* 'to exist (for an inanimate subject)' (= *takasa-an* → *taka-san*). Thus, the predicative adjective conjugates according to the paradigm for *an*.

- *an* (non-PST)   *atan* (PST)   *nee(ra)n* (NEG)   *nee(ra)ntan* (NEG.PST)
- *magisan*   *magisatan*   *magikoonee(ra)n*   *magikoonee(ra)ntan*

Note the formation of the negative finite forms. The Negative Form is constructed with its Adverbial Form (*-ku*) followed by the contrastive topic marker (*ya*), yielding *koo* (← *ku + ya*), which is then followed by the negative forms of *an* (i.e., *-nee(ra)n* and *-nee(ra)ntan*). Note that the Adverbial Form ends with *-ku* for Type A and *-shiku* for Type B.

- (Type A) *maasa-* → *maaku-* → *maaku + ya* → *maa koo* → *maa koo nee(ra)n*
- (Type B) *ichunasha-* → *ichunashiku-* → *ichunashiku+ya* → *ichunashi koo* → *ichunashi koo nee(ra)n*

For Type C, the Negative Form seems to fluctuate between *wakkoo nee(ra)n* and *warukoo nee(ra)n* in Naha (OGJ2, p. 312).

The table below shows a comparison of the Plain and Polite Forms.

	NONPAST	PAST	NEGATIVE	NEG-PAST
Plain form	*maasa-n*	*maasa-tan*	*maakoo nee(ra)-n*	*maakoo nee(ra)n-tan*
Polite form	*maasa-ibiin*	*maasa-ibiitan*	*maakoo nee-biran*	*maakoo nee-bi(ra)n-tan*

- *Kunu tui ya churasan*   'This bird is beautiful.'
- *Kunu muuchii ya maakoo neeran*   'This *muuchii* is not tasty.'
- *Chuuya ippee hiisatan*   'It was very cold today.'

4.2. Adnominal Form

The Adnominal Form is used when adjectives modify a noun. The Adnominal Form ends in *-s(h)aru* instead of *-s(h)an* (the first example). The Negative Form does not have a different Adnominal Form, and the same form is used (the second example). (See Topic 8 for the use of Adnominal Form in focus sentences.)

- *Anu churasaru tui ya nuu ndi ii ga?*   'What is that beautiful bird called?'
- *Maakoo neeran muuchii.*   'a *muuchii* that is not tasty / a poor-tasting *muuchii*'

In addition to the Adnominal Form, the Adjectival Root can be used to modify a noun directly. This is a productive word formation process in Okinawan, but not in Japanese.

Adjectival Root	vs.	Adnominal Form	
• *magi iyu*	vs.	*magisaru iyu*	'big fish'
• *guma saba*	vs.	*gumasaru saba*	'small slippers'

Sometimes, there is a semantic contrast between the two morphological processes. See below.

Adjectival Root	vs.	Adnominal Form	
• *guma jin* 'small change'	vs.	*gumasaru jin*	'small coin (in size)'
• *ufu tchu* 'adult'	vs.	*ufusaru tchu*	'many people, crowd'

However, the above contrast does not always appear. In the following examples, only the Adjectival Root is used to modify a noun. (Further exploration is necessary to uncover the form-meaning correlation.) In the following examples, ˣ indicates ungrammatical forms.

Adjectival Root	vs.	Adnominal Form	
• *mii mun*	vs.	ˣ*miisaru mun*	'new thing'
• *furu ganchoo*	vs.	ˣ*furusaru ganchoo*	'old glasses'

There is an interesting pair, *yii* and *yutasan*. Both mean 'good', but the former appears as an Adjectival Root only (Miyara 2019:163).

- *yii ʔwaachichi* — 'nice weather'
- *yii mun* — 'a good thing'
- *yii kangee* — 'a good idea'

The adjective *yutasan/yutasaru* is limited in usage.

- *yutasami?* — 'Is it okay?'
- *yutasaru gutu unigeesabira.* — 'Please take good care of me' (greeting expression)

4.3. Adverbial Form

The Adverbial Form of an adjective ends with *ku* (Type A) or *shiku* (Type B). As discussed above, the Adverbial Form is used in the formation of negative adjectives, but it is also used to modify a verb as a regular adverb.

(Type A)

- *maasan* → *maaku* 'voraciously'
- *magisan* → *magiku* 'big (adv.)'

(Type B)

- *uturashan / uturusan* → *uturushiku* 'fearfully'
- *ichunashan / ichunasan* → *ichunashiku* 'busily'

Here are some examples of adverbial use.

- *Kunuguroo ichunashiku soon.* 'I have been busy these days.'
- *Kuchi magiku akiti kwimisheebiri.* 'Please open your mouth wide.'

The Adverbial Form appears with *nain* 'become' to indicate a changed state.

- *Gooyaachanpuruu ya maaku natoon.* 'The gooyaachampuru has become tasty.'
- *Kunu usajee ujiraashiku natoon.* 'This rabbit has become cute.'
- *Munu nu dee ya takaku naibitii?* 'Has the price gone up?' (Hanazono 2020:69)

4.4. Apocopated Form

The Apocopated Form is used in a number of constructions. This form is made by dropping *n* from the Dictionary Form (e.g., *achisa* ← *achisa-n*) and other Finite Forms.

(a) The Apocopated Form functions as a noun and can take the topic particle *ya* (e.g., *achisa* + *ya* → *achisaa*) in the construction with *a shiga* 'although it is…'

- *Achisaa a shiga…* 'Though it is hot…'
- *Fusaa a shiga…* 'Though I want it…'
- *Uturusaa a shiga…* 'Though I am afraid…'

(b) The Apocopated Form of 'sensation/emotion' adjectives [L10(B4)] can appear with the verb *sun* to indicate a speaker's inference of the third person's internal state (e.g., *Achisa soon* 'He/she seems hot' / 'He/she is showing signs of feeling hot').

- *Fusa sun.* 'He/she seems to want…' (Miyara 2000:52)
- *Hajikasa sun.* 'He/she seems embarrassed/ashamed.' (Miyara 2000:52)
- *Warabee maasa mun kadi ussa soon.* 'Eating delicious food, the child looks happy.'
- *Tanmee tu ʔnmee ya ʔnmaga kanasa sooibiin.* 'Grandpa and Grandma love their grandchildren.' (Hanazono 2020:152)

This construction turns adjectives into verbs, i.e., 'to do something in such a way'. For example, the adjective *atarasan* means 'precious, valuable', and *atarasa sun* means 'cherish, value highly, or 'in a manner you cherish it' as in the next example. Note that *sshi* is the G.FORM of *sun*.

- *Deedakasaru munu yakutu **atarasa sshi** chikariyoo.*   'This is an expensive thing; please use it sparingly.'

(c) The Apocopated Form can also be followed by the nominalizer *shi* (e.g. *maasa shi*), which represents nominal concepts, such as 'person', 'thing', 'place', 'time', etc. The entire phrase can be followed by the particle *ya* (e.g. *maasa shi ya* → *maasashee*) when it serves as a topic of a sentence [L4(B3)].

- *Ichiban maasa **shee** kunu iyu yaibiin.*   'The **one** that is most delicious is this fish.'
- *Achisa **shee** hachigwachi yan.*   'The **one** that is hot is August.'

(d) The Apocopated Form can be followed by *nu* to make a reason clause.

- *Kunu ushiroo achisa**nu** numaran.*   'Because this soup is hot, I cannot drink it.'
- *Saataa nu amasa**nu**…*   'Sugar is sweet, so…'

TOPIC 5

Questions

Questions are divided into two types: yes/no-questions and wh-questions. The yes/no-question is marked by a sentence final particle (SFP), -i or naa, while the wh-question is marked by ga. Both -i and naa appear after the Finite Form. The wh-question is marked by ga, which appears after the Apocopated Form. There are also self-directed questions ('I wonder if / wh- etc.') which are marked with gayaa. These SFPS are obligatory to mark a question. [Abbreviations in the table: H=Hanazono 2020, M=Miyara 2019]

Preceding Element	Question Particle	Example	Type of Question	English Example	Lesson
FIN.FORM	*-i*	kamum-i	Yes/no-question	'Do you…?' 'Are you…?'	L3[B2–3] M (95–96)
FIN.FORM	**naa**	kaman naa	Yes/no-question (soft)	'Do you…?' 'Are you…?'	L5[C4] H (L8)
APO.FORM	**ga**	kamu ga	Wh-question	'Wh-…?'	L1[B4] M (96–97)
APO.FORM	**gayaa**	kamu gayaa	Self-doubt	'I wonder if / wh-'	L3[B5]

5.1. Yes/No-Question Particles

(1) *-i*: This question particle is used for yes/no questions. It triggers a morphophonological change when it follows non-past affirmative forms of verbs and adjectives (both plain and polite): the final *n* of the non-past affirmative form will change to *m*, making the final element of a question *m-i*.

- *Kuree ?yaa mun ya**m**-i?* (← ...ya**n**-i)   'Is this yours?'
- *Achaa ichu**m**-i?* (← ...ichu**n**-i)   'Are you going tomorrow?'
- *Kunu gurukunoo maasa**m**-i?*   'Is this *gurukun* fish tasty?'
  (← ...maasa**n**-i)
- *Shinshii ya yamatunchu yaibii**m**-i?*   'Is the teacher a Japanese person?'
  (← *yaibii**n** -i*)

However, the *n* of the negative form (e.g., *ikan* 'do not go') does not change to *m* (e.g., *ikan-i*). A negative question is often interpreted as an invitation ('Don't you want to go?') or a rhetorical question ('You really can't do it?') (see the last example below).

- *Kuree ?yaa mun ya **aran**-i?*   'Isn't this yours?'
  (← ...**aran**-i)
- *Shinshii ya yamatunchu ya **aibiran**-i?*   'Isn't the teacher a Japanese person?'
  (← *aibiran -i*)
- *Kunu gurukunoo **maakooneen**-i?*   'Isn't this *gurukun* fish tasty?' (asking
  (← ...**maakooneen**-i)   someone who refuses to eat the fish)
- *Majun ika**n**-i?*   'Won't you go together?' (invitation)
- *Junni Eegoo nara**n**-i?*   'You really can't speak English? (I
     think you can.)' (rhetorical question)

In the case of past-tense questions, *-i* is attached to the G.FORM of both PAST-1 ('Did you do...?') and PAST-2 ('(Did you see) me/him/her do...?') as well as the past negative ('Didn't you/he etc....?'). It can also follow the past adjective G.FORM as well.

- *Munu ka**di**-i?*   (← ...*kad-an*, PAST-1)   'Did **you** eat?'
- *Munu kamu**ti**-i?*   (← ...*kamut-an*, PAST-2)   'Did (you see) **me/him** eating?'
- *Munu kaman**ti**-i?*   (← ...*kamant-an*, PAST-1)   'Didn't **you** eat?'
- *Kunu gurukunoo maasa**ti**-i?*   (← ...*maasat-an*)   'Was this *gurukun* fish tasty?'

The table below summarize these different forms for verbs and adjectives.

Verbs

	NON-PAST	NEGATIVE	PAST-1	PAST-2	NEG-PAST
Statement	kamun	kaman	kad-an	kamut-an	kamant-an
Question	kamum-i	kaman-i	kadi-i	kamuti-i	kamanti-i

Adjectives

	NON-PAST	NEGATIVE	PAST	NEG-PAST
Statement	*maasan*	*maakoonee(ra)n*	*maasat-an*	*maakoonee(ra)nt-an*
Question	*maasa**m-i***	*maakoonee(ra)**n-i***	*maasa**ti-i***	*maakoonee(ra)**nti-i***

This particle can also appear directly after a noun without the copula.

- *Taruu-i?*   'Is it Taro?' (Sakihara 2018:271)
- *ʔyaa-n chui-i?*   'Are you alone, too?' (ibid.)
- *Makutu-i?*   'Is it true?' (ibid.)
- *Ganjuu-i?*   'Are you well?'

(2) **naa**: This is another particle used for yes/no questions. Compared to an *-i*-marked question, *naa*-marked questions are softer. The speaker of the first example may be assuming the addressee will go back to his village directly after sightseeing and is checking if his assumption is correct. The second question is from the song "Haisai Ojisan." A young man is asking the old man next door if he has any leftover *awamori*. *Naa* questions are more appropriate in these friendly contexts.

- *Anshi unu atu shima nkai muduti ichun **naa**?*   'And after that (sightseeing), are you going back to your village?' (Sakihara 2018:285)
- *Yuubi nu sangoobin gwaa nukutoon **naa**? Nukutoora wanni wakiran **naa**?*   'Do you still have the three-*goo* (i.e., small) bottle (of *awamori*)? If there is some left, would you share some with me?'

Comparing the two negative questions below, the first with *-i* has a stronger coercive tone than the *naa*-marked version.

- *Kaman-i?*   '(Oh,) you don't eat?' (among friends)
- *Kaman naa?*   'Won't you eat?'

5.2. Wh-Questions

ga: This particle appears at the end of a wh-question with an interrogative word, such as *taa* 'who', *nuu* 'what', *maa* 'where', *ichi* 'when', *nuunchi* 'why', *chaa* 'how', and *chassa* 'how much'. It appears after the Apocopated Form of verbs (nonpast, PAST-1, and PAST-2) or adjectives.

- *Kunu toofoo chassa yaibii **ga**?*   'How much is this tofu?'
- *Ichi Tookyoo nkai ichu **ga**?*   'When are you going to Tokyo?'
- *Chinuu nuu kada **ga**?*   'What did you eat yesterday?'
- *Ittaa ya nuu soo **ga**?*   'What are you guys doing?'
  (Sakihara 2018:306)

5.3. Self-addressing Questions

gayaa: This particle expresses the speaker's self-doubt (i.e., 'I wonder'). It follows the Apocopated Form of the past and non-past forms of verbs and adjectives. It can appear with both yes/no- ('I wonder if…') and wh- ('I wonder wh-…?') questions.

- *Wannee kunu hunoo naa yuda **gayaa**.*   'I wonder if I already read this book.'
- *Aree kunu hun yuda **gayaa**.*   'I wonder if he read this book.'
- *Jiroo umusa **gayaa**.*   'I wonder which one is interesting.'
- *Acha aree maa nkai ichu **gayaa**.*   'I wonder where he will go tomorrow."

TOPIC 6

Clause Combining

When combining clauses, the initial clause is marked by a specific verb form such as the Gerund Form or a conjunctive word attached to a specific verb form. In the discussion below, the following notation is used:

[A __x (+ y)] [B]
(A=first clause, B=second clause, x=verb form, y=conjunctive word)

There are two major types of clause combining in Okinawan: (1) simple clause combining and (2) adverbial clause combining. The former connects two clauses with a simple 'and' relation.

6.1. Simple Clause Combining

The Gerund Form or the *(y)aani* form is used to combine clauses with a simple semantic relationship. To arrive at a specific interpretation, a number of semantic and pragmatic factors must be considered.

6.1.1. 'and' (1): [A ___G.FORM] [B] 'A and B' [L3(A1)]

(a) Sequential Actions: The same actor is engaged in two sequential actions.

- *Sannin nu faa nkai **chichidi**, ʔnbusun.* 'We will wrap it up with *sannin* leaves and steam them.'

The tense of the entire sentence is determined by that of the verb in sentence clause (B), as the Gerund Form in clause (A) in Modern Okinawan does not indicate tense. Compare *ʔnbusu* (nonpast) above and *ʔnbuchan* (PAST-1) below.

- *Sannin nu faa nkai **chichidi**, ʔnbuchan.* 'We wrapped it up with *sannin* leaves and steamed them.'

To clarify the sequential relation, the conjunctive particle *kara* can be added after the Gerund Form, or a conjunctive *anshi kara* 'and then' can be added at the beginning of the second clause.

- *Sannin nu faa nkai **chichidi kara**, ʔnbusu sa.*   'We will wrap this up with *sannin* leaves, and then steam them.'
- *Sannin nu faa nkai **chichidi, anshikara**, ʔnbusu sa.*   'We will wrap this up with *sannin* leaves, and after that, steam them.'

(b) Parallel Actions: Different actors are engaged in two separate actions at the same time.

- *Kazuko sanoo sanshin **fichi**, Taruu ya mooin.*   'Kazuko plays the *sanshin*, and Taro dances.'
- *Kazuko sanoo sanshin **fichi**, Taruu ya mooitan.*   'Kazuko played the *sanshin*, and Taro danced.'

(c) Manner: When one actor is engaged in two actions simultaneously, the first action is usually taken to indicate a manner in which the second action is carried out.

- *Nakamura sannoo isu nkai **yichi**, hun yumun.*   'Ms. Nakamura sits on a chair and reads a book.'

(d) Cause/Reason: The first clause (A) with the Gerund Form can be interpreted as a reason or cause for the second clause (B) as in the first example below, but this usage is limited. Cause/reason is normally expressed with a clause with *kutu/gutu* as in the second example [L4(B1)]. See the contrast between the Gerund Form (*kooti*) and the particle *kutu* (*koota kutu*) in expressing a reason.

- *Ufooku **kadi**, wata mitchoon.*   'I am full because I ate a lot.'
- *Chuu ya dateen {ˣ **kooti** / **koota kutu**}, achaa ya kooran.*   'I bought too much today, so I will not buy it tomorrow.'

6.1.2. 'and' (2): [A___B.ROOT + *(y)aani*] [B] 'A and B' [L6(A3)]

(-y appears with V-verbs, but not with the C-verbs.)

The -(y)aani form can be used instead of the Gerund Form to indicate sequential actions and manner (Nishioka and Nakahara 2006:72–73).

(a) Sequential

- *Amirika nkai **ʔnjaani** eego narain.*   '(He) will go to America and study English.'

(b) Manner

- *Shiitu nu chaa ya ama nkai **tachaani** yuntaku soon.* 'The students are standing there talking.'

6.2. Adverbial Clause Combining

Various conjunctive particles and verb forms are used to combine clauses with a variety of semantic relations. There are four main categories: temporal, logical, purpose, and conditional relations.

6.2.1. Temporal Relations

'When'   [A__ADNOM.FORM + **basu / tuchi** (**nee**)] [B] 'do B **when** doing A'
         [A__ADV.FORM + (**i**)**nee**] [B] 'do B **when** doing A'   [L10(B2)]
'Before' [A__ADNOM.FORM + **mee**] [B] 'do B **before** doing A'
'After'   [A__G.FORM + **atu**] [B] 'do B **after** doing A'
         [A__G.FORM + **kara**] [B] 'do B **after** doing A'   [L10(A2)]
'While'   [A__ADNOM.FORM + **ʔweeda/ʔweema**] [B] '**while** doing A, do B'   [L10(C1)]
         [A__ADV.FORM + **gachii/ganaa**] [B] '**while** doing A, do B'   [L8(C1)]
'And so forth' [A__ G.ROOT + (**t**)**ai**] [B__ G.ROOT + (**t**)**ai**] + **sun** 'doing A, B, **and so forth**'
                                                                                  [L6(A4)]

For the 'when' relationship, a *basu (nee) / tuchi (nee)* clause is used. Both nonpast and past tense Adnominal Forms can be used in (A), but their interpretations would be different. The same temporal relation can be also expressed by the Adverbial Form with (*i*) *nee*.

- *Chuugoku nkai **ichuru basu** nee / **ichii** nee visa turanee naran.* 'When (you) go to China, (you) must obtain a visa.' (i.e. You obtain a visa **before** going to China.)
- *Hawai nkai **ʔnjaru basu** nee / **ʔnjai** nee 'Kona coffee' nudan.* 'When (I) went to Hawaii, I drank Kona coffee.' (i.e., I drank Kona coffee **after** I got to Hawaii.)
- *Wannee chaa munu **kamuru basu** nee nmeeshi chikain.* 'When I eat food, I use chopsticks.'
- *Munu **kadooru basu** denwa nu kakatichan.* 'When I was eating food, the phone rang.'

For the *mee* clause, only the nonpast tense adnominal form is used in [A].

- *Wannee chaa munu **kamuru mee** tii arain.* 'I wash my hands before I eat.'

Both *gachii* and *ganaa* are possible for the temporal relation 'while'. The form to be used before this conjunctive particle is the Adverbial Form.

- *Kwaashi **kami gachii**, yuntaku sun.* 'While eating snacks, we chat.'

6.2.2. Logical Relations

'So'	[A__APO.FORM ***kutu/gutu***] [B]	'A, **so** B'	[L4(B1)]
'So'	[A__ADNOM.FORM + ***munnu***] [B]	'A, **so** B'	[L9(A3)]
'So'	[A__APO.FORM (adjective)-***nu***] [B]	'A (adj.), **so** B'	[L4(B2)]
'But'	[A__APO.FORM + ***shiga***] [B]	'A, **but** B'	[L4(B1)]
'But'	[A__ADNOM.FORM + ***munnu***] [B]	'A, **but** B'	[L9(A3)]

The conjunctive particle *kutu/gutu* following the Apocopated Form indicates the 'so' relation while *shiga* indicates the 'but' relation.

- *Achaa shiken ya **kutu** chuu ya ashibii gaa ikan* 'There is a test tomorrow, so I will not go out to play today.'
- *Ken sanoo biiru kooita **shiga**, numantan.* 'Ken bought beer, but did not drink it.'
- *Eego ya wakaran **shiga** amirika nkai ichibusan.* 'I don't understand English, but I want to go to America.'

Munnu can be interpreted as either 'so' or 'but' depending on the context.

- *Chuu ya achisaru **munnu**, yaa nkai utoochu sa.* 'It is hot today, so I will stay home.'
- *Hiisataru **munnu**, umi nkai ichutan.* 'It's cold, but he went to the beach.'

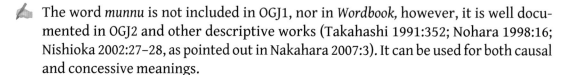
The word *munnu* is not included in OGJ1, nor in *Wordbook*, however, it is well documented in OGJ2 and other descriptive works (Takahashi 1991:352; Nohara 1998:16; Nishioka 2002:27–28, as pointed out in Nakahara 2007:3). It can be used for both causal and concessive meanings.

- *Kunu futonoo yafarasa**nu**, ninjiyassan.* 'This futon is soft, so it is easy to sleep.'
- *Kainanoo nama michi nu wassa**nu**, tuuig-urisaibii sa.* 'As for the Kainan area, its road is bad, so it is difficult to go through.

6.2.3. Purpose Relations

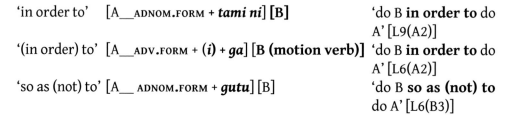

'in order to' [A__ADNOM.FORM + ***tami ni***] [B] 'do B **in order to** do A' [L9(A2)]

'(in order) to' [A__ADV.FORM + (***i***) + ***ga***] [B (motion verb)] 'do B **in order to** do A' [L6(A2)]

'so as (not) to' [A__ADNOM.FORM + ***gutu***] [B] 'do B **so as (not) to** do A' [L6(B3)]

There are two constructions that indicate 'in order to' relations. The first is the use of *tami ni* following the Adnominal Form, and the second is the use of *ga* after the Adverbial Form. The extra *i* appears after the Adverbial Form for C-verbs [L6(A2)].

- *Eego **narairu tami ni**, Amirika nkai ichun.*   'In order to study English, I will go to America.'
- *Machi-gwaa nkai shishi **kooi ga** ichun.*   'I go to the market to buy meat.'
- *Dushi gwaa ga saki **numii ga** chan.*   'My friend came to drink *sake*.'
- *Nakijin (n)kai sakura **nnjii ga** ika yaa.*   'Let's go to Nakijin to see the cherry blossoms.'

A somewhat similar relation can be also expressed by *gutu*.

- *Yii daigaku nkai iiru **gutu** kami sama nkai unigeesun.*   'I pray (to a god) so as to get into a good university.'
- *Guburii naran **gutu** kii chikiri yo.*   'Be mindful not to be rude.'

6.2.4. Conditional Relations

(a) The *(r)ee* Conditional
    'if'   [A__***(r)ee***] [B]   '**If** A, then B'   [L6(B2)]
    'unless'   [A__ N.FORM + {***dee / daree***}] [B]   '**If not** A, then B'   [L6(B2)]

This is a common conditional sentence type. Depending on the certainty of occurrence of event A, *(r)ee* is interpreted as either 'if' or 'when'. If A certainly will occur, the interpretation is 'When A happens, B happens', but if A's occurrence is not certain, the interpretation is 'If A, then B.'

- *Inagungwa ga **kuree** majun munu kamarii shiga yaa.*   'When/If the daughter comes back, we can eat meals together.'
- *Ari ga **iree**, muru chichu sa.*   'If he tells (us to do it), everyone will listen.'
- *Kunu hun **yumee** wakai shiga, **yuman dee / daree**[1] wakaran.*   'If you read this book, you will understand it. If you don't read it, you will not.'

[1] The negative counterpart of *ree* is *dee/daree*. *Daree* could be hypothesized to have derived from *du + a + ree* 'focus particle + a (← an) + ree' as follows: *du a ree → da ree → daree*.]

(b) The Concessive (*tin*) Conditionals
    'even if' [A__ G.FORM + ***n***] [B] '**Even if** A, B' [L9(C2)]

- *Achaa ya ami **futi n**, ichun.*   'Even if it rains tomorrow, I am going.'
- *Warabi (ga) **yati n**, nain doo.*   'Even if (s)he is a child, (s)he can do it.'

- ***Taa yati n** nain doo.*   'Whoever it is, (s)he can do it.' (i.e., 'Anyone can do it.')
- ***Takasati n**, kooin.*   'Even if it is expensive, I will buy it.'
- ***Yashikooneenti n**, kooin.*   'Even if it is not cheap, I will buy it.'

(c) The Provisional (*raa*) Conditionals
'If…is the case' [A__ APO.FORM + ***raa***] [B] '**If** A is the case, then B' [L8(B3)]

The Provisional Conditional is used on the basis of some premise, e.g., after he/she heard some information most probably from the addressee, such as 'it will rain tomorrow.' Following a premise, the speaker expresses his/her will or issues an invitation or command.

- A: *Achaa ya ami fuin ndi ii ssaa.*   'They said it will rain tomorrow.'
  B: *Ami **fuiraa** ikan.*   'If it rains tomorrow (as you said), I am not going.'
- A: *Wannee yaanoo Hawai nkai ichun.*   'I will go to Hawaii next year.'
  B: *Hawai nkai **ichuraa**, Kona coffee numi yoo.*   'If you are going to Hawaii (as you said), drink Kona coffee.'

(d) The Habitual (*nee*) Conditional
'If/when/whenever…,…' [A__ ADV.FORM + ***(i) nee***] [B] '**If/when/whenever** A, B never fails to happen' [L10(B2)]

The Habitual Conditional is formed with the Adverbial Form followed by *nee*. The vowel *i* appears after the Adverbial Form of a C-verb, i.e., the Adverbial Form has a long *ii* ending (see *ga* in 6.2.3). This extra vowel does not appear in V-verbs, some irregular verbs (*an*, *yan*, *wun*), and adjectives (e.g., *achisainee* 'if / when / whenever it is hot').

- *Chiburu yami-**i nee**, kusui numun.*   'Whenever I have a headache, I take medicine.'
- *Muuchii nai **nee**, fiiku nain.*   'Whenever *muuchii* (season) arrives, it becomes cold.'
- *Achisai **nee**, umi wutooti ʔwiijun.*   'If / when / whenever it is hot, I will swim in the ocean.'

TOPIC 7

Sentence Final Particles

Sentence Final Particles (SFPs) appear at the end of a sentence and inform the listener how to interpret the utterance. Furthermore, strictly speaking, SFPs do not communicate 'meanings', but instruct the recipient of a sentence how to interpret the information conveyed in it (cf. Blakemore 2000). SFPs can be broadly classified into two types depending on the propositions they are attached to: (1) Information Oriented Particles and (2) (Inter)action Oriented Particles. The former type indicates the speaker's stance towards the information that is being communicated, while the latter clarifies the meaning of a sentence involving the speaker's or addressee's actions. Although these two categories are defined separately here, the boundaries are not definite and some particles' functions may cross the two categories. Morphologically, some sentence final particles are bound morphemes that appear after, for example, the Apocopated Form, while some others are not, as they appear after a Finite Form. It should be noted that the list of SFPs in this section is by no means exhaustive (see Nishioka 2002, Nohara 1986, 1998, and Sakihara 2018 for more discussion). One important exclusion is *naa*, which is attached to a sentence ending in the Finite Form to form a yes/no-question. This SFP is discussed separately in Topic 5. (H in the last column in the two tables below refers to the lesson in Hanazono [2020].)

Table 1. Information Oriented Particles

PRECEDING ELEMENT	SFP	EXAMPLE	PROCEDURAL MEANING	APPROXIMATE ENGLISH EXPRESSIONS	LESSON
FIN.FORM	*doo*	*achisan doo*	Speaker's (= S's) information	'I tell you'; 'Believe me' 'You know?'	L1[A5]
APO.FORM	*sa*	*achisa sa*	Light assertion; discovery	'I tell you'; 'You know…'; 'Oh…'	L2[B7] H (L9)
APO.FORM	*ssaa*	*achisa ssaa* *nai ssaa*	S's information; emphatic assertion; experience-based	'Oh, boy!'; 'Indeed…'	L4[A5] H (L14)
FIN.FORM	*yaa* (1)	*achisan yaa*	Shared information	'Right?'; 'I know you agree with me'	L1[A5]
APO.FORM	*(ee) sani*	*chee (ee) sani* *nai sani*	Counterargument; agreement-seeking	'See?'; 'I told you so'; 'Don't you agree?'	L9[C3]
FIN.FORM	*tee*	*achisan tee* *nain tee*	Inference	'I believe…'	L4[A5]

Table 2. (Inter)action Oriented Particles

PRECEDING ELEMENT	SFP	EXAMPLE	PROCEDURAL MEANING	APPROXIMATE ENGLISH EXPRESSIONS	LESSON
INT.FORM	*na* (1)	*nudi nda na*	Speaker intention	'I will do it.'	L5[C4] H (L26)
INT.FORM	*na* (2)	*dii numa na*	Invitation	'Let's do it.'	L5[C4]
INT.FORM	*yaa* (2)	*kurasa yaa*	Invitation	'Let's do it, shall we?'	

7.1. Information Oriented Particles

This group of particles code the speaker's relation to the information conveyed. They are particularly sensitive to how the information is acquired and/or how much it is shared between interlocutors. While some information is naturally shared (e.g., today's weather), some others are privileged information which can be shared only through communication (e.g., what I ate this morning) (see Kamio 1994). Some information is already part of the speaker's knowledge, while other information has been newly obtained, and yet some others are obtained inferentially.

(a) **Doo** marks the information as exclusively and firmly belonging to the speaker. The speaker can strongly assert the statement with this particle (Sakihara 2018:25–26). It follows a Finite Form.

- *Kunu gurukunoo maasan **doo**.*   '(You may not know, so let me tell you) this *gurukun* fish is tasty.'
- *Asatu shinshii n mensheen **doo**.*   '(You may not know, so let me tell you) Asato sensei is also coming.'
- *Wannee ichun **doo**. ʔyaa n ikani?*   'I'm going. Aren't you going?'

(b) **Sa** is similar to *doo* in the force of assertion (Sakihara 2018:26–32). The statement may be based on the immediate experience or may be based on the speaker's conjecture. The first example below can be said by someone who has just tasted the fish or by someone who knows that the dish was prepared by a good chef. While *doo* follows any Finite Form, *sa* follows Apocopated Forms.

- *Kunu gurukunoo maasa **sa**.*   '(Just want to tell you) this *gurukun* fish is tasty.'
- *Asatu shinshii n menshee **sa**.*   '(Just want to tell you) Asato sensei is also coming.'
- *Anshee nuigusui mutchi chaabii **sa**.*   'I will bring ointment.' (Sakihara 2018: 203)
- *Makutu sookee nankuru nai **sa**.* (Proverb)   'If you do the right thing, things will be all right, you see.'

(c) **Sa** may indicate the speaker's sudden realization of something (see the first sentence below). It often appears with the resultative/evidential marker (*-(t)een*) [L7(C1)] and may be followed by *yaa* (Sakihara 2018:111–113).

- *Ai, achisa **sa**.*   'Oh, it's hot.' (Uttered when a mother touched her sick baby's head, and unexpectedly found out he has a fever. It could be used in a manner to alert others.)
- *Iina urijin natoo **sa** (yaa)!*   'Oh, it's already the *urijin* season! (Right?)'
- *Taruu ya chee **sa** yaa!*   'Oh, Taro is here!' (The speaker realized Taro arrived based on visual or hearsay evidence.) (*chee* is the *(t)een* form of *chuun* 'come'; originally from Kudo et al. (2007:152) cited by Sakihara (2018:112).)

(d) **Ssaa** is like *sa* above, but it indicates that the speaker has processed the new information more firmly. It is very often used in soliloquy with adjectives of emotion and sensation, but may also present information as something new for the addressee (the last example). It follows the Apocopated Form.

- *Wannee kurujaataa ya mashi yaibii **ssaa**.*   'I prefer brown sugar (*muuchii*).'
- *Hiisa ndi umuta shiga, chin dateen chichoo kutu achisa **ssaa**.*   'Although I thought it would be cold, but since I'm wearing a lot of clothes, it's so hot!'
- *Duu nu amakuma ʔwiigoosa **ssaa**.*   'I am itchy all over my body.' (A patient talking to a doctor) (Sakihara 2018:203)

(e) **Yaa** (1) indicates that the speaker wants to share the information with the addressee.

- *Kunu gurukunoo maasan **yaa**.*   'This *gurukun* fish is tasty, right?'
- *ʔami nu futooibiin **yaa**.*   'It is raining, right?"
- *Kuree achaa shi n shimabiin **yaa**.*   'We can do it tomorrow, right?'

(f) **Sani** or **eesani** is used when the speaker responds to the addressee's previous utterance or assumption.

- A: *Taruu n chuumi?*   'Is Taro also coming?'
  B: *Aree ichunasa kutu, kuun **eesani**.*   '(No,) I assume he is not coming since he is busy.'
- *ʔyaa-n ichu **eesani**.*   '(Just to be sure,) aren't you also going?'
- *Uri, ataranta (ee) **sani**.*   'See, you didn't win (a lottery ticket).'

If *sani* or *eesani* is pronounced with a rising intonation, the speaker requests the addressee's agreement on the information.

- *Uri, ataran (ee) **sani**?*   '(I believe) (the lottery tickets) won't hit a jackpot. Don't you agree?'

(g) **Tee** following the Finite Form (e.g., the nonpast form) presents information as the speaker's inference. It may present information as an explanation for the preceding information (see the last example) (Sakihara 2018:106, Shinzato 1991:4).

- *Kunu u-cha achisan **tee**.*   '(I believe) this tea is hot (because steam is coming out).'
- *Asatu shinshii n mensheen **tee**.*   '(I believe) Asato sensei will also come.'

- *Waa ga sun **tee**.*   'I will do it.' (This does not simply mean 'I will do it,' but it is the speaker's conclusion based on the circumstances. E.g., 'You don't do it? Ok, so the only option left is that *I* must do it' with a tone of mild frustration (Sakihara 2018:208)

7.2. (Inter)action Oriented Particles

This type of particle is attached to a sentence indicating the speaker's own action, which may involve the addressee directly or indirectly. What precedes these particles is the Intention Form of verbs (e.g., *kaka* < *kakan*).

(a) ***Na (1)*** often appears with a sentence showing the speaker's intention to do some action. The sentence marked with *na* may be self-directed speech, and the addressee may not be affected at all.

- *Kunu hun yudi nda **na**.*   'I will try reading this book!'
- *Ichika Hawai nkai ika **na** ndi umutoon.*   'I think I want to go to Hawaii someday!'
- *Kutuwaki shi unigee shi nda **na*** (Sakihiara 2018:198)   'With an explanation, I will ask (them to let me sleep tonight).'

(b) ***Na (2)*** often appears with a vocative marker such as *dii* when the speaker invites the addressee to do something together.

- *Dii, majun ika **na**.*   'Let's go together.'
- *Dii, uchinaaguchi sshi hanasi gwaa sa **na**.*   'Let's speak in Okinawan.' (Sakihara 2018:214)

(c) ***Yaa (2)*** involves the addressee in the decision making.

- *Majun kurasa **yaa**.*   'Let's live together. (Okay?)' (Sakihara 2018:216)
- *Suu ni nigayai miitu nara **yaa**.*   'Let's ask the father and get married. (Okay?)' (ibid., p. 216)
- *ittaa nkai ishiushi kwira **yaa**.*   'I will give you a stone grinder.' (ibid., p. 199)

TOPIC 8

Focus Concord

Okinawan has unique syntactic agreement patterns of 'Focus Concord' (henceforth, FC), known as *kakari musubi* in traditional Okinawan (and Old Japanese) grammar (Shinzato 2020a, Shinzato and Serafim 2013, Serafim and Shinzato 2021). Structurally, special focus particles *du* and *ga* call for unique conjugational forms other than the normal finite forms to end sentences for special rhetorical effects. Functionally, what comes before the focus particle is focused information (or new, highlighted/emphatically stressed information for the hearer), and the predicate part constitutes a presupposition (old, shared information). This syntactic agreement is known to exist only in a few languages in the world (Whitman 1997:173).

More specifically, the focus particle *du* triggers the Adnominal Form (or the *-ru* ending form) to make an emphatic statement, while the particle *ga* prompts the *Ra* Form to express doubts/self-inquiry (i.e., 'I wonder').

- …[X]Focus *du* …[(Predicate) ADNOMINAL.FORM] Presupposition   (Emphatic Statement)
- …[X]Focus *ga*…[(Predicate) RA.FORM] Presupposition   (Doubts/Self-inquiry)

8.1…du…ru

The Adnominal Form is made by changing the **n** of the Finite Form to **ru**:

- Copulas: {*yan* / *yaibiin*}   change n → ru   {*yaru* / *yaibiiru*}
- Verbs: {V-**n** / V-*biin*}   change n → ru   {V-**ru** / V-*biiru*}
- Adjectives: {A-*san* / A-*saibiin*} change n → ru   {A-*aru* / A-*saibiiru*}

8.1.1. Focusing on a Noun

Here are some examples. The sentences on the left side of the arrow are regular sentences, while those on the right side are the FC sentences. In a FC sentence, the focused element before the particle *du* is contrastively emphasized. For instance, *mijun* in the first sentence below is emphasized as an item selected vis-à-vis other types of fish, which are excluded. In the last sentence, *ya* changes to *ga* when followed by *du*; ˣ*ya du* is not permissible.

- *Kuree mijun {yan / yaibiin}.* → *Kuree mijun du {yaru / yaibiiru}.*
  'This is sardine.' 'This is *sardine* (not any other type of fish).'

- *Nama sutumiti mun {kamun / kamabiin}.* → *Nama du sutumiti mun {kamuru / kamabiiru}.*
  'I will eat breakfast now.' 'I will eat breakfast *now* (not any other time).'

- *Yuna ya {churasan / churasaibiin}.* → *Yuna ga du {churasaru / churasaibiiru}.*
  'Yuna is beautiful.' '*Yuna* is beautiful (not any other person).'

To put the second *du…ru* sentence above in context, see the next exchanges between A and B. A, upon seeing B eating a meal at around noon, assumes that B is eating lunch. B may deny this assumption (presupposition) in two different ways. B's first response emphasizes *nama* 'now', as in: 'I am eating breakfast *now* (because I was too busy this morning and did not have time to eat it till now).' B's second response emphasizes *sutumiti mun* 'breakfast', denying A's presupposition: 'I am eating *breakfast* (not lunch) now.'

- A: *Naa asaban jibun yan yaa.* (Seeing B eating a meal around noon) 'It is lunch time already.'
  B: (i) *Yii yii, nama du sutumiti mun kamuru.* 'No, I am eating breakfast **now**.'
  (ii) *Yii yii, nama sutumiti mun du kamuru.* 'No, it's **breakfast** that I'm eating now.'

The FC pattern can also be used in a yes/no-question. Below are three versions of a yes/no-question:

- *Ama wuti takarakuji utoomi?* 'Are they selling lottery tickets over there?'
- *Ama wuti takarakuji du utoorui?* 'Is it *lottery tickets* that they are selling over there?'
- *Ama wuti du takarakuji utoorui?* 'Is it *over there* that they are selling lottery tickets?'

The first question above is a simple yes/no-question. There is no presupposition in this sentence. The second one, on the other hand, consists of a presupposition and a focus. The presupposition is that 'they sell *something* over there', and the focus is on 'something'. That is, the speaker wants to know if 'something' is 'lottery tickets'. In contrast, the third sentence has a different presupposition: 'Lottery tickets are sold *somewhere* around here. (My friend told me so.)' The speaker wants to know if 'somewhere' (focus) is '(a store) over there' where lottery tickets are sold, which he perhaps assumes because he sees a long line of people.

In the wh-question below, '*someone* is coming' is known and presupposed. What is unknown is this 'someone'. Thus, the wh-word corresponding to this 'someone' is the interest of the question. In A's follow-up question, this 'someone' is a focus and is marked with *du*. This is a FC sentence highlighting the subject *Shogo ga* against the presupposition 'someone is coming'.

- A: *Achaa ya **taa** ga chuu ga? Shogo ga **du** chuu**rui**?*   'Who's coming? Is it *Shogo* that is coming?'
- B: *Wuu wuu, aibiran. Kenta ga **du** chaabii**ru**.*   'No, it's not. It is *Kenta* that is coming.'

8.1.2. Focusing on a Predicate

All the focused items so far have been nouns. However, it is possible to highlight a predicate (both adjectives and verbs). In this case, *du* attaches to the Apocopated Form of an adjective and the Adverbial Form of a verb. *Du* is then followed by *aru* (←*an*) and *suru* (←*sun*), respectively.

- *achisan* → *achisa du aru*.   (APOCO   + ***du*** + ***aru***)
- *kamun* → *kami du suru*   (ADV.FORM   + ***du*** + ***suru***)

The semantic difference between a noun-focus and a predicate-focus sentence is illustrated below. Bold type in the English translations indicates emphasis.

- *Uree achisan* → (i) *Uri ga **du** achisaru*. 'It is *that* **one** that is hot.'
  (ii) *Uree achisa **du** aru*. 'That is **hot** (not cold).'

The predicate-focused FC is also used in questions. Unlike regular *-i* questions, FC questions are used when the speaker assumes a certain context. In the FC version below, the speaker may have noticed that the addressee is sweating, and on the basis of this fact, he/she asks the question:

- *Achisam**i**?*   'Are you hot? (I have no idea; I am just asking.)'
- *Achisa **du** arui?*   'Are you hot? (I am asking because, e.g., you are sweating.)'

Here are the same parallels with a verbal predicate.

- *Saataa iri***imi**? 'Shall I put sugar (in it)? (I have no idea; I am just asking.)'
- *Saataa irii **du** surui*? '(So) shall I put sugar (in it)? (Since that's what you always ask me to.)'

8.2. Quasi-Focus Concord

In addition to the particle *du*, the adverb *anshi* 'extremely' also calls for the Adnominal Form (see the first version below). We call this phenomenon 'Quasi-Focus Concord.' As the second version shows, the Finite Form *achisan* is ungrammatical in the presence of *anshi*. However, that is not the case with a semantically similar adverb, *ippee* 'extremely,' which does not trigger the Adnominal Form. The ˣ indicates ungrammatical sentences.

- *Chuu ya **anshi** achisa**ru**.* 'Today it is very hot!' (***anshi***—Adnominal Form)
- ˣ *Chuu ya **anshi** achisan.* 'Today it is very hot!' (***anshi***—Finite Form) = ungrammatical
- ˣ *Chuu ya **ippee** achisa**ru**.* 'Today it is very hot!' (***ippee*** and Adnominal F.) = ungrammatical
- *Chuu ya **ippee** achisan.* 'Today it is very hot!' (***ippee*** and Finite Form)

8.3. ...ga...ra

The ***ga...ra*** pattern turns a statement into one of doubt or self-inquiry: 'I wonder if / I wonder wh-....' This is not directly addressed to the hearer so the hearer is not obliged to respond, though it is possible he/she does. The end form is called the *Ra* Form and is distinguished from the Intentional Form (i.e., NEGATIVE ROOT + *(r)a*) in this book (cf. Shinzato and Serafim 2013:57). It is of note that both of these are often and indiscriminately referred to as *mizen-kei*, or the *irrealis* form in the traditional Okinawan grammar (Uchima 1994:194). The *Ra* Form is made by simply changing ***n*** to -*ra*.

- Copulas: {*yan* / *yaibiin*}   change *n* → *ra* {*yara* / *yaibiira*}
- Verbs: {V-*n* / V-*biin*}   change *n* → *ra* {V-*ra* / V-*biira*}
- Adjectives: {A-*san* / A-*saibiin*}   change *n* → *ra* {A-*sara* / A-*saibiira*}

Here are some examples:

- *Anu tchoo Gushiken san **ga** {ya**ra** / yaibii**ra**}.* 'I wonder if that is Mr. Gushiken.'
- *Aree ichi **ga** {chuu**ra** / chaabii**ra**}.* 'I wonder when he will come.'
- *Ama ga **ga** {yassa**ra** / yassabii**ra**}.* 'I wonder if that place (store) is cheap.'

8.3.1. Focusing on a Noun

Putting the *ga…ra* construction into conversational contexts:

- A: *Tchu nu dateen wun yaa. Anu tchoo Osaka Naomi **ga** ya**ra**?* 'There are many people (around her). I wonder if that is Naomi Osaka.' (*Naomi Osaka* = a famous tennis player)

  B: *Naomi san yaibii sa.* 'It is Naomi.'

- A: *Aree akabanaa **ga** ya**ra**, diigu **ga** ya**ra**.* (pointing to red flowers) 'I wonder if that over there is hibiscus or *Erythrina*.'

  B: *Diigu yaibiin.* 'It is *Erythrina*.'

The focus particle *ga* can also appear after a wh-word, such as *ichi* 'when' and *taa ga* 'who + subject marker'.

- A: *Ushiimii ya ichi **ga** su**ra**. ?yaa wakaimi?* 'I wonder when the *Ushiimee* is. Do you know?'

  B: *Kundu nu nichiyoo yaibiin.* 'It is this Sunday.'

- A: *Taa ga **ga** chuu**ra**, yaa.* 'I wonder who is coming.'

  B: *Nna chaabiin doo.* 'Everyone is coming.'

8.3.2. Focusing on a Predicate

As in the case of *du* focus, adjectives and verbs can also be focused with the particle ***ga*** breaking the predicate as below:

- *achisan* → *achisa **ga** ara.* (APOCO + ***ga*** + *ara*)
- *kamun* → *kami **ga** sura* (ADV.FORM + ***ga*** + *sura*)

Compare the two different focus construction sentences in conversations below. In the first exchange, it is the nouns (*suba* 'noodle', *nuushi* 'owner') that are focused for a comparison, while in the second one, it is the predicate, *maasan*, and subsequently the clause as a whole that is focused.

- A: *Ama nu suba yaa ya chaa u-chaku nu mandoon yaa.* 'That noodle shop always has customers.'

  *Suba nu **ga** maasa**ra**, nuushi ga **ga** yutasa**ra**.* (*nuushi* = owner) 'I wonder if the noodles are good, or if the owner is good.'

  B: *Suba nu ippee maasa kutu du yaibiiru.* 'It is because their noodles are very good. (That's why they have many customers.)'

(That noodle shop has always many customers.)

- A: *Suba nu maasa **ga** ara.*   'I wonder if it (= the reason) is that the noodles are good.'

  B: *Uu, ama nu subaa ippee maasaibiin doo.*   'Yes, their noodles are very good.'

Here is another example with a verb in focus (*yumi **ga** sura* ← *yumun*) in B's utterance.

A: *Aree nama manga **ga** yudoora, sumuchi **ga** yudoora.*   'Is it the *comics* that he is reading? Is it the *book* that he is reading?'

B: *Sumuchee yumi **ga** sura?*   'I wonder if he reads books (because his tests are terrible).'

APPENDIX 1

VOCABULARY LIST

Abbreviations

add = additional vocabulary
Adj. = adjective
Adv. = adverb
Conj. = conjunction
Inj. = interjection
N = noun
N-proper = proper noun
N-wh = noun wh-word

Prel. = Preliminary Lesson
Pron. = pronouns
PRT = particle
SFP = sentence final particle
V-c = consonant verbs
V-hon. = honorific verbs
V-IRG = irregular verbs
V-v = vowel verbs

 Verbs and adjectives are listed in their dictionary forms. The polite prefix *u-* as in *u-cha* is not added except for conventionalized cases. Formulaic expressions are not given minor morpheme boundary breaks, e.g., *Uwakaku namisoochi.*

Word	Class	Meaning	Lesson
aakeejuu	N	'dragonfly'	2B(add)
Aashi	N-proper	'Awashi' (place name)	7A
achaa	N	'tomorrow'	2C(add)
achisan	Adj.	'hot'	1A(add)
achun	V-c	'to open (INTR)'	3A(add)
afakee	N	'clam'	7B
afasan	Adj.	'bland'	6A(add)

Word	Class	Meaning	Lesson
again[1]	V-v	'to rise (INTR)'	3A(add)
again[2]	V-v	'to be fried (INTR)'	3A(add)
again[3]	V-v	'to stop (INTR)' (used for 'rain')	6B(add)
agari	N	'east'	9B
agiin[1]	V-v	'to raise', 'to fry (food) (TR)'	3A(add)
agiin[2]	V-v	'to fry (food) (TR)'	3A(add)
ai	Inj.	(exclamation)	1B
ainaa	Inj.	(exclamation)	1B
ajimaa	N	'intersection'	5B
akaa	N	'red (N)' [*akasan* (Adj)]	6B
akagai	N	'light'	6B
aka-jin	N	'red clothes'	10A
akasan	Adj.	'red'	6B
akiin	V-v	'to open (TR)'	3A(add)
amasan	Adj.	'sweet'	6B(add)
Amawari	N-proper	'Amawari' (name of a historical figure)	9B
ami	N	'rain'	6B
an suraa	Conj.	'in that case' ← *an su-raa*	8B
an[1]	V-IRG	'to exist', 'there is'	2B
an[2]	V-IRG	'(an event) happens in/at [Place]'	9A
anmasan	Adj.	'sick'	4B
anshee	Conj.	'then'	1B
anshi	Adv.	'very' [*anshi*…ADNOM.FORM]	5C
anshikara	Conj.	'then'	1A
ansuka	Adv.	'that much'	4A
araimun	N	'laundry, something (to be) washed'	4A(add)

Word	Class	Meaning	Lesson
arain	V-v	'to wash'	10A(add)
ari	Pron.	'that (over there)'	1A(add)
ashibun	V-c	'to play'	7B(add)
ataimee	N	'no question', 'of course'	10C
atain	V-v	'to be hit', 'win'	6B(add)
atarasan	Adj.	'precious'	9A(add)
atchun	V-c	'to walk'	5A(add)
attaa	Pron.	'they'	2C
atu	N	'after' [G.FORM + *atu* = 'after...doing']	10C
atu	N	'later'	5B
awatiin	V-v	'to get excited', 'to panic'	10C(add)
ayaa	N	'mother'	2A(add)
ayakaain	V-v	'to share' [*ayakarachi* (G.FORM) 'let me receive']	10A
basu	N	'bus'	5A
bento	N	'boxed lunch'	3A(add)
bideogeemu	N	'video game'	1B(add)
biiru	N	'beer'	1A(add)
bikaan	PRT	'only'	7B
bikeen	PRT	'only'	7B
bingata	N	'textile with Ryukyuan motifs and designs'	8C(add)
boojishi	N	'pork loin'	5C
booshi	N	'cap', 'hat'	10A(add)
-busan	Suffix	'want to'	6A
cha	N	'tea' (→ *u-cha*)	1A(add)
-chaa	Suffix	'plural suffix used as in kinship terms'	2C
chaa[1]	Adv-wh	'how?'	1B

Word	Class	Meaning	Lesson
chaa[2]	Adv.	'always'	10A
chaa matooba	Adv.	'straight on'	5B
chaabira tai/sai	Greeting	'I am here (a greeting at the door when visiting someone)'	8B(add)
chaain	V-v	'(lights) to be turned off (INTR)'	6B(add)
chaasun	V-c	'to turn off (TR)'	6B(add)
chakushi	N	'the eldest son'	9B
chassa	N-wh	'how much?'	5B
chibiraasan	Adj.	'splendid', 'brisk', 'energetic'	9B
chiburu	N	'head'	4A
chichasan	Adj.	'close', 'near'	7A
chichi	N	'time' ← 'month' ('moon')	7A
chichiatai	N	'T-section (at the end of a road)'	5B
chichihi	N	'time' ← 'months and days'	10A
chichimun	V-c	'wrap'	3C
chichun[1]	V-c	'hear, listen'	1B(add)
chichun[2]	V-c	'(lights) to turn on (INTR)' [*chichi* (G.FORM), *chikiin* (TR)]	6B
chideekuni	N	'carrot'	5C
chiin	V-v	'to wear' [*chichi* (G.FORM)]	10A
chiiruu	N	'yellow' (also *kiiruu*)	6B
chikain	V-v	'to use' [*chikai* (ADV.FORM)]	7B
chikariin	V-v	'can be heard'	9B
chikiin[1]	V-v	'to soak'	7C
chikiin[2]	V-v	'to turn on (lights)' cf. *chichun*[2]	6B
chimu	N	'liver'	5C
chimu shinji	N	'soup with pork liver'	5C

Word	Class	Meaning	Lesson
chin	N	'clothes' (cf. *aka-jin* 'red clothes')	3C(add)
china	N	'rope', 'tug of war'	9A
chinbooraa	N	'sea snail'	7A
chinshi	N	'knee'	4A(add)
chinuu	N	'yesterday'	3B(add)
chira	N	'face'	4A(add)
chirudai sun	V-IRG	'get disappointed'	9C
chitu	N	'gift'	3A(add)
choodee	N	'siblings'	2C
chui	N	'one person'	2C
chu-keen	N	'once' [*ta-keen* 'twice']	9C
chukuin	V-v	'to make'	5C
chukuin	V-v	'to make' [*chukura* [5C]]	3A
churasan	Adj.	'beautiful' [*churasa ree* (COND) [L6(B2)]]	1A(add)
chuu	Adj.	'today'	2C(add)
chuubaa	N	'tough person'	5C
chuun	V-IRG	'to come' [*kuu* (IMP)]	5A
chuusan	Adj.	'strong'	4B(add)
daigaku	N	'university'	3C(add)
dakudakuu	Adv.	'heart pounding' (onomatopoeia)	9C
dariin	V-v	'to feel tired'	4B
dateen	Adv.	'a lot'	4B(add)
deekuni	N	'radish'	3C(add)
diigu	N	'*Erythrina*' (prefectural flower of Okinawa)	7C(add)
dikiyaa	N	'smart person/student'	7A(add)
dikka	Inj	'Let's' (same as *ditcha*)	5C(add)

Word	Class	Meaning	Lesson
ditcha	Inj	'Let's' (same as *dikka*)	5C(add)
doo	SFP	'I tell you'	1A
doyoobi	N	'Saturday'	6A
du	PRT-focus	Focus PRT [*du…ru* (ADNOM.FORM)]	4A
dushi	N	'friend'	2A
duu	N	'body'	4A
duu chui	Idiom	'by oneself'	7B(add)
duu humii	Idiom	'self-praise'	7C(add)
duu shi	Idiom	'by oneself'	7C
ee	Inj.	'interjection, attention-getter'	9B
ee sani	SFP	'didn't I say so?', 'wouldn't you agree?'	9C
Eego	N-proper	'English language'	1A(add)
faa	N	'leaf'	3C
fee	N	'south'	9C(add)
feesan	Adj.	'fast'	1B
fee-ʔnma	N	'fast horse'	10A
fichun	V-c	'to pull' [*fikee* (IMP)]	9C
fiisan	Adj.	'cold' (same as *hiisan*)	3A
fijai	N	'left'	5B
firumasan	Adj.	'surprising', 'strange'	7C
fudi	N	'brush'	7B(add)
fuin	V-v	'to fall (rain)'	6B
fujun	V-c	'to be satisfied'	9C
futon	N	'bedding'	5A(add)
fu(u)san	Adj.	'want'	6A (add)
ga[1]	PRT-focus	FOCUS CONSTRUCTION: *ga*…-RA.FORM	7A

Word	Class	Meaning	Lesson
ga[2]	PRT	'in order to...'	6A
gaa	PRT	'ga + ya'	7C
-gachii	Suffix	'while doing A, do B'	8C
gakkoo	N	'school'	2C
ganchoo	N	'eyeglasses'	10A(add)
gani	N	'crab'	8A(add)
ganjuu	N	'be in good health'	9A
gayaa	SFP	'I wonder'	3B
geta	N	'clogs' (Jp. loan)	10A(add)
-gisan	Suffix	'looks like'	10C
gohan	N	'rice'	7A(add)
gooyaa	N	'bitter melon'	1B(add)
Gosamaru	N-proper	'Gosamaru' (name of a historical figure)	9B
gumasan	Adj.	'small'	4A(add)
guree	PRT	'about'	10B
-gurisan	Suffix	'hard to V'	5A
gurukun	N	'type of popular fish in Okinawa'	1B(add)
gutee nu mandoon	Idiom	'very strong'	4B(add)
gutu	PRT	'like'	6B
-gwaa	Suffix	DIM (diminutive suffix)	5A
haabeeruu	N	'butterfly'	2B(add)
haarii	N	'boat race'	8B(add)
hachimachi	N	'headband'	10A
hachun	V-c	'to wear'	10A(add)
hain	V-v	'to run'	7A

Word	Class	Meaning	Lesson
haji	N	'It is expected that…'	8B
hajikasan	Adj	'embarrassing'	10A
hajimain	V-v	'to start (INTR)' [*hajimiin* (TR)]	9C
haka	N	'grave'	8A
hakama	N	'Japanese formal garments worn from waist down' (Jp. loan)	10A(add)
hama	N	'beach'	7A
hama uri	N	family outing in the spring (lit. going to the beach) (see Cultural Note [7(1)])	7A
hanafichi	N	'(have) a cold'	4A
haniin	V-v	'to run over'	10C(add)
hantushi	N	'half-year'	10A(add)
hashiru	N	'sliding door'	6A(add)
hatachi	N	'twenty years old'	2B
Hawaigo	N-proper	'Hawaiian language'	1A(add)
heein	V-v	'to spread widely', 'to be in fashion' (or *feein*)	8C(add)
hiisan	Adj.	'cold' (same as *fiisan*)	3A
hikooki	N	'airplane'	5A(add)
hikusan	Adj.	'low'	4A(add)
hiru	N	'garlic'	5C
hisa	N	'foot', 'legs'	4A(add)
huka	N	'outside'	8C(add)
hun	N	'book'	1A(add)
hushi	N	'stars'	1A(add)
-i	PRT	'question particle'	3B
ichain	V-v	'to meet' [*ichati* (G.FORM)]	10B

Word	Class	Meaning	Lesson
ichariba choodee	Idiom	'once we met, brothers/sisters forever'	10C
ichi ichi madi n	Idiom	'many years to come'	10A
ichiban	N	'best'	7A(add)
ichun	V-IRG	'to go' [*ichi* (ADV.FORM), *ika* (int), *ichuru* (ADNOM)]	5A
ichunasan	Adj.	'busy'	7A(add)
ifi	Adv.	'a little'	5C
ii	Response	'yes' (plain)	3A
iin[1]	V-v	'to enter', 'be put in (INTR)' [*itch-oon* (ASP)]	3B
iin[2] (*ʔyun, iyun*)	V-IRG	'to say'	1A
iina	Adv.	'already'	7A
ikirasan	Adj.	'few', 'small quantity'	2C
ikuchi	N-wh	'how old?'	2B
ikutai	N-wh	'how many (people)?'	2C
imisheen	V-hon.	'to say' (EXAL.FORM of *i-in*)	5C
in	N	'dog'	2A(add)
inchasan	Adj.	'short'	4A(add)
ippee	Adv.	'very'	1B
irichii	N	'simmered vegetables'	1B
irii	N	'West'	9B
iriin	V-v	'to put in (TR)' [*iri-tan/ittan* (PAST-1), *irii-tan* (PAST-2)]	3B
isatuu	N	'praying mantis'	2C(add)
ittaa	Pron.	'you' (plural-plain)	2B
iyu	N	'fish'	1A
ji	N	'o'clock'	7C(add)

Word	Class	Meaning	Lesson
jifi	Adv.	'by all means'	6B
jiru	N-wh	'which?' [*jiroo* ← *jiru* + *ya* (TOP)]	5A
joogu	N	'like…', 'person who likes a particular food (WB)'	7C
jooi	Adv	'by far', 'out of the question'	9A(add)
jooji	N	'skillful', 'good'	2A
jootuu	Adj.	'great', 'fantastic'	4B
junni	Adv	'really'	3B(add)
juu	N	'stacked bento boxes'	8C
ka(a)shii	N	'help' [*ka(a)shii sun* 'help (TR)']	9A
kaagi nu mandoon	Idiom	'very handsome', 'beautiful'	4B(add)
kachun[1]	V-c	'to write'	2C(add)
kachun[2]	V-c	'to win' [*kata nee naran* 'must win' [L6(C3)]]	9A
kadu	N	'corner'	5B
kafuu na mun	N	'lucky guy'	10B
kafuushi	N	'thanks' (said to someone younger)	10A
kain[1]	V-v	'to borrow'	4B(add)
kain[2]	V-v	'to cut' [*kati* (G.FORM)]	8A
kaji[1]	N	'number'	3C
kaji[2]	N	'wind'	8B(add)
kajimayaa	N	'97th birthday celebration (by lunar calendar)'	10A
kaki	N	'persimmon'	8A(add)
kakiin	V-v	'to wear'	10A(add)
kamun[1]	V-c	'to eat' [*kaman* (NEG)]	4A
kamun[2]	V-c	'(animal) to bite'	10C(add)
kanain	V-v	'to not be able to work'	8B

Word	Class	Meaning	Lesson
kanasan	Adj.	'lovely', 'dear' [*kanasa sun* 'love']	10B
kangeein	V-v	'to think'	10C(add)
kanji	N	'Chinese character' (Jp. loan)	7A(add)
kanjun	V-c	'to wear'	10A(add)
-kantii sun	Suffix	'difficult to...'	10B
kanzashi	N	'hair ornament' (Jp. loan)	10A(add)
kara[1]	PRT	'by means of (transportation)'	5A
kara[2]	PRT	'through'	5A
kara[3]	PRT	G.ROOT + *kara* = 'after...'	10A
karasan	Adj.	'spicy'	6B(add)
karasun	V-c	'to lend'	8A(add)
kata	N	'shoulder'	4A(add)
katamiin	V-v	'to carry on the shoulder'	9B
katasan	Adj	'hard'	5A(add)
katchun	V-c	'to win'	9A
keein	V-v	'to return' (INTR)	5C(add)
kii	N	'tree'	6B
kii chikiin	Idiom	'pay attention', 'be careful'	5C(add)
Kirin	N-proper	'Kirin beer'	2B
koo	N	'incense' (→ *u-koo*)	8C(add)
kooin	V-v	'buy' [*koora* 'will buy']	5C
kubi	N	'neck'	4A(add)
kubushimi	N	'cuttlefish', often served as sashimi	1B
kugani kutuba	N	'words of wisdom'	10C
kuji	N	'lottery'	6B(add)
kuju	N	'last year'	9A

Word	Class	Meaning	Lesson
kumu	N	'clouds'	6B(add)
kumun	V-c	'wear'	10A(add)
kunchi	V-c	'stamina'	5C(add)
kundu	N	'this coming…'	6A
kuneein	V-v	'to put up with', 'to forgive'	9B(add)
kunjun	V-c	'to tie', 'to chain' [*kundan* (NEG)]	3C
kuri	Pron.	'this'	1A(add)
kuruma	N	'car'	1B(add)
kurusan	Adj	'black'	6B
kusa	N	'grass'	8A
kushi[1]	N	'lower back'	4A(add)
kushi[2]	N	'back' (opposite of 'front')	5C(add)
kusui	N	'medicine'	4B
kutsu	N	'shoes' (Jp. loan)	10A(add)
kutu	PRT-Conj.	'so', 'because'	4B
kutu nu/ga an	Construction	'have done…' [*kutu ya neen* (NEG)]	10C(add)
kutushi	N	'this year'	9A
kuujun	V-v	'to row'	10B(add)
kwaashi	N	'sweets'	2A
kwatchii	N	'feast'	1B
kwatchii sabira	Greeting	(expression said before meal)	1B
kweeyun	V-c	'to become fat'	9C(add)
-kwiin	Suffix	with G.FORM 'do…for someone'	8A
-kwimisheen	Suffix	'benefactive' (EXAL) [*-misooran* (NEG)]	8C
-kwimisooree	Suffix	'please do…'	5B

Word	Class	Meaning	Lesson
maa	N-wh	'where?'	4A
maada	Adv.	'not yet' (same as *naada*)	10B
maagana	N	'somewhere'	4A
maasan	Adj	'delicious'	1A(add)
maasu	N	'salt'	6A
machigeein	N	'make mistakes'	9B(add)
Machigwaa	N-proper	'Makishi market'	5A
machiya	N	'small shop'	5A(add)
machun[1]	V-c	'to wait'	5A(add)
machun[2]	V-c	'to spray', 'to sprinkle'	10C(add)
madi	PRT	'as far as'	5A
madu[1]	N	'time'	6B(add)
madu[2]	N	'window'	4B(add)
magain	V-v	'to turn'	5B
magisan	Adj	'big'	4A(add)
majun	Adv.	'together'	6B(add)
makasun	V-c	'to beat'	9A(add)
makiin	V-v	'to lose'	9A
maniaain	V-v	'to be on time'	10B(add)
mashi	N	'better'	4B
mayaa	N	'cat'	2B(add)
mee[1]	N	'front'	5C(add)
mee[2]	PRT	'before'	10C
mensheen	V-hon.	'to go/come/stay (EXAL)'	5A
mensooree	V-hon. (greeting)	'Welcome!'	5C

Word	Class	Meaning	Lesson
michain	V-v	'to close (INTR)'	3A(add)
michi	N	'road'	5A
mi-chichi	N	'three months'	10B
michiin	V-v	'to close (TR)'	3A(add)
mii	N	'eye(s)'	4A(add)
mii nada guru-guruu sun	Idiom	'tears welling up in the eyes'	10C
miiduusan	Adj.	'long time no see'	9A
miiyun	V-c	'can be seen'	9B
miji	N	'water'	6A(add)
mimi	N	'ear(s)'	4A(add)
miruku	N	'milk', 'cream'	3A(add)
mooki	N	'profit'	5C
muchikasan	Adj.	'difficult'	1A(add)
muchun	V-c	'to have, hold'	2C
muduin	V-v	'to return' [*muduti* (G.FORM)]	10C
mun	N	'thing'	2C(add)
munnu	N	'because', 'although'	9A
munu	N	'thing', 'food'	4A
munu wakain	Idiom	'to become reasonable (after passing the teenage years)'	7B(add)
mun[u]ii	N	'local dialect', 'the way of saying'	8B(add)
murasachi	N	'purple'	3C
muru	N, Adv.	'all'	9C(add)
muuchii	N	'rice cake'	3A
muuchii biisa	N	'cold wave'	3A

Word	Class	Meaning	Lesson
n[1]	PRT	'also'	2A
n[2]	PRT	*yati n* = 'even if it's …', N + *ga n* = 'even for N', *tiichi n* = 'not even one' [7C]	7B
na	SFP	'will do', 'let's …'	5C
naa[1]	PRT	'already'	10A
naa[2]	SFP	'Is it the case that …'	5C
naa[3]	N	'name'	3B(add)
naa[4]	Adv.	'more'	3B
naada	Adv.	'not yet' (same as *maada*)	10B
Naafa	N-proper	Naha, the capital of Okinawa	1A(add)
naagi	N	'gift'	3A(add)
naahin	Adv.	'more'	8C(add)
Nachijin	N-proper	'Nakijin' (place name)	6A
nachun	V-c	'to chirp', 'cry'	7A(add)
nada	N	'tears'	10C
nagasan	Adj.	'long'	4A(add)
nagiin	V-v	'to throw'	8A(add)
nain	V-v	'to become', 'can do' [3B]	2B
nakami	N	'pig intestines'	1B
nama	N	'now'	3A(add)
narabiin	V-v	'to line … up', 'to arrange …' (TR)	8C
narabun	V-c	'to line up (INTR)' [*naradi* (G.FORM)]	8C
narain	V-v	'to learn'	6B(add)
-natee naran	Construction	'should not become …'	10C
-ndee	Suffix	with G.FORM 'try …'	9B
ndi	PRT	'that' (complementizer)	1A

Word	Class	Meaning	Lesson
ndiin	V-v	'to get wet'	7C(add)
-nee	PRT	'if/when…'	10B
-nee sun	Suffix	'have a feeling that'	6B
neen	V-IRG	negative of *an* (same as 'neeran')	2C(add)
-neen	Suffix	with G.FORM 'end up…'	9C
neeran	V-IRG	negative of *an* (same as 'neen')	2C(add)
nengajoo	N	'New Year's Greeting Card' (Jp. loan)	6B(add)
nichi	N	'fever'	4A
nichi ʔnjasun	V-c	'to run a fever'	5C
nifee deebiru	Greeting	'thank you'	1B
nifee doo	Greeting	'thank you' [less formal than *nifee deebiru*]	2A
nijiri	N	'right'	5B
nijuuichi	N	'twenty-one'	2B
-nin	Suffix	CLASSIFIER (for people)	2C(add)
ninjun	V-c	'to sleep'	5C
Ninufabushi	N-proper	'pole star', 'the North Star'	1B(add)
nishi	N	'North'	9C(add)
nji	PRT	'at' (same as *wuti*)	II (Topic 2)
nkai	PRT	'to'	5A
nkai[1]	PRT	'in', 'at'	2B(add)
nkai[2]	PRT	'into', 'with'	3C
nkashi	N	'long time ago'	9B
nnjun	V-c	'to see'	6A
n(n)na	N	'everyone'	5C
n(n)su	N	'miso', 'fermented soybeans'	3C(add)

Word	Class	Meaning	Lesson
nooin	V-v	'to recover (INTR)' [*noosun* (TR)]	6A
noosun	V-c	'to fix (TR)' [*nooin* (INTR)]	6A(add)
-nu	PRT	Adj…*sa* + *nu* (cause)	4B
nu[1]	PRT	genitive particle (GEN)	1B
nu[2]	PRT	subject particle	2B
nuin	V-v	'to ride'	8C (add)
nukuin	V-v	'to be left'	5C(add)
numun	V-c	'to drink'	3A(add)
nurain	V-v	'to scold'	8A(add)
nuu n neen	Idiom	'there is nothing' [G(C2)]	7C
nuudii	N	'throat'	4A(add)
nuugana	N	'something'	4B
nuunchi	N-wh	'why?'	9A
Oojima	N-proper	'Oojima' (place name)	7A
ooruu	N	'blue/green'	6B
Orion	N-proper	'the name of a popular Okinawan beer' (also the Orion constellation)	1A(add)
paarankuu	N	'percussion'	9B
rafutee	N	'a traditional Okinawan dish in which chopped pork is slow cooked with soy sauce, sugar, and awamori liquor'	1B
-(r)an nee naran	Suffix	'must'	6B
-(r)ariin[1]	Suffix	POTENTIAL: SITUATIONAL POSSIBILITY	7B
-(r)ariin[2]	Suffix	PASSIVE	8A
-(r)ee	Suffix	'if/when'	6B
sa	SFP	'I tell you', 'you know', 'I assume'	2B

Word	Class	Meaning	Lesson
saani	PRT	'by' (same as sshi)	6A
saaru	N	'monkey'	8A(add)
saasaa	Adv.	'heart pounding' (onomatopoeia), cf. dakudaku	9C
saataa	N	'sugar'	3B
saba	N	'slippers'	10A(add)
sabiin	V-hon.	'to do' [sabira (INT.FORM), sabiran (NEG)]	8B
sabiran	V-IRG	'do not' (POLITE NEGATIVE of sun)'	4B
sachi	N	'later', 'ahead'	10B
sagain	V-v	'come down' [sagati (G.FORM)]	4B
sai	Suffix	polite suffix—male (cf. Preliminary)	2A
saki	N	'sake', 'rice wine' (cf. u-jaki [8C])	1A(add)
sakkwii	N	'cough'	4B
sakura	N	'cherry blossoms'	6A
sangwachi	N	'March'	7A
sanmin	N	'calculation'	10A(add)
sannichi	N	'third day of the month'	7A
sannin	N	'*Alpinia zerumbet*' (name of plant in the ginger family)	3C
sashimi	N	'sashimi (raw fish cuisine)'	1A(add)
sawajun	V-c	'to make a racket'	10C(add)
shi[1]	PRT	'nominalizer' [shee ← shi + ya]	4B
shi[2]	PRT	'within' [ichi jikan shi 'within one hour']	7C
shi[3]	PRT	'by means of'	1A
shichi[1]	N	'like', 'fond of'	9A
shichi[2]	N	'time', 'season'	10B
shiga	PRT-Conj.	'however', 'but'	4B

Word	Class	Meaning	Lesson
shigu	Adv.	'right away'	5A(add)
shiija	N	'older siblings'	2C
shiisaa	N	'lion-dog statue'	1B(add)
shiisan	Adj.	'sour'	6B(add)
shiitu	N	'student'	1A(add)
shikaraasan	Adj.	'lonely'	4B(add)
shikuchi	N	'work'	8C(add)
shima	N	'Okinawan-style sumo wrestling'	4B(add)
shimiin[1]	V-v	'to close'	6A(add)
shimiin[2]	V-IRG	'to do (causative)'	9B
shimiin[3]	V-v	'to wear (on head, around the neck)'	10A
shimun[1]	V-c	'to complete (without a problem)' [*shimun doo* 'OK; sure' is often used to agree to do something:]	8A
shimun[2]	V-c	G.FORM + *shimun* = 'OK to do; permission'	10C
shinshii	N	'teacher'	1B(add)
shiran (t)chu	Idiom	'stranger'	10C
shiru	N	'soup' (→ *u-shiru*)	1A(add)
shishi	N	'meat'	5A(add)
shitaku	N	'people on the rope'	9B
shiwa	N	'worry'	8A(add)
shiwaashi	N	'December'	6B(add)
shokudoo	N	'cafeteria'	5C(add)
sooti chuun	V-IRG	'to bring (a person)' [*sooti chooru* (ADNOM.FORM)]	8A(add)
sooti ichun	V-IRG	'to take someone' [*sooti ʔnji* (G.FORM)]	8A(add)
ssaa	SFP	'exclamatory remark'	4A
sshi	PRT	'by' (same as *saani*)	6A

Word	Class	Meaning	Lesson
suba	N	'noodles'	7A(add)
suguin	V-v	'to hit'	8A(add)
sukaato	N	'skirt' (Jp. loan)	10A(add)
sumuchi	N	'book'	1A(add)
sun	V-IRG	'to do' [san (NEG), sshi (G.FORM)]	3A
sunui	N	'*mozuku* seaweed'	7B
surii	N	'procession'	9B
sushi	N	'sushi'	1A(add)
sutumiti mun	N	'breakfast'	10A(add)
suuji	N	'celebratory gathering'	10A(add)
suujuusan	Adj.	'salty'	6B(add)
ta chichi	N	'two months'	10B
taa	N-wh	'who?'	2C
taachi mee	Pron. + N	'the second one from here'	5B(add)
taarii	N	'father', 'dad'	2A
tachichi	N	'next month'	10B
tai[1]	Suffix	polite suffix—female (cf. Preliminary)	2A
tai[2]	N	'two people' (see also *tchai* and *ttai*)	2C
takasan	Adj.	'expensive', 'tall', 'big (nose)'	4A(add)
taki	N	'height'	6B(add)
tako raisu	N	'taco rice—Okinawan-American dish with a taco shell replaced by rice'	1A(add)
takushii	N	'taxi'	5A
tami (ni)	N	'for the sake of', 'in order to'	8A(add)
tanmee	N	'grandfather'	2A(add)
tanushimi	N	'fun'	6A(add)

Word	Class	Meaning	Lesson
tchai	N	'two people' (see also *tai*[2] and *ttai*)	2C
tchu	N	'person', 'people'	2C
tee	SFP	'I assume', 'I guess'	4A
-(t)een	Suffix	'has…ed' (RES)	7C
tideein	V-v	'prepare food for a special occasion' [*tideeti* (G.FORM)]	8C
tigami	N	'letter'	3A(add)
tiganee	N	'help'	3C
tii	N	'hand'	4A(add)
tii	N	'karate'	7A(add)
tiichi	N	'one'	7C
tiida	N	'the sun'	2C(add)
tinchi yohoo	N	'weather forecast'	8B(add)
tinjoo	N	'ceiling'	3C
tinpura	N	'tempura'	3A(add)
tinsagu	N	'balsam flower'	1B(add)
too too	Inj.	'OK', 'Come on!'	8C
too too (too)	Inj.	(exclamation)	2B
-toochun	Suffix	'preparatory aspect'	7C
ttai	N	'two people' (see also *tai*[2] and *tchai*)	2C
tu	PRT	'and'	2C
tu	PRT	'with', 'as' (compare with *tu* 'and'[L2G(C6)])	7B(add)
tuchi	N	'time'	9B(add)
tui	N	'bird'	2B(add)
tuin	V-v	'to take', 'to catch' [*tura* 'will get', *turaran* (NEG)]	2C(add)
tuji	N	'wife'	7C(add)

Word	Class	Meaning	Lesson
tumain	V-v	'(something) to stop' (INTR)	5B(add)
tumiin	V-v	'to stop (something)' (TR)	5B(add)
turasan	V-c	'to give'	8B
tushi	N	'age'	3C
tuuin	V-v	'to go through'	5A
u-	Prefix	POLITE PREFIX	1B
uchain	V-v	'to suit', 'to be becoming'	10A
Uchinaaguchi	N-proper	'Okinawan language'	1A
uchun	V-c	'to bite'	10C(add)
ufee	Adv.	'a little'	3B
ufooku	Adv	'a lot' (see *ufusan*)	7A(add)
ufu tanmee	N	'great-grandfather'	8C(add)
ufu ʔnmee	N	'great-grandmother'	10A
Ufugushiku	N-proper	'Ufugushiku' (family name)	8B
ufusan	Adj.	'many', 'much' [*ufooku* (Adv)]	2C
ufutchu	N	'adult'	3C(add)
ugushiku	N-proper	'Shuri Castle'	2B(add)
uin	V-v	'to sell'	5C(add)
ujiraasan	Adj.	'cute'	2C(add)
ukaji	N	'help'	6A
ukiin	V-v	'to get up (INTR)'	10A(add)
ukusun	V-c	'to wake up (TR)'	10A(add)
umi	N	'ocean'	1A(add)
umuin	V-v	'to think'	1A(add)
umus(s)an	Adj.	'interesting'	1A
unchikee-sun	V-hon.	'to bring someone' [G(B2)]	8B

Word	Class	Meaning	Lesson
uni	N	'ogre'	8A(add)
unjoo	Pron.	'you' (topic)' (singular-polite)	2B(add)
unju	Pron.	'you' (singular-polite)	2B(add)
unju naa taa	Pron.	'you' (plural-polite)	2B(add)
unnukiin	V-hon.	'say' (humble verb)	10A
uri[1]	Pron.	'that'	1A
uri, uri[2]	Inj.	'here, here'	1B
urizin	N	'spring-like season in Okinawa'	7A
usaasun	V-c	'to press', 'with *tii* ('hands')', 'to pray'	8C
usagain	V-hon.	'to eat/drink (EXAL)' [*usagati* (G.FORM), *usagamisheen*]	5C(add)
usaji	N	'rabbit'	6B(add)
usandee	N	'food offering to ancestors to be consumed [*usandee sun*] by the family later (WB)'	8C
ushiimii	N	'the day to pay respect to one's ancestors'	8A
usu	N	'salt water'	7C
uta	N	'song'	3A(add)
utabimisheen	V-hon.	'to give' [*utabimisheebiri* (IMP)]	10A
-utabimisheen	Suffix	'benefactive (EXAL)' [*-utabimisheebiri* (IMP)]	8C
utain	V-v	'to sing'	3A(add)
uttii	N	'day before yesterday'	3B(add)
uttu	N	'younger sibling'	2A (add)
uturusan	Adj.	'scary'	8B(add)
uu	Response	'yes' (plain)	Prel.
Uwakaku nai-misoochii?	Greeting	'You grew younger?'	1A
uya	N	'parents'	2C

Word	Class	Meaning	Lesson
waa	Pron.	'my'	2A
wakasan	Adj.	'young'	1A
wan	Pron.	'I, my'	1A(add)
wannee	Pron.	'I (topic)'	2A
warabi	N	'child'	2B(add)
warabi-n-chaa	N	'children'	2B(add)
warain	V-v	'to laugh'	8A(add)
wassan	Adj.	'bad'	5A
wata	N	'stomach', 'belly'	4A
wattaa	Pron.	'we, our'	2A
wikiga uttu	N	'younger brother'	2A(add)
winagu uttu	N	'younger sister'	2A(add)
wubamaa	N	'aunt'	2A(add)
wujasaa	N	'uncle'	2A(add)
wun	V-IRG	'to exist (for animates)'	2B(add)
wuti	PRT	'at' (same as *wutooti*)	5B
wutooti	PRT	'at' (same as *wuti*)	5B
wutu	N	'husband'	7C(add)
wuu wuu	Response	'no' (polite)	Prel.
ya	PRT	Topic-marking particle	1A
yaa[1]	N	'house', 'family'	2B(add)
yaa[2]	SFP	'right?'	1A
yaan	N	'next year'	9A(add)
-(y)aani	Suffix	'V_1 and V_2'	6A
yaaninju	N	'family'	2C
yaaruu	N	'gecko'	2C(add)

Word	Class	Meaning	Lesson
yaasan	Adj	'hungry'	4B(add)
yafarasan	Adj	'soft'	5A(add)
yagamasan	Adj	'noisy'	6A(add)
-(y)ai	Suffix	'doing V_1 and doing V_2'	6A
yaka	PRT	'rather than'	7A
yaku ni tachun	Idiom	'contribute', 'be of use'	6B(add)
Yamatuguchi	N-proper	'Japanese language'	1A(add)
yamisheen	V-hon.	COPULA (EXALTATION FORM)	5C
yamun	V-c	'to hurt', 'to have pains'	4A
yan	V-copula	'be', 'am', 'are'	1B
yashiga	Conj.	'but'	10C
yashimiin	V-v	'to reduce the price'	5C
yashimun	V-c	'to rest', 'to skip (school, etc.)'	4B
yassan	Adj	'cheap'	5C
-yassan	Suffix	'easy to V'	5A
yatchii	N	'older brother'	2C
yii kaagi	Idiom	'handsome', 'beautiful'	4B(add)
yii soogwachi deebiru	Greeting	Okinawan New Year greeting	1A
yii yii	Response	'no' (plain) (→ see also Preliminary Lesson)	3B
yin	N	'yen' (Japanese currency)	4A(add)
yinu saku	Idiom	'same amount' (same as *yunu saku*)	7C
yoo[1]	SFP	(imperative, request, 'please do something')	8A(add)
yoo[2]	SFP	(expressing surprise, exclamation)	9B
yoo[3]	SFP	(call for attention, 'you know')	9B
yoonnaa	Adv.	'slowly'	10A

Word	Class	Meaning	Lesson
yubun	C-v	'to call someone'	3A
yuin	V-v	'to stop by'	10A(add)
yuku	Adv.	'even', 'still more'	7C
Yunabaru	N-proper	'Yonabaru' (place name)	9A
yuntaku	N	'chitchat'	8C(add)
yunu saku	Idiom	'same amount' (same as *yinu saku*)	7C
yuru	N	'evening'	6B
yutasan	Adj.	'fine, good'	2B
yuttai	N	'four people'	2C
yuu	Adv.	'often'	8B(add)
yuufuru	N	'bath'	3C(add)
-yuusun	Suffix	'can'	7B
yuuwee	N	'congratulatory remarks'	10A
zubon	N	'pants' (Jp. loan)	10A(add)
ʔnbusun	V-c	'to steam'	3C
ʔnjasun[1]	V-c	'to take out (TR)'	3A(add)
ʔnjasun[2]	V-c	'to put out (TR)' [ʔnjachi (G.STEM)]	5C
ʔnji-in	V-v	'to come out', 'run'	4A
ʔnjiin[1]	V-v	'to go/come out (INTR)' [ʔnjiti (G.STEM)]	3A(add)
ʔnjiin[2]	V-v	'to leave', 'to graduate' [ʔnjiti (G.STEM)]	3C(add)
ʔnma	N	'horse'	7A
ʔnmee	N	'grandmother'	2A(add)
ʔnmii	N	'older sister'	2C
ʔnmu	N	'potato'	3C
ʔwaa	N	'pig'	1A
ʔwaachichi	N	'weather'	6B

Word	Class	Meaning	Lesson
ʔweeda	N	'during the time'	10C
ʔwenchu	N	'mouse'	2B(add)
ʔwiijun	V-c	'to swim'	3A
ʔwiirikisan	Adj.	'fun'	3C(add)
ʔyaa	Pron.	'you' (singular-plain)	2B(add)

APPENDIX 2

CONSTRUCTION LIST

ADNOM = Adnominal Form
ADV.FORM = Adverbial Form
APOCO = Apocopate Form
B.ROOT = Basic Root
FINITE = Finite Form

G.FORM = Gerund Form
G.ROOT = Gerund Root
INT.FORM = Intentional Form
N.FORM = Negative Form
N.ROOT = Negative Root

1. Sorted by Lesson

Name	Building Block	Construction	Meaning	Lesson(s)
Polite	B.ROOT	tu-ibiin tach-abiin	'will take' 'will stand'	L1(B1, 2), L2(B4)
Negative	N.ROOT	tu-ran tut-an	'not take' 'not stand'	L2(A3)
Progressive /Result	G.ROOT	tu-toon tatch-oon	'be taking/have taken' 'be standing/have stood'	L3(A3)
PAST-2[1]	APOCO	tui-tan tachu-tan	'took, and I saw it' 'stood, and I saw it'	L3(B1)
PAST-1[1]	G.ROOT	tu-tan tatch-an	'took' 'stood'	L3(B1)
Cause-Effect	APOCO	tui-kutu tachu-kutu	'take, so…' 'stand, so…'	L4(B1)
Concessive	APOCO	tui-shiga tachu-shiga	'take, but…' 'stand, but…'	L4(B1)

Appendix 2

Name	Building Block	Construction	Meaning	Lesson(s)
Nominalization	APOCO	*tui-shi* *tachu-shi*	'the one that takes…' 'the one that stands…'	L4(B3)
Adverbial	B.ROOT	*tu-i* *tach-i*	'to take' 'to stand'	L5(A1)
'Easy to do'	ADV.FORM	*tui-yassan* *tach-yassan*	'easy to take' 'easy to stand'	L5(A2)
'Hard to do' (1)	ADV.FORM	*tui-gurisan* *tachi-gurisan*	'hard to take' 'hard to stand'	L5(A2)
Request	G.FORM	*tuti-kwimisooree* *tatchi-kwimisooree*	'please take it' 'please stand'	L5(B3)
Desiderative	ADV.FORM	*tui-busan* *tachi-busan*	'want to take' 'want to stand'	L6(A1)
Purposive	ADV.FORM	*tui-ga* *tachi-i-ga*	'in order to take' 'in order to stand'	L6(A2)
***Aani* form**[2]	B.ROOT	*tu-yaani* *tach-aani*	'take, and' 'stand, and'	L6(A3)
Representative	G.ROOT	*tu-tai* *tatch-ai*	'taking, etc.' 'standing, etc.'	L6(A4)
Obligation	N.FORM	*turan-daree/nee naran* *tatan-daree/nee naran*	'must take' 'must stand'	L6(B1)
(R)ee Conditional	N.ROOT	*tu-ree* *tat-ee*	'if…take' 'if…stand'	L6(B2)
'So as to'	ADNOM	*tuiru gutu* *tachuru gutu*	'so as to get' 'so as to stand'	L6(B3)
Conjecture	FINITE	*tuin nee sun* *tachun nee sun*	'have a feeling that…take' 'have a feeling that…stand'	L6(B4)
'do and go/come'	G.FORM	*tuti-ichun* *tatchi-ichun*	'get and go' 'stand and go'	L7(A1)
Potential (ability)†	ADV.FORM	*tui-yuusun* *tachi-yuusun*	'can take it' 'can stand'	L7(B1)

Name	Building Block	Construction	Meaning	Lesson(s)
Potential (situation)†	INT.FORM	*tura-riin* *tata-riin*	'possible to take it' 'possible to stand'	L7(B1)
Resultative	G.ROOT	*tu-teen* *tatch-een*	'have taken it' 'have stood'	L7(C1)
Preparatory Aspect	G.ROOT	*tu-toochun* *tatch-oochun*	'take it for now/future' 'stand for now/future'	L7(C2)
Benefactive	G.FORM	*tuti-kwiin* *tatchi-kwiin*	'take for someone' 'stand for someone'	L8(A2)
Imperative	N.ROOT	*tu-ri yoo* *tat-i yoo*	'Take!' 'Stand!'	L8(A3)
Imperative	N.ROOT	*tu-ree* *tat-ee*	'Take!' 'Stand!'	L8(A3)
Passive	INT.FORM	*tura-riin* *tata-riin*	'be taken' 'be stood (up)'	L8(A5)
Exalting	ADV.FORM	*tu(i)-misheen* *tachi-misheen*	'(honorable person) takes' '(honorable person) stands'	L8(B1)
Provisional Conditional	APOCO	*tui-raa* *tachu-raa*	'if it's the case that…take' 'if it's the case that…stand'	L8(B3)
Conjecture	ADNOM	*tuiru-haji* *tachuru-haji*	'it may take' 'it may stand'	L8(B4)
Simultaneous	ADV.FORM	*tui-gachii* *tachi-gachii*	'while taking' 'while standing'	L8(C2)
Purpose	ADNOM	*tuiru tami ni* *tachuru tami ni*	'in order to take it' 'in order to stand'	L9(A2)
Contrast/Reason	ADNOM	*tuiru munnu* *tachuru munnu*	'take it so/but…' 'stand so/but…'	L9(A3)
Causative	INT.FORM	*tura-sun* *tata-sun*	'make someone take' 'make someone stand'	L9(B1)

Name	Building Block	Construction	Meaning	Lesson(s)
Causative-Passive	INT.FORM	*tura-sariin* *tata-sariin*	'be made to take' 'be made to stand'	L9(B2)
Completive Aspect	G.FORM	*tuti-neen* *tatchi-neen*	'end up taking it' 'end up standing'	L9(C1)
Concessive Conditional	G.FORM	*tuti n* *tatchi n*	'even if one takes it' 'even if one stands'	L9(C2)
After/since	G.FORM	*tuti-kara* *tatchi-kara*	'after taking' 'after standing'	L10(A2)
Habitual Conditional	ADV.FORM	*tui-nee* *tachi-i-nee*	'when(ever)…take' 'when(ever)…stand'	L10(B2)
'Hard to do' (2)	ADV.FORM	*tui kantii sun* *tatchi kantii sun*	'difficult to take' 'difficult to stand'	L10(B3)
'before'	ADNOM	*tuiru mee* *tachuru mee*	'before taking' 'before standing'	L10(C1)
'while'	ADNOM	*tuiru ʔweeda/ʔweema* *tachuru ʔweeda/ʔweema*	'while taking' 'while standing'	L10(C1)
'after'	G.FORM	*tuiti-atu* *tatchi-atu*	'after taking' 'after standing'	L10(C1)
Permission	G.FORM	*tuiti n shimun* *tatchi n shimun*	'OK to take' 'OK to stand'	L10(C2)
Exemption	G.FORM (negative)	*turanti n shimun* *tatanti n shimun*	'don't have to get' 'don't have to stand'	L10(C2)
Prohibition	G.FORM	*tutee naran* (*tuti ya > tutee*) *tatchee naran* (*tatchi ya > tachee*)	'cannot take' 'cannot stand'	L10(C2)
Experiential	ADNOM (PAST-1)	*tutaru kutu nu an* *tatcharu kutu nu an*	'have gotten it' 'have stood (there)'	L10(C3)
Visual evidential	ADV.FORM	*tui-gisan* *tatchi-gisan*	'looks as if…take' 'looks as if…stand'	L10(C4)

2. Sorted by Building Blocks

Building Block / Name	Construction	Meaning	Lesson(s)
ADNOM			
'So as to'	*tuiru gutu* *tachuru gutu*	'so as to get' 'so as to stand'	L6(B3)
Conjecture	*tuiru-haji* *tachuru-haji*	'it may take' 'it may stand'	L8(B4)
Purpose	*tuiru tami ni* *tachuru tami ni*	'in order to take it' 'in order to'	L9(A2)
Contrast / Reason	*tuiru munnu* *tachuru munnu*	'take it so/but...' 'stand so/but...'	L9(A3)
'before'	*tuiru mee* *tachuru mee*	'before taking' 'before standing'	L10(C1)
'while'	*tuiru ʔweeda/ʔweema* *tachuru ʔweeda/ʔweema*	'while taking' 'while standing'	L10(C1)
ADNOM (PAST-1)			
Experiential	*tutaru kutu nu an* *tatcharu kutu nu an*	'have gotten it' 'have stood (there)'	L10(C3)
ADV.FORM			
'Easy to do'	*tui-yassan* *tachi-yassan*	'easy to take' 'easy to stand'	L5(A2)
'Hard to do' (1)	*tui-gurisan* *tachi-gurisan*	'hard to take' 'hard to stand'	L5(A2)
Desiderative	*tui-busan* *tachi-busan*	'want to take' 'want to stand'	L6(A1)
Purposive	*tui-ga* *tachi-i-ga*	'in order to take' 'in order to stand'	L6(A2)
Potential (ability)†	*tui-yuusun* *tachi-yuusun*	'can take it' 'can stand'	L7(B1)
Exalting	*tu(i)-misheen* *tachi-misheen*	'(honorable person) takes' '(honorable person) stands'	L8(B1)

Building Block / Name	Construction	Meaning	Lesson(s)
Simultaneous	*tui-gachii* *tachi-gachii*	'while taking' 'while standing'	L8(C2)
Habitual Conditional	*tui-nee* *tachi-i-nee*	'when(ever) … take' 'when(ever) … stand'	L10(B2)
'Hard to do' (2)	*tui kantii sun* *tatchi kantii sun*	'difficult to take' 'difficult to stand'	L10(B3)
Visual evidential	*tui-gisan* *tatchi-gisan*	'looks as if … take' 'looks as if … stand'	L10(C4)
APOCO			
PAST-2[1]	*tui-tan* *tachu-tan*	'took, and I saw it' 'stood, and I saw it'	L3(B1)
Cause-Effect	*tui-kutu* *tachu-kutu*	'take, so …' 'stand, so …'	L4(B1)
Concessive	*tui-shiga* *tachu-shiga*	'take, but …' 'stand, but …'	L4(B1)
Nominalization	*tui-shi* *tachu-shi*	'the one that takes …' 'the one that stands …'	L4(B3)
Provisional Conditional	*tui-raa* *tachu-raa*	'if it's the case that … take …' 'if it's the case that … stand'	L8(B3)
B.ROOT			
Polite	*tu-ibiin* *tach-abiin*	'will take' 'will stand'	L1(B1, 2), L2(B4)
Adverbial	*tu-i* *tach-i*	'to take' 'to stand'	L5(A1)
***Aani* form**[2]	*tu-yaani* *tach-aani*	'take, and' 'stand, and'	L6(A3)
FINITE			
Conjecture	*tuin nee sun* *tachun nee sun*	'have a feeling that … take' 'have a feeling that … stand'	L6(B4)

Building Block / Name	Construction	Meaning	Lesson(s)
G.FORM			
Request	tuti-kwimisooree tatchi-kwimisooree	'please take it' 'please stand'	L5(B3)
'do and go/come'	tuti-ichun tatchi-ichun	'get and go' 'stand and go'	L7(A1)
Benefactive	tuti-kwiin tatchi-kwiin	'take for someone' 'stand for someone'	L8(A2)
Completive Aspect	tuti-neen tatchi-neen	'end up taking it' 'end up standing'	L9(C1)
Concessive Conditional	tuti n tatchi n	'even if one takes it' 'even if one stands'	L9(C2)
'after/since'	tuti-kara tatchi-kara	'after taking' 'after standing'	L10(A2)
'after'	tuti-atu tatchi-atu	'after taking' 'after standing'	L10(C1)
Permission	tuti n shimun tatchi n shimun	'OK to take' 'OK to stand'	L10(C2)
Exemption	turanti n shimun tatanti n shimun	'don't have to get' 'don't have to stand'	L10(C2)
Prohibition	tutee naran (tuti ya > tutee) tatchee naran (tachi ya > tachee)	'cannot take' 'cannot stand'	L10(C2)
G.ROOT			
Progressive /Result	tu-toon tatch-oon	'be taking/have taken' 'be standing/have stood'	L3(A3)
PAST-1[1]	tu-tan tatch-an	'took' 'stood'	L3(B1)
Representative	tu-tai tatch-ai	'taking, etc.' 'standing, etc.'	L6(A4)
Resultative	tu-teen tatch-een	'have taken it' 'have stood'	L7(C1)

Building Block / Name	Construction	Meaning	Lesson(s)
Preparatory Aspect	*tu-toochun* *tatch-oochun*	'take it for now/future' 'stand for now/future'	L7(C2)
INT.FORM			
Potential (situation)[3]	*tura-riin* *tata-riin*	'possible to take it' 'possible to stand'	L7(B1)
Passive	*tura-riin* *tata-riin*	'be taken' 'be stood (up)'	L8(A5)
Causative	*tura-sun* *tata-sun*	'make someone take' 'make someone stand'	L9(B1)
Causative-Passive	*tura-sariin* *tata-sariin*	'be made to take' 'be made to stand'	L9(B2)
N.FORM			
Obligation	*turan-daree/nee naran* *tutan-daree/nee naran*	'must take' 'must stand'	L6(B1)
N.ROOT			
(R)ee Conditional	*tu-ree* *tat-ee*	'if…take' 'if…stand'	L6(B2)
Imperative	*tu-ree* *tat-ee*	'Take!' 'Stand!'	L8(A3)

[1] For further study, see Shinzato (1991 and 2003a).
[2] See Nishioka and Nakahara (2000: 72).
[3] For further study, see Shinzato (2008).

REFERENCES

RESOURCES IN ENGLISH

Bhowmik, Davinder, L. 2008. *Writing Okinawa: Narrative Acts of Identity and Resistance.* London: Routledge.

Blakemore, Diane. 2000. "Indicators and Procedures: *Nevertheless* and *But*." *Journal of Linguistics* 36 (3): 463–486.

Gillan, Matt. 2015. Ryukyuan Languages in Ryukyuan Music." In *Handbook of the Ryukyuan Languages: History, Structure, and Use,* edited by P. Heinrich, S. Miyara, and M. Shimoji, 685–702. Berlin/Boston/Munich: Walter de Gruyter.

Heinrich, Patrick. 2008. "Establishing Okinawan Heritage Language Education." In *Japanese as Foreign Language in the Age of Globalization*, edited by P. Heinrich and Y. Sugita, 65–86. München: Iudicium.

———. 2015. "Language Shift." In *Handbook of the Ryukyuan Languages: History, Structure, and Use*, edited by P. Heinrich, S. Miyara, and M. Shimoji, 613–630. Berlin/Boston/Munich: Walter de Gruyter.

Hijirida, Kyoko, and Tomoko Oshiro. 2011. *Language Handbook.* Accessed February 21, 2022. http://manoa.hawaii.edu/okinawa/wordpress/?page_id=135.

Ishihara, Masahide. 2014. "Language Vitality and Endangerment in the Ryukyus." In *Language Crisis in the Ryukyus*, edited by M. Anderson and P. Heinrich, 140–168. Newcastle, UK: Cambridge Scholars Publishing.

Kamio, Akio. 1994. "The Theory of Territory of Information: The Case of Japanese." *Journal of Pragmatics* 21 (1): 67–100.

Matisoff, James. 1986. "Hearts and Minds in South-East Asian Languages and English: An Essay in the Comparative Lexical Semantics of Psycho-Collocations." *Cahiers de Linguistique—Asie Orientale* 15 (1): 5–57.

Moseley, Christopher. 2010. *Atlas of the World's Languages in Danger*, 3rd ed. UNESCO Publishing, Online version. Accessed February 21, 2022. http://www.unesco.org/culture/en/endangeredlanguages/atlas.

Sakihara, Masashi, Shigehisa Karimata, Moriyo Shimabukuro, Lucila Etsuko Gibo, and Brandon Akio Ing. 2017. *Rikka, Uchinaa-nkai! Okinawan Language Textbook for Beginners.* Accessed February 22, 2022. https://liuchiuan.files.wordpress.com/2017/09/rikka_2nded_final.pdf.

Serafim, Leon A., and Rumiko Shinzato. 2021. *The Language of the Old-Okinawan Omoro Sōshi: Reference Grammar with Textual Selections.* Kent, UK: Global Oriental/Brill.

Shinzato, Rumiko. 1991. "Epistemic Properties of Temporal Auxiliaries: A Case Study from Okinawan, Japanese and Old Japanese." *Linguistics* 29 (1): 53–77.

———. 2003a. "Experiencing Self vs. Observing Self: The Semantics of Stative Extensions in Japanese." *Language Sciences* 25 (2): 211–238.

———. 2003b. "Wars, Politics, and Language: A Case Study of the Okinawan Language." In *At War with Words*, edited by M. N. Dedaić and D. N. Nelson, 283–313. Berlin/New York: Mouton de Gruyter.

———. 2008. "From 'Emergence' to 'Ability': A Case of Japanese *naru* and *dekiru*." In *Proceedings from the Main Session of the Fortieth Meeting of the Chicago Linguistic Society: Volume 40-1*, edited by Nikki Adams, Adam Cooper, Fey Parrill, and Thomas Wier, 365–379. Chicago: Chicago Linguistic Society.

———. 2020a. "Focus-Predicate Concord (*Kakari Musubi*) Constructions in Japanese/Okinawan." *Oxford Research Encyclopedia of Linguistics.* Oxford: Oxford University Press.

———. 2020b. "Passives as Unmarked Voice: A Case of 'Warning' Passives in Okinawan." *Language Sciences* 80. Accessed February 22, 2022. https://doi.org/10.1016/j.langsci.2020.101276.

Shinzato, Rumiko, and Leon A. Serafim. 2013. *Synchrony and Diachrony of Okinawan Kakari Musubi in Comparative Perspective with Premodern Japanese.* Kent, UK: Global Oriental/Brill.

Whitman, John. 1997. "*Kakarimusubi* from a Comparative Perspective." *Japanese/Korean Linguistics*, vol. 6, edited by Ho-min Sohn and John Haig: 161–78. Stanford: Center for the Study of Language and Information.

Yamanokuchi, Baku. 2000. "Shell-Shocked Island." Translated by Rie Takagi. In *Southern Exposure: Modern Japanese Literature from Okinawa*, edited by M. Molasky and S. Rabson, 49. Honolulu: University of Hawai'i Press.

RESOURCES IN JAPANESE

Hanazono, Satoru 花薗悟. 2020.『初級　沖縄語』東京：研究社 (*Elementary Okinawan.* Tokyo: Kenkyūsha).

Hokama, Shuzen 外間守善. 1971.「沖縄方言形容詞の史的変遷」『沖縄の言語史』pp. 101–128. 東京：法政大学出版局 (Historical Development of Adjectives in Okinawan. *Language History of Okinawan.* Tokyo: Hōsei Daigaku Shuppankyoku).

———. 1976.「おもろ語「うりずん」と「若夏」」沖縄文化研究 3: 244–257 ("*Urizun*" and "*Wakanachi*" in the Omoro Language. *Okinawa Bunka Kenkyū* 3).

Ifa, Fuyū 伊波普猷. (1929) 1974.『校注琉球戯曲集』那覇：榕樹書林 (A Collection of Ryukyuan Dramas with Annotations. Naha: Yōju Shorin).

Ikegami, Yoshihiko 池上嘉彦. 1981.『「する」と「なる」の言語学：言語と文化のタイポロジーへの試論』東京：大修館 (*'DO-Language' and 'BECOME-Language': Two Contrasting Types of Linguistic Representation*. Tokyo: Taishūkan).

Ishikawa, Akiko 石川明子. 1996.「琉球那覇方言の主格助詞について－共時的観点から」上田功、砂川有里子、高見健一、野田尚史、蓮沼昭子（編）『小泉保博士古希記念論文集：言語探求の領域』pp. 35–41. 東京:大学書林 ("On the Subject Particles in the Naha Dialect of the Ryukyuan – from a Synchronic Perspective." In *Festschrift for Professor Koizumi on His Seventieth Birthday for Professor Koizumi Tamotsu: Areas in Language Research*, edited by I. Ueda, Y. Sunakawa, K. Takami, H. Noda, and A. Hasunuma, Tokyo: Daigaku Shorin).

Kinjō, Chōei 金城朝永 (1944) 1974.「那覇方言概説]大藤時彦、外間守善（編）『金城朝永全集1 言語·文学篇』pp. 1–150. 沖縄：沖縄タイムス社 ("A General Description of the Naha Dialect." In *The Complete Works of Kinjō Chōei*, Vol. 1. Language and Literature, edited by T. Ōfuji and S. Hokama, Okinawa: Okinawa Taimusu-sha).

———. (1950) 1974.「北を西と呼ぶ話：方位と風の琉球語」大藤時彦、外間守善（編）『金城朝永全集１言語文学編』pp. 258–261. 沖縄：沖縄タイムス社 ("A Story of Calling *Kita* (North) *Nishi* (West): Direction and Wind in Ryukyuan." In *The Complete Works of Kinjō Chōei*, Vol. 1. Language and Literature, edited by T. Ōfuji and S. Hokama, Okinawa: Okinawa Taimusu-sha).

Kudō, Mayumi 工藤真由美, Yoriko Takaezu 高江洲頼子, and Hiromi Yagame 八亀裕美. 2007.「首里方言のアスペクト・テンス・エヴィデンシャリティー」大阪大学大学院文学研究科紀要. ("Aspect, Tense and Evidentiality in Shuri Dialect in Okinawa Prefecture" in *Memoirs of the Graduate School of Letters, Osaka University* 47).

Miyara, Shinshō 宮良信詳. 2000.『うちなーぐち講座：首里ことばのしくみ』那覇：沖縄タイムス社 (*Lectures on Uchinaa-guchi: The Structure of the Shuri Language*. Naha: Okinawa Taimususha).

———. 2019.『ウチナーロ: しくみと解説』沖縄：時事出版 (*Uchinaa-guchi: Its Structure and Description*. Naha: Okinawa Jiji Shuppan).

Nakahara, Jō 仲原穣. 2007.「沖縄県那覇市首里方言の原因・理由表現」『全国方言辞典《原因・理由表現編》』科学研究費補助金研究成果報告書 ("Expressions of 'Cause' and 'Reason' in the Shuri Dialect of Naha, Okinawa Prefecture" in *A Report for the Grant-in-Aid for Scientific Research*). Accessed February 22, 2022. http://hougen.sakura.ne.jp/shuppan/2007/2-9shuri.pdf.

Nakasone, Seizen 仲宗根政善. (1979) 1987.「なかべきよら御城]『琉球方言の研究』収録, pp. 283–293. 東京：新泉社 ("The Fine Castle in the Beautiful Sky." Reprinted in *A Study of Ryukyuan Dialects*. Tokyo: Shinsensha).

Nishioka, Satoshi 西岡敏. 2002.「沖縄語首里方言の終助詞付き用言語彙資料」『琉球方言の研究』26: 17–46 ("Reference Material for Predicates with Sentence Final Particles in the Shuri Dialect of Okinawan." *A Study of Ryukyuan Dialects*. Tokyo: Shinsensha).

Nishioka, Satoshi 西岡敏, and Jō Nakahara 仲原穣. (2000) 2006.『沖縄語の入門：たのしいウチナーグチ』東京：白水社 (*Introduction to the Okinawan Language: Enjoyable Uchinaaguchi*. Tokyo: Hakusuisha).

Nohara, Mitsuyoshi 野原三義. 1986.『琉球方言助詞の研究』 東京：武蔵野書院 (*A Study of Particles in Ryukyuan Dialects*. Tokyo: Musashino Shoin).

———. 1998.『新編 琉球方言助詞の研究』東京：沖縄学研究所（*A Study of Particles in Ryukyuan Dialects* (New Edition). Tokyo: Okinawagaku Kenkyūjo).

Okinawa Prefecture 沖縄県. 2019. 「平成31年住民基本台帳年齢別人口」 (The Population Size by Age Groups. Basic Resident Register, 2019). Accessed February 21, 2022. https://www.pref.okinawa.jp/site/kikaku/shichoson/2422.html.

———. 2020. 「後期「しまくとぅば」普及推進行動計画―県民への定着にむけて―（令和元年度―令和４年度）」 (Planning of Activities Promoting *Shimakutuba*: Towards Spreading *Shimakutuba* among Prefectural Citizens – the Second Phase [2019–2022]).

Onochi, Ken 小野地健. 2008. 「クシャミと人類文化：身体音からの人類文化研究の体系化のための試論」『非文字資料研究の可能性：若手研究者研究成果論文集』 横浜：神奈川大学２１世紀COEプログラム「人類文化研究のための非文字資料の体系化」研究推進会議 ("Sneezes and Human Cultures: An Exploratory Study of Systematization of Cultural Anthropology Based on Bodily Sounds." In *Collected Papers of Young Researchers: The Possibility of the Study of Unwritten Materials,* edited by the Committee for Research Promotion of the Study of Unwritten Materials for the Study of Human Cultures. Yokohama: Kanagawa University, 21st Century COE Program). Accessed February 21, 2022. http://www.himoji.jp/jp/publication/pdf/seika/801_01/02-089-107.pdf.

Sakihara, Masashi. 2018. 崎原正志『琉球語沖縄首里方言のモダリティ：叙述・実行・質問のモダリティを中心に』琉球大学、博士論文 (*Modality in the Shuri Dialect of the Ryukyuan Language: With Focus on Descriptive, Speech Act, and Question Modalities*. Doctoral dissertation. The University of the Ryukyus). Accessed February 22, 2022. http://ir.lib.u-ryukyu.ac.jp/handle/20.500.12000/40991.

Sanada, Shinji and Kenji Tomosada 真田信治・友定賢治. 2007.『地方別方言語源辞典』東京：東京堂出版 (*An Etymological Dictionary of Dialects*. Tokyo: Tōkyōdō Shuppan).

Shimoji, Michinori. 2021. 下地理則 琉球諸語における除括性 (clusivity)：調査票の提案と今後の展望。令和3年度第2回「日本の消滅危機言語・方言の記録とドキュメンテーションの作成」オンライン研究発表会（Clusivity in Ryukyuan Languages: A Suggestion for a Questionnaire and Its Prospects. An Online PowerPoint Presentation at the Second Meeting in 2021 for "Recording of Endangered Languages and Dialects in Japan and Making of Documentation" Sponsored by the National Institute for Japanese Language and Linguistics (NINJAL), December 12, 2021).

Takahashi, Toshizō. 1991. 高橋俊三「助詞「こと」「もの」考」」『おもろさうしの国語学的研究』pp. 334–354. 東京：武蔵野書院 ("A Look at *Koto* and *Mono*": *A Language Study of Omoro Sōshi*. Tokyo: Musashino Shoin).

Takara, Ben 高良勉. 2005a.『ウチナーグチ（沖縄語）練習帳』東京：NHK出版 (*A Practice Guide for Uchinaaguchi* (the Okinawan Language). Tokyo: NHK Publishing).

———. 2005b. 高良勉『沖縄生活誌』東京：岩波書店 (*Okinawa Lifestyle Magazine*, Tokyo: Iwanami Shoten, 62–63).

Tsuhako, Toshiko. 1992. 津波古敏子「沖縄語の中南部方言」『言語学辞典』河野六郎, 亀井孝, 千野栄一 （編）, pp. 829–848 ("The Central and Southern Dialects of Okinawa." In *A Dictionary of Linguistics*, edited by R. Kono, T. Kamei, and E. Chino. Tokyo: Sanseido).

Uchima, Chokujin 内間直仁. 1994.『琉球方言助詞と表現の研究』東京：笠間書院 (*A Study of Ryukyuan Particles and their Expressions.* Tokyo: Kasama Shoin).

———. 2011.『琉球方言とウチ・ソト意識』東京：研究社 (*Ryukyuan Dialects and Inside-Outside Consiousness.* Tokyo: Kenkyūsha).

Yabiku, Hiroshi 屋比久浩. 1963.「「イッター」と「ワッター」：接続形式の一考察」沖縄文化１３号, pp.159–163 ("*Ittaa*" and "*wattaa*" – An Inquiry on Combining Forms. *Okinawa Bunka* 13).

DICTIONARIES

Sakihara, Mitsugu. 2006. *Okinawan-English Wordbook: A Short Lexicon of the Okinawan Language with English Definitions and Japanese Cognates.* Edited by Stewart Curry. Honolulu: University of Hawai'i Press.

Handa, Ichirō 半田一郎. 1999.『琉球語辞典』東京：大学書林 (*Ryukyuan Dictionary.* Tokyo: Daigaku Shorin).

Miyara, Shinshō. 2021. 宮良信詳.『うちなーぐち活用辞典』国立国語研究所 (*A Usage Dictionary of Okinawan.* Tokyo: National Institute of Japanese Language and Linguistics).

Uchima, Chokujin 内間直仁 and Mitsuyoshi Nohara 野原三義. 2006.『沖縄語辞典：那覇方言を中心に』. 東京：研究社 (*Okinawan Dictionary: Naha Dialect.* Tokyo: Kenkyusha).

Uemura, Yukio 上村幸雄. 1963.『沖縄語辞典』国立国語研究所 （編集） 東京：大蔵省印刷局 (*A Dictionary of the Okinawan Language.* Edited by Kokuritsu Kokugo Kenkyūjo. Tokyo: Department of the Treasury, Printing Division).

ABOUT THE AUTHORS

Rumiko Shinzato is professor emerita in the Department of Modern Languages at the Georgia Institute of Technology.

Shoichi Iwasaki is a professor in the Department of Asian Languages and Cultures at the University of California at Los Angeles.